# Campaign Contributions and Legislative Voting

# Campaign Contributions and Legislative Voting

## A NEW APPROACH

STACY B. GORDON

ROUTLEDGE
NEW YORK AND LONDON

Published in 2005 by
Routledge
Taylor & Francis Group
270 Madison Avenue
New York, NY 10016
www.routledge-ny.com

Published in Great Britain by
Routledge
Taylor & Francis Group
2 Park Square
Milton Park, Abingdon,
Oxon, OX14 4RN U.K.
www.routledge.co.uk

10 9 8 7 6 5 4 3 2 1

Library of Congress Cataloging-in-Publication Data
    Gordon, Stacy B., 1965–
        Campaign contributions and legislative voting : a new approach/Stacy B. Gordon.
          p. cm.
        Includes bibliographical references and index.
        ISBN 0-415-94977-7 (hc : alk. paper) — ISBN 0-415-94978-5 (pb : alk. paper)
        1. Campaign funds—California. 2. Political action committees—California. 3. Legisla-
tion—California. 4. California. Legislature—Voting. 5. Campaign funds—United States. 6.
Political action committees—United States. 7. Legislation—United States. I. Title.

      JK1991.5.C2G67 2004
      328.794'0775—dc22

                                              2004011917

*For Zachary and Claire*

# Table of Contents

# Acknowledgments

In the years spent working on this project, one constant has been individuals coming forward to provide emotional and intellectual support at just the time when I needed them most. Throughout, I have gained much from my professors and colleagues at the University of California–Davis and the University of Nevada–Reno and my friends who worked at the state capitol in Sacramento. It was the intersection of these groups of smart, interesting, and thoughtful people that planted the seed for this project, and it was their continued support over the last decade that led to its final form. Given the litany to follow, one might think that no mistakes could possibly remain. However, some clearly do and they remain my own.

Important methodological suggestions (and patient explanations) were offered by Professors A. Colin Cameron and James Spriggs III, both of the University of California–Davis. Monica Barczak, Stephen Nicholson (currently of Georgia State University), and Rebecca Britton, fellow graduate students at the University of California–Davis, and Professor William L. Eubank (of the University of Nevada–Reno) all endured the roughest versions of this work and were still able to make insightful comments. In the case of Rebecca, she also suffered through my angst that this would never get published and humored my thoughts of an alternate career.

Additional thanks go to Professor Robert W. Jackman of the University of California–Davis. His patient reading, listening (over the entire ten years), and perceptive comments always improved the manuscript and its author. Special thanks are also extended to Professor Gary M. Segura of the University of Iowa, whose friendship, advice, patience, and faith were, and continue to be, invaluable to this work and my career more generally. Professor Walt Stone's review of the manuscript was extremely helpful and in the end his suggestions made it significantly better than it was before.

My friends at the capitol, Alan Gordon, Sandy Fried, Corey Brown, and the many people they introduced to me, reinforced my belief that a new understanding of the contributions relationship had to be developed. The anecdotes they shared with me and the trends that they saw in their daily work refined my argument and the model that ultimately resulted. Without their insight and guidance—and that of Dan Dunmoyer and Ken Mandler—much of the nuance of this argument would be lost. In particular, I want to thank former Senator Barry Keene. He has put so much thought into these issues and was able to provide me with insights that no one else could. He generously gave his time each time I asked and his help is greatly appreciated.

I spent much of the first summer on this effort in the state archives with the extraordinarily knowledgeable staff there. Their understanding of the available data was a great help and their willingness to search for information went beyond the call of duty. The same goes for Rob Tempio, my editor at Routledge. He has provided me with so much support and was critical to helping this process move forward.

I want to thank my family for their patience. They put up with me sleeping through most family events during a period when I decided I had to have a tenure-track position, a child, and a manuscript all at the same time. Without their love and support, I would not have made it through any of this successfully, much less with most of my sanity intact. And, last, but not least, thanks to my daughter Claire. Her love and her four-year-old insight into what is important make my work worth doing.

# 1

# Interest Groups and Policy Making

"You take the king's shilling, you do the king's bidding."

Barry Carmody of the Association of California Insurance Carriers

Barry Carmody's complaint reflects a common view of the policy making process in the United States today: simply put, money matters. Indeed, the cost of campaigns has been increasing exponentially in recent years—with a large percentage of the money for those campaigns coming from interest groups—and citizens are less convinced that they are represented by the people they elect. The impression is growing that money has an undue influence on policy making.

With the increase in the cost of campaigns, the ability to raise money to engage in those campaigns becomes critical. Without significant financial support, most candidates cannot make a realistic run for public office (Jacobson and Kernell 1981). Between the 1972 and the 1980 election cycles, campaign spending by the U.S. House of Representatives candidates increased 450 percent and spending by Senate candidates increased 600 percent. The total expenditures in 2002 of $930 million (opensecrets.org) dwarf the $66 million spent in the 1972 elections (Brooks et al. 1998).

Although the amount of money needed for modern campaigns has attracted significant public comment, where the bulk of the money comes from is telling as well. In 1996, political action committee (PAC) money made up 41 percent of the money raised by incumbents in the U.S. House of

Representatives campaigns and 20 percent of the money raised by U.S. Senate incumbents (Common Cause 1997), leading many to conclude that, increasingly, it is the special interests to which elected officials cater, not their geographic constituencies.

As these numbers have been growing and shifting, numerous scandals have broken in both state and federal government that add to the impression that money plays an inappropriate role. A Federal Bureau of Investigation (FBI) sting operation in California led to the conviction of many state legislators, staff members, and lobbyists. Former Senator Joseph Montoya and former Assemblyman Frank Hill were videotaped taking money from undercover FBI agents in exchange for votes on a bogus piece of legislation (Walsh 1997). Lobbyist Clay Jackson and former Senators Paul Carpenter and Alan Robbins were convicted of attempting to funnel insurance industry money to Robbins (then chair of the Senate Insurance, Claims, and Corporations Committee) through Carpenter's campaign committee (Walsh 1996).[1]

At the federal level, former Senator Robert Packwood's (D-OR) diaries revealed that his legislative activities bordered on the indictable. He sought campaign contributions and other financial help from people who could gain from his legislative position and did favors for them in return. He often judged the value of meetings and legislative decisions by how much money they would bring in (Kemper 1995).

In 1997, accusations were made that the Chinese government made illegal contributions to U.S. congressional and presidential campaigns in attempts to influence federal policy. President Clinton was accused of being unlawfully involved in the fund raising of the Democratic National Committee (DNC) by "selling" overnight stays in the Lincoln bedroom and directing DNC activities. Even Representative Dan Burton (R-IN), the leader of the House inquiry into Democratic campaign fund raising, was accused of misconduct. He allegedly asked a lobbyist to raise money from Pakistani-Americans and then threatened the lobbyist when he refused to do so (Carr 1997). During 2003, inquiries into potential contributions irregularities occurred at the state level in Texas (Oppel 2004) and at the local level in Washington state (Kershaw 2003) among others.

Although these activities may seem extreme and rare, some have found that even the simplest of campaign finance laws are skirted on a regular basis. Federal Election Commission (FEC) requirements that donor names, addresses, and occupations be reported are often ignored by candidates and such requirements are not enforced by the Commission. Information on up to 57 percent of all contributors to the National Republican Campaign Committee was not properly disclosed in the 1994 elections (Roeder 1997).

These scandals have hardly gone unnoticed by the public. In a 1997 *New York Times* survey, 89 percent of people questioned stated that significant and fundamental change is needed in our campaign financing system (Endicott 1997). In 2000, another national study by National Public Radio, the Kaiser Family Foundation, and the Kennedy School of Government found that 89 percent of those surveyed believed that government corruption was a very important or somewhat important problem.

Efforts at reform are increasing in number. For example, in April 1997, there were fifty-seven campaign finance reform bills pending in the U.S. Congress (Endicott 1997). But the future of those efforts looked dim, even at the time, because many in Congress are resistant to changes in the current system (O'Rourke 1997). And, although small alterations to the current system managed to pass one house of Congress or the other, ultimately, no meaningful campaign finance reform was accomplished in the 105th or 106th Congresses. It was not until the 107th Congress passed the McCain–Feingold Campaign Finance Reform Act in 2003 that reform efforts were successful at the federal level.

Because the public perceives a conflict of interest when legislators attempt to regulate their own behavior, or because citizens have lost faith in the system as a whole, the public has gotten into the reform mood. In 1997, campaign finance reform issues were on the ballot in seven of the twenty-four states with the initiative, and all but one passed (Alexander and Weiler 1997).[2] In one of the most overwhelming victories, an initiative in Nevada won with 71 percent of the vote (Alexander and Weiler 1997). The success of those reforms followed eight initiatives on the ballot in seven states in the 1994 election cycle, all but two of which passed (Alexander and NyBlom 1996).[3]

However, not all feel that limiting donations is the answer to the problem. Former Speaker of the California Assembly Jesse Unruh is often credited with commenting on interest group influence in the following manner, "If you can't take their money, eat their food, drink their booze ... and vote against them the next day, you don't belong in this business." Some practitioners agree and argue that the amount of money given is not problematic, as long as the public is aware of the source of the donations. Representative John Doolittle (R-CA) believes that as long as the public knows who is giving how much to the candidates (his own reform bills have required daily updates of donations via the Internet), the limits on contributions and public financing of campaigns are immaterial (Endicott 1997).

What is important to note is that most of the reform movements (except Doolittle's) assume that money is the problem. The most common argument is that members require money to gain public office and much of that money comes from interest groups; therefore, legislators are concerned with representing the interests of contributing groups in order to secure or protect contributions for future races. However, the hypothesis that contributions negatively affect the representative link between legislators and constituents has not received sufficient support. Until we know not only whether this relationship exists, but the character of the relationship, any attempts to address it with legislation are doomed to disappoint.

This effort endeavors to resolve both issues. It is important to first determine whether or not a direct relationship between campaign contributions and legislative voting behavior can be identified. And, if this connection is found to exist, we must understand its basic nature. Ultimately, it becomes clear that it is the nature of the relationship between money and votes that makes the relationship between these two important activities so difficult to detect.

Campaign donations are not traded for votes as part of a market exchange, which is why they have not been found to affect a large number of votes. Instead, contributions are gifts given for the purpose of developing and maintaining personal relationships and, as are most gifts, they are self-interested: given to create an obligation on behalf of the recipient (Clawson et al. 1998). If this is a correct conceptualization, then interest group contributions should only influence votes in specific and relatively rare circumstances. Votes should be affected only when the situation is appropriate: when the legislator desires to provide the vote for the group, not when he feels coerced to do so. More specifically, contributions affect votes only when they are critical to the outcome of legislation. It is by separating these votes from those that are less crucial that the connection becomes clear. However, the fact that the impact is infrequent and not coerced does not mean that political donations do not have important substantive and normative consequences for policy making. Those rare votes can have a cumulatively large impact on public policy because they determine the difference between the passage and failure of new policy.

## 1. The Role of Interest Groups in the Policy Making System

Interest in the general influence of interest groups on democratic representation is clearly not new. It is well known that James Madison was worried about the effects of faction on popular governments, because groups are concerned with their interests, often to the detriment of the rest of society (Madison 1787 [1982], 43). But he knew that political freedom was necessary as well. "It could not be a less folly to abolish liberty, which is essential to political life, because it nourishes faction, than it would be to wish the annihilation of air, which is essential to animal life, because it imparts to fire its destructive agency." Although he believed that groups did pose a threat to the interests and needs of all other citizens, he understood that it would be impossible to eliminate them without undermining democratic freedom as well.

Groups enhance the representative nature of democracy in four ways. First, interest groups signal to representatives which issues are salient and to whom. Even potential groups—those not yet organized—are able to affect policy if only because the threat of their development has an effect similar to an actual, currently organized group (Truman 1951). And, according to pluralists, not organizing is as much of a signal to members as organizing. It illustrates to policy makers that the issue is not important to affected groups.

Second, groups may also indicate the intensity of preferences regarding a particular issue. Dahl (1956) argues that the American system of interest group pluralism automatically controls for intensity through the participation of interest groups, because the only way to determine relative intensity is through overt activity, as observed through group participation. To the extent that group activity often has a significant effect on the outcome of policy, "[a]ll other things being equal, the outcome of a policy decision will be determined by the relative intensity of preference among the members of a group" (Dahl 1956, 135). Thus, interest groups positively affect the representative nature of the policy process by reflecting relative intensity of preferences of those groups that are potentially affected.

Third, interest groups also act to lower information costs to policy makers. Because the individuals who make up groups are experts in their area of interest, they often provide this information to legislators. Groups competing within an issue area can give concise and complete information surrounding the technicalities, opinions, and concerns regarding complex affairs (Milbrath 1963; Ornstein 1978).

Finally, groups provide information to legislators regarding oversight. Because their interests are focused on the policy effects of legislative outcomes and not just the political benefits of legislation, groups have significant incentives to make sure that the policies they support are duly instituted by the executive branch. In contrast to groups, "members intervene effectively in the bureaucracy on [implementation] matters where they can claim credit for intervention" (Mayhew 1974, 125). Where there is no credit to be claimed nor reelection benefits to gain, legislators have little or no incentive to participate in oversight (Ogul 1976; Scher 1963).[4] Although disinterest in implementation among legislators may be the rule rather than the exception, groups with an interest in implementation "can almost always find a sympathetic member of Congress to take up their cause" if they provide background information and can tie the implementation issue to a constituent interest (Wilson 1989, 85). Thus, interest groups often provide the needed political incentive for Congressmembers to provide oversight on the executive branch (Aberbach 1990).

In summary, interest groups have the ability to provide important and necessary services in the political system and many argue that these services increase the level of responsiveness of democratic government. However, the impact of interest group participation is not one-sided. Those concerned about bias argue that there are significant costs to accompany these benefits and that these costs outweigh the advantages provided by group activity.

## 2. Interest Group Bias in the Representative System

Even though much of the concern centers on money, it is important to remember that there are numerous ways in which interest groups can bias representation. What are these other forms of bias and why have financial advantages so engaged our interest?

Mancur Olson (1965) outlines how organizational costs cause bias in the interest group system of representation. Pluralists and others who support interest group participation in government argue that even if groups do bias representation, increased competition between groups and overlapping group memberships of individuals limit the effects of that bias (Denzau and Munger 1986; Truman 1951). On the other hand, Olson contends that we should be aware that groups are made up of individuals and that a group's strength (and even its existence) is largely determined by the costs and benefits to individuals of joining and participating. Olson posits that small groups, in particular, are more easily organized than large groups. This is because small groups are less likely to be affected by free-riders.[5] To the extent that all groups are not as easily organized, then the signaling of interest and the information provided by groups is biased toward some groups (small groups) more than others.

Not only is it easier for smaller groups to organize because the costs are lower, but also because the benefits that they gain from organization may be greater. Parker (1996) argues that it is often the case that the smaller a group, the less the relative costs to society when that group achieves its policy goals and, thus, the less societal opposition to its success. Although I do not agree that Parker's argument will hold under all conditions, a governmental program for a small group will be less expensive to the public as a whole than that same program for a much larger group.

More directly related to the issues addressed here, strong arguments have been made that significant resources vary across interest groups, causing variations in power. One such group resource is membership. Because of a candidate's electoral incentive to maximize votes, an interest group with a large membership may have more political clout than a group with a small membership. The group's power is particularly strong if the membership covers many electoral districts: "Beyond the direct political translation of size into votes, a large group representing many citizens has a built-in legitimacy; it 'speaks' for a sizeable part of America, not just for a handful of individuals" (Ornstein 1978, 73). In his survey of legislators, Kingdon finds that members of Congress do not take pressure from an interest group seriously unless there is a link between the group's interest and the legislator's constituency (1989, 150–52).

This is one crucial advantage for school people, for instance. Said one congressman, "Schools affect everybody. All congressmen have schools in abundance, and parents are affected, which means everybody" (Kingdon 1989, 153).

Milbrath goes so far as to assert that "the influence of groups is derived from the fact that members of groups are citizens and the political system is designed to respond to the influence of their votes" (1963, 342). Therefore, to Milbrath and Kingdon, membership is critical.

This is not to say that membership biases are not a concern. In "Federalist 10," Madison clearly points out his problems with majority factions. These are particularly dangerous, he argues, because they, through legitimate channels, "sacrifice to [their] ruling passion or interest, both the public good and the rights of other citizens" (Madison 1787, 45). And though minority factions can, for the most part, be controlled by the system of majority rule, majority factions may actually gain more control than even their majority status would entitle them (see also Guinier 1994). The risk in this, at its most extreme, is that the majority might work to eliminate the political rights of the minority; examples include the disenfranchisement of Southern blacks prior to the 1965 Voting Rights Act. Situations such as these result in substantial and enduring biases toward the interests of large groups.

If both group size and organizational capabilities cause biases in policy making, why is the influence of money considered to be particularly negative when compared with the impact of other group resources? First, regardless of the costs of organizing, if the costs of not organizing rise to a certain level, organization will occur, even among groups that Olson and others argue have the fewest organizational incentives (for an example, see Piven and Cloward 1977). Second, there are additional incentives to organization overlooked by Olson (e.g., see Berry 1997; Chong 1991), so more groups may organize than Olson predicts. Third, even taking into account Madison's concern with majority factions, one could argue that any additional attention a representative gives to the public policy concerns of interest groups with large memberships is, at the least, consistent with majority rule. Verba et al. (1995) provide the best argument why the American public would be more comfortable with the fact that only a few people spend a lot of time as campaign volunteers, while most spend very little time, than with the fact that some give a lot of money while others give little or none.

> [T]he challenge to democratic equality is not as serious if those who are not active abstain voluntarily and choose freely to put their eggs in another basket. If, however, those who are inactive cannot take part —because they lack the means or face intimidation or other barriers, rather than because they do not want to—then participatory inequalities constitute a more serious affront to democratic norms (pp. 29–30).

If money biases representation, it is probably because people are failing to participate because they are incapable, not because they choose not to. This has negative, normative implications that the other forms of bias do not.

## 2.1 How Money Biases the Representative System

Although this effort focuses on the influence of campaign contributions on legislative voting behavior—both because the relationship has been so ambiguous and because it appears so obviously unethical—it is important to note that the financial advantages of some groups can bias the level of representation in many ways. First, the source of a group's financial resources influences the menu of pressure tactics from which they may choose. If a group cannot raise the money it needs from its own members, it has to turn to others to help the group achieve its policy goals. Where a group ends up getting its money from can often determine its tactics and strategies and, thus, its success (Hayes 1981; Walker 1991).

Walker (1991) observes that many group patrons (e.g., government agencies) are unlikely to support groups that demonstrate, protest, or engage themselves in controversial issues. Those groups must use inside rather than outside lobbying techniques, even when using outside strategies might improve their chances of success by increasing the arena of conflict and influencing public opinion. On the other hand, professional groups that are maintained by dues use inside strategies because they desire specific benefits and little conflict. In addition, citizen groups relying on dues use outside sources of lobbying to achieve larger, collective goals and gain from an expanded arena of conflict. And, given that inside lobbying strategies may be more successful than outside strategies when attempting to achieve specific types of group objectives (Milbrath 1963; Ornstein 1978), funding sources and their impact on different strategies can have the effect of influencing the success of group goals.

Sources of funding also help determine the type of benefits that a group seeks, which can affect a group's policy success. Hayes (1981) argues that voluntary organizations need concrete and immediate benefits to maintain their memberships, so much of their money is spent on various incentives to organization, such as material side payments. In contrast, smaller organizations with more specific interests that can maintain a permanent staff can focus their money and effort on purely purposive benefits. They thus obtain more policy effect for the amount of money spent. Therefore, even groups with relatively similar financial resources are not created equal. Large groups still get less policy output per dollar they raise compared with small groups.

Once a group has money, that money can be used to attract other resources that help a group to achieve its policy aims.

With substantial monetary resources, the American Petroleum Institute maintains impressive offices in downtown Washington staffed with lobbyists, public relations officials and petroleum engineers to supply information to Congress and the executive branch, to monitor relevant government activity, and to finance magazine and newspaper advertise-ments giving the viewpoints of the oil industry…. On the other hand, groups with fewer monetary resources may rely heavily on volunteers, have storefront offices, obtain public attention through press releases, and give no campaign contributions to legislators.

(Ornstein 1978, 70)

This implies that interest groups with money can buy the types of resources that are naturally available to other groups. They can create grass roots support where none previously existed if they have money to buy television time and newspaper space and contact prospective supporters (Smith 1988). They can use money to provide material side payments to increase their membership size or to collect information for legislators more readily than groups without.

In particular, money can be used by a group to provide votes to candidates, a service we would expect to be provided primarily by large membership groups. The impact of group contributions and candidate campaign spending on electoral success has been well documented (Jacobson 1978 and 1980; Jacobson and Kernell 1981). This implies that a small group with access to financial resources can, in effect, deliver more votes to a particular candidate than a large membership group. Thus, money can even buy a relatively small group many of the advantages of a large group.

Finally, money can affect the legislative process directly. For instance, it can buy access.

"The PAC, let's face it, gives you more visibility in a town with very, very competitive interests," he [Clifford Gibbons, a lobbyist at the law firm Hogan & Hartson] confessed to the *National Journal*. If a lobbyist doesn't help a lawmaker raise money, he added, "chances are you are not going to get your phone calls returned. Maybe once, but you are not going to be on anyone's short list." Another lobbyist put it this way: Members of Congress might forget who gave to their last campaign, but "their schedulers don't."

(Birnbaum 1992, 165)

Birnbaum (1992) notes that money does not just generate entrance into a member's office to speak about bills, but allows a group's lobbyists into parties and political fundraisers where much of the social lobbying occurs. If a group does not buy tickets to fundraisers, its members or lobbyists will not have an opportunity to speak with numerous legislators or possible issue-coalition allies outside of the more formal office setting. And, if face-to-face contact is as critical a part of advocacy as some say, then groups with access can more easily obtain their policy goals than groups without.

As noted previously, many who study legislative voting behavior find this relationship highly intuitive. Since 1974, the percentage of campaign financing dollars given by PACs has increased dramatically, while that of individual donors has dropped. Not only has the aggregate amount of money that changes hands increased, but individual groups have increased their contribution spending. On the presumption that these groups are not economically irrational, we expect that they are getting a return on their investment. In other words, this increased activity suggests that groups who are better off financially are also privileged when participating in the political process. This hypothesis has been supported, in part, by Hall and Wayman (1990) and Evans (1996).

The problem that campaign contributions and, by implication, the power they buy poses for democracy is put best by Ginsberg and Green (1986):

> The dependence of candidates on private contributions may allow well-heeled special interests an opportunity to influence unduly the outcomes of electoral contests and the content of national policy. This potential result is certainly incompatible with the democratic ideal of the vote as a mechanism through which each individual can exercise an equal measure of influence on the governmental process (p. 76).

Other theories of how campaign contributions affect policy making are discussed in detail in the next chapter. However, the major point is that groups that are financially well endowed have many ways to use their money to maximize their success in the policy making arena. This is not to suggest that the only threat to fair democratic representation is money. Other interest group characteristics obviously generate policy biases that favor organized group interests. Money is nevertheless different and considerably more problematic primarily because contributions seem to be the most direct way for groups to affect legislative decision making. In addition, while one arguably might claim positive consequences from other forms of group influence, few would wish to defend the claim that increased representation of wealthier groups *simply because they are wealthier* helps achieve a more egalitarian level of representation overall.

## 2.2 Summary

It is not overstating the issue to say that the general view of the public is that interest groups control the political process. And, as scholars, we have attempted to sort out the conditions under which groups either hinder or help legislators in their efforts to represent citizens. But while it is clear that interest groups can and do provide some positive incentives for legislators during policy making, it is equally as clear that these honorable aspects of the interaction between groups and policy makers are counterbalanced by the bias toward organized interests that can result.

With this in mind, it is my purpose to address a single aspect of this relationship—the effect of group donations on legislative voting behavior. There are many tools and methods used by groups to achieve their legislative goals, but the direct connection between money and votes is considered to be among the most difficult to identify and the most ethically and legally questionable if found to exist.

## 3. Theoretical Summary and Outline of the Book

In Chapter 2, I discuss the effects of money more specifically. There are numerous studies, both anecdotal and scientific, testing whether there is, indeed, a relationship between the amount of money contributed to members of the legislature during their campaigns and subsequent legislative behavior.

Scholars study whether the amount of contributions affect the level of access allowed to groups (Austen-Smith 1995; Birnbaum 1992; Grenzke 1989; Wright 1990), the amount of effort that legislators put forth on legislation (Evans 1996; Hall and Wayman 1990), or the actual voting behavior of members (Etzioni 1984; Langbein and Lotwis 1990; Stern 1988; Wilhite and Theilmann 1987) and under what circumstances these relationships hold (Jones and Keiser 1987). These studies show that money does have an observable and clear impact on both access and effort, but support for the hypothesis that money directly influences votes is less clear.

This potential conflict in findings exists because we have not provided a sufficient explanation for why contributions affect votes. The best analogy for campaign contributions is not bribery, as we tend to believe, but, as Clawson et al. (1998) suggest, contributions are more like gifts. As such, contributions do not "buy" votes, but "are given to establish a personal connection, open an avenue for access, and create a generalized sense of obligation" (Clawson et al. 1998, 61). If this is the case, then once a contribution is given, a vote has not been bought, instead the expectation is that at some point some equivalency will be reciprocated. Contributions, then, do not necessarily precede a legislator voting consistently with a group. Instead, money is given in the hopes of creating the bond or obligation which will be repaid however or whenever the legislator can do so. We must attempt to figure out where the obligation to reciprocate is the strongest or the least risky for legislators. Sometimes that means a legislator will provide effort on behalf of the group's interests. Sometimes it means that the legislator will vote with the group on low visibility issues (Clawson et al. 1998). It is also probable that the legislator will reciprocate on critical votes.

Understanding contributions and votes this way illustrates why we have failed to isolate the true effect of donations on the voting behavior of legislators: we have focused our studies of contributions and votes too narrowly, usually studying aggregate member voting scores or individual legislative votes on a small number of bills. However, this new conceptualization suggests that context will affect the relationship.[6] If this is indeed the case, we must both broaden and narrow the focus of our studies. We must broaden our studies by moving beyond federal data to look for other sources that allow the analysis of larger numbers of bills. Concurrently, we must narrow our studies to include a large number of individual votes (as opposed to aggregate vote scores that compile these individual votes into a single measure) that cross both issue area and context. Once each of these aspects of the political context are included in a single model, it becomes clear that what is important is not the number of votes that contributions change, but which votes are changed. Wealthier groups have a disproportionate impact on policy outcomes because their contributions affect those few votes that change the outcome of legislation.

Unfortunately, identifying this type of behavior is extremely difficult. There are two reasons for this. First, even if direct influence peddling does occur, it is illegal for a legislator to allow campaign contributions to directly buy his vote and it is illegal for contributors to make any connection between their donations and specific pieces of legislation. Therefore, both legislators and lobbyists are quite circumspect about even the appearance that money might purchase particular votes.

Second, a *quid pro quo* relationship between legislators and lobbyists probably does not exist except in rare and unusual circumstances. When testifying on behalf of Proposition 208 (a campaign finance reform measure in California) Barry Keene, the former Democratic Majority Leader of the California State Senate, put it this way, "I believe a lot of it is unconscious. Over a period of time, you build up denial mechanisms for what you're doing or why you're doing it ... It's almost Pavlovian. The more you do it, the less wrong it seems to feel" (Bernstein 1997). In other words, legislators and lobbyists are not disingenuous when they argue that money does not buy votes. Contributions can have an independent influence on voting behavior even when participants are not aware of it. The theory presented here identifies the manner in which there can be a connection between money and votes even without conscious participation by either party.

Finally, because of the ambiguous nature of gifts and reciprocity, specific instances of such behavior are difficult to identify in the legislative arena—especially in the U.S. Congress. Therefore, this analysis uses data from the California State Senate, where the information needed to identify the relationships of interest is more readily available. The justification for the use of California data is discussed in Chapter 2.

In addition, the ambiguity of the gifts relationship means that several types of evidence must be presented in support of the theory. In Chapter 3, evidence is provided supporting this theory of legislative behavior by presenting a case study involving former State Senator John Doolittle, currently a U.S. congressman, and the California Trial Lawyers Association (CTLA). During the 1987–88 electoral cycle, Doolittle received $40,000 from the CTLA. This amount is remarkable primarily because of who Doolittle is: a very conservative Republican not known for his cooperation or flexibility. To make the situation even more atypical, the CTLA tends to support liberal Democrats and it was the 1987–88 election cycle when Doolittle had his most serious Democratic challenger, Roy Whiteaker. Although Doolittle spent just over one million dollars to defend his seat, Whiteaker still received 46 percent of the vote. Theoretically, the CTLA could have spent their money to defeat rather than support Doolittle and they had every reason to want to do so. In the 1987–88 session, he supported their agenda in the Judiciary Committee less often than any other member of the committee. Why would they have contributed so much money to him under these conditions?

Evidence suggests that, although Doolittle failed to support the CTLA most of the time, it was because he could do so without threatening its interests. On most of the CTLA bills that received a vote in the Judiciary Committee in 1987–88, Doolittle's vote was not required for the lawyers to achieve their goals on tort reform, because they were Democratic supporters who generally got their way in the Democratically controlled Senate. However, it appears that Doolittle was willing to abstain from legislation when the CTLA needed him to do so. An anecdote regarding a single bill suggests that Doolittle was willing to provide the trial lawyers with a critical abstention when their Democratic supporters on the committee were unable or unwilling to cast their vote with the CTLA on a tort issue. These rare critical votes on tort reform would have been sufficient reason for the CTLA to support Doolittle's campaign.

Did this relationship exist because they were buying his votes in a *quid pro quo* exchange? It is possible. But, although Doolittle rarely supported the CTLA interests, many of those around the capitol considered him to be a friend of the trial lawyers—even given the meager assistance he offered. Although he was quite conservative and rarely provided vote support for the group, he was an attorney and was made a member of the Judiciary Committee during his first term in office. Because of this, it is likely that the trial lawyers initially contributed to him to develop a relationship with someone to whom they might want access. Perhaps it was this friendship, built upon campaign contributions, which led to his willingness to provide help when they required it.

Although the gift relationship can create friendships like those between Doolittle and the CTLA, these types of relationships do not just occur between a single legislator and a single interest group. It could occur between almost any legislator or interest group when the situation is right. When legislators know how important a vote is to a contributing group's goals, they are more responsive to that pressure because, to continue the analogy, the desire to reciprocate will be the strongest in that situation. It makes sense that the more important his vote to a favorable outcome of the bill (as defined by the donor), the more responsibility he feels to respond to the group's concerns. Under these circumstances and the corresponding increased pressure, members will be less willing to vote against contributor interests than on bills when their votes are not critical.

In Chapter 4, I present four additional case studies to illustrate this point. The first two show the subtlety of this relationship and how the vote context can affect the connection between money and voting behavior. In the first case, although pressure was strong from groups on both sides of Assembly Bill (AB) 1500, it was clear to legislators to which group the bill was most important. However, even though the bill was voted on in both houses of the California legislature, contributions only appear to influence votes in the Senate, where the bill passed by the smallest possible margin, a simple majority. In the Assembly, where the bill passed by a larger margin, contributions were not a significant factor in the decision making process. In the second case, two similar bills were introduced into the senate and, once again, contributions only appear to have had an influence on voting in the critical vote situation.

The final two cases illustrate situations where money did not influence voting behavior, even when the votes were critical. In the first, groups avoided a policy change for almost a decade, but when public opinion shifted and the issue became highly visible to the constituencies of the voting legislators, the groups were unable to influence the necessary critical votes. The last case describes a critical vote on a bill where contributions are determined not to be a deciding factor in the vote decision because of the unique relationship the dominant group had with the majority party.

However, it is not enough to show that the relationship between contributions and votes existed between one member and one group or even on a set of critical case studies. For contributions to have a significant impact on legislative outcomes over time, there must be a general pattern of behavior that covers many groups and legislators. In Chapter 5, I use the California data to examine whether the behavior exhibited in the Doolittle case and the critical case studies is generalizable by using votes on 102 bills from the California Senate Committee on Governmental Organization. I show that, controlling for other factors affecting legislative votes, contributions do have an independent impact on behavior when we study a large number of bills. However, what is more important for the purposes of this study, I show that the relationship between contributions and votes is driven by the critical nature of those votes. Once critical votes are separated from those that are not critical, it is clear that contributions only influence behavior when a member's vote is crucial to the outcome of legislation and have no effect on noncritical votes at all.

Committee characteristics, such as jurisdiction and types of clientele groups, also affect the relationship posited here. That is why, in Chapter 6, I present additional analyses using randomly selected bills from all but one of the eighteen Senate committees.[7] These analyses highlight an important point: contributions affect voting in all committees. What differentiates committees is how readily this relationship is revealed. Although critical votes are influenced by contributions in all committees, in some committee types that influence is obvious even when analyzing all votes.

Finally, in Chapter 7, I outline the implications of this research for our understanding of the role of interest groups in policy making and for the future of campaign finance and legislative reform. The manner in which contributions influence legislative behavior has ramifications for the way we attempt to deal with the problem. For example, if there is an obvious and direct connection between money and votes, Representative Doolittle's suggestion regarding the immediate disclosure of contributions in a way that is both accessible and useful to constituents may be sufficient to deal with the problem. If, however, the relationship is more complex, as suggested here, then providing more information to citizens will not be enough. In that case, only changing the finance system in significant and rudimentary ways can alter the relationship.

## 4. Conclusion

The general public and political observers believe that campaign contributions have a significant and negative effect on the level of representation received by the general public and this perception is fed by the increasing number of scandals involving contributors and politicians. Moreover, political scientists have found a relationship between campaign contributions and the level of access accorded to various groups and the amount of effort that legislators put forth on behalf of those same contributors. However, we have not determined whether there is a consistent relationship between contributions and legislative voting behavior. And, until we understand this relationship in greater detail, we will have difficulty understanding the true impact groups have on policy making. Neither will we know how to institute reforms to alter this negative bias while retaining the positive role that interest groups play in the representative process.

The ambiguous findings on voting behavior are the result of an incorrect conceptualization of the relationship. We assume that the relationship resembles a market and, therefore, unless contributions have a consistent impact on legislative voting behavior, their effect is irrelevant. This is not the case. Contributions, for whatever reason they are given, create a relationship between the relevant actors much like gifts create relationships between individuals. Consequently, contributions influence only a few votes. However, they are a significant and potentially negative factor because the votes they affect are critical to the outcome of legislation.

If this theory is correct, it not only clarifies the relationship that political scientists and other observers of the political process find so compelling, but it also provides some explanation as to why the connection between contributions and votes is so difficult to identify: we assume that a large number of votes must be changed and that the decision to trade money for votes must be a conscious decision. However, there is nothing in the conception of the political world presented here that requires that the connection between contributions and votes be conscious on anyone's part. Only four simple political truths must be accepted.

First, some governmental advocates believe that their political contributions provide them with something—usually access—and, therefore, contribute to political campaigns. Second, those same advocates lobby especially hard when a bill is marginal than when it is almost surely going to succeed. Third, advocates lobby especially hard those legislators they believe can be persuaded to align themselves with the lobbyists. To this end, they increase pressure on those to whom they have contributed to play on the sense of obligation created by their contributions. Fourth, and finally, the legislators take account of the relationship that they have developed with interest groups when making their decision and are especially concerned with this when their vote is critical.

Past studies imply that for money to buy votes in a manner that undermines democratic equality, the parties involved must knowingly participate. This is not the case. Money can advantage wealthier groups to the disadvantage of society as a whole even when those participating are not knowingly involved in vote buying. If the activities are unconscious even to the participants, then we must be able to independently identify when contributions are likely to be a deciding factor in decision making.

Finally, the relationship between contributions and votes has been difficult to identify because the instances where they are directly connected are relatively rare. Critical votes make up a small percentage of the votes cast by legislators, but this does not make them irrelevant to policy outcomes. Because critical votes by definition determine the outcome of policy, a single vote can change the political realities of an interest group or a large segment of society. Cumulatively, critical votes are a significant aspect of legislative policy making because they determine the passage or failure of legislation.

# 2

# The Effects of Contributions on the Representative Process

"A gift that does nothing to enhance solidarity is a contradiction."

Mary Douglas[1]

In this chapter, I discuss the campaign contributions literature in more detail, focusing on the relationship between interest group donations and legislative voting behavior. I argue that we misunderstand the relationship between contributions and votes because both our conceptualization of the relationship and our normative views of contributions are incomplete. In turn, our limited theoretical and normative outlook is sustained by serious deficiencies in the available data.

The initial problem is the assumption that the relationship between campaign contributions and legislative votes is similar to a market relationship, where the two actors explicitly agree upon an exchange. If it is a market relationship, contributions will influence a large number of votes or legislators' aggregate vote scores, because the contributions are supposed to be buying those votes as part of a *quid pro quo* agreement. Normatively, we assume that if contributions have a negative effect on representative democracy, they must influence a large number of votes or a legislator's voting patterns.

However, the relationship between contributions and votes is not a *quid pro quo* market interaction between donor and recipient, but instead the more appropriate analogy is the less concrete and longer term relationship of obligation and reciprocity (Clawson et al. 1998). If this is the case, then contributions will not change aggregate vote scores or even a large number of a legislator's votes, but will affect a change in voting behavior in specific and relatively rare circumstances. Contributions will only influence votes that are of high value to interest groups and, at the same time, are potentially less costly to legislators because these are the situations that will most logically cue the obligation to reciprocate.

Unfortunately, because of the difficulties inherent in collecting information on money and voting, most studies focus on a small number of interest groups or votes and, therefore, are unable to identify how the voting environment influences this relationship. Once a large number of bills are included in the analysis, models can take account of how the value or costs of a vote influence the connection between money and voting. When this is done, it becomes clear that, from a normative viewpoint, contributions are a significant problem not because of the number of votes they change, but because of which votes they change. Contributions are problematic because the votes they affect are critical to policy outcomes.

In summary, I present a theory that not only clarifies the relationship between contributions and legislative voting, but also has important implications for campaign finance reform. As long as there are differences in the ability of groups to contribute to political campaigns, there is a bias toward larger donors, thus reducing the power of some political groups simply because they lack sizable financial resources.

This chapter is organized into three parts. First, I summarize the many studies of campaign contributions and legislative behavior and illustrate that although we have a well-developed understanding of the effect of contributions on many aspects of legislative behavior, the one connection we have difficulty making is that between money and votes. Second, I argue that the underlying reason this association has not been made (even while making the connection between contributions and other behaviors) is because the prevailing conceptualization of the relationship between contributions and legislative behavior is incorrect. This affects two common expectations about the relationship. This assumption also influences our research designs. Therefore, it is in this second section that I outline the data limitations mentioned above, how they influence our conclusions, and why California data is so well suited for testing this type of relationship. Third, I explain the theory that informs this analysis and discuss what types of votes should be affected if contributions are, in fact, gifts and not bribes.

### 1. Contributions and Legislative Behavior

Political scientists hypothesize four relationships between campaign contributions and legislative action. First, contributions can have an electoral effect. PACs attempt to affect legislative outcomes by helping those who hold issue positions similar to their own gain public office (Saltzman 1987; Wright 1985). Organized interests give money to legislators who hold sympathetic issue positions in an attempt "to employ the legislator or group of legislators that are the least-cost suppliers of [a] desired policy" (Grier and Munger 1986, 352). In this setting, then, contributions do not change behavior, but reward "good" behavior. Legislator characteristics such as committee assignment, party, electoral security, and seniority influence a member's expected votes and actions and these votes and actions are, in turn, a determinant of the campaign contributions a candidate receives from a particular group (Grier and Munger 1986; Wright 1985).

In the second relationship, contributions have an access effect. They facilitate access to officeholders so groups may express their issue positions to members (Austen-Smith 1995; Grenzke 1989; Wright 1990). Although contributions may be given to an individual who is not expected to support a particular interest group, the group still donates money because that individual is expected to win and, because lobbyists require access to be politically effective (Berry 1997; Milbrath 1963), the group will need access to that member once elected.

Using testimony in committees as a measure of access, Leyden (1995) finds that if a group has various "costly resources,"[2] the probability that the group will be able to contact a committee and provide a reason why they should be able to testify on a particular bill increases as well. Contributions, then, do not affect the decision making process except through a group's persuasion techniques.

In the third posited relationship, campaign contributions do not have an impact on votes, per se, but on another important aspect of the policy making process, legislative effort. Hall and Wayman (1990) find that, controlling for all other factors, campaign contributions buy time. In other words, monetary help by interest groups may buy a member's involvement in the bill's movement through committee—debate, amendment activity, etc. (see also Evans 1996). By looking solely at votes, these scholars argue, we miss this more subtle relationship.

In the fourth relationship, contributions have a vote effect (Etzioni 1984; Langbein and Lotwis 1990; Stern 1988; Wilhite and Theilmann 1987).[3] Controlling for the influence of other variables on individual votes (e.g., ideology, party, constituent interest, etc.), campaign contributions have an independent impact on the voting decisions made by members.

This is the relationship that many scholars find particularly interesting because, besides being illegal in many cases, it holds the most negative implications for our understanding of democratic representation. Public policies supported by wealthier groups are more likely to be passed than those preferred by groups with fewer financial resources.

Do the data support these four relationships? There is reason to believe that the contributions/electoral outcome relationship exists. Because contributions to a candidate seem to attract more contributions (Jacobson and Kernell 1981) and campaign spending has a significant impact on election outcomes, particularly for challengers (Jacobson 1978 and 1980), it seems that contributing in an attempt to control election outcomes is a logical strategy. And, with some exceptions (Gopoian 1984; Welch 1980), those who study the electoral effect agree that groups do sometimes use contributions with this strategy in mind (Grier and Munger 1986; Saltzman 1987; Wright 1985).

The access and effort effects have also been widely supported.[4] Not only do those who specifically address access (Austen-Smith 1995; Grenzke 1989; Wright 1990) or effort (Evans 1996; Hall and Wayman 1990) find a relationship, but those who study lobbying strategies find that advocates tend to lobby those who hold similar issue positions to their own, not those who disagree with them (Bauer et al. 1963; Dexter 1969; Matthews 1960; Milbrath 1963; Wright 1990).[5] These lobbying patterns suggest that access and effort are the key components, not changing a member's vote. Empirically, the effort effect is the most strongly supported impact of contributions to date.

However, the results regarding contributions and votes are ambiguous at best. On an anecdotal level, many of those involved in the process believe that contributions influence votes (Birnbaum 2000; Jackson 1990; Stern 1988). Each year, Common Cause cites policies that it believes have been influenced by large donors. For example, in *Paying the Price* (Common Cause 2000), that organization notes that tobacco, gun, gaming, and alcohol groups spent $268 million on lobbying and campaign contributions from 1989 to 2000 and were successful at blocking legislation threatening their interests. In fact, it has almost become a requisite part of the election process for journalists to summarize what policy benefits wealthy donors have received and poorer groups have failed to receive in the past congressional session.[6]

Even some academic studies find support for the connection between money and congressional voting. Frendeis and Waterman (1985) determine that contributions did have a significant effect on vote decisions regarding the passage of trucking deregulation. Wilhite and Theilmann (1987) and Saltzman (1987) find that the impact of labor contributions on labor legislation was both strong and consistent. In addition, Langbein and Lotwis (1990) find evidence for the thesis that contributions affect votes even on highly visible issues like gun control and Fleisher (1993) finds a relationship between contributions and the votes of ideologically moderate members on defense legislation.

Gopoian (1984) studies the contributions patterns of thirty-three different PACs and finds that PACs do not attempt to maximize power or access exclusively, but instead contribute to realize both narrow parochial policy concerns and broad ideological agendas. The contribution patterns he discovers suggest that economic interest groups try to achieve a vote or effort effect. Welch (1980, 115) agrees, stating that the results of his study tend "to support the assumption that an economic interest group contributes in order to obtain political favors, not to affect electoral outcomes."[7]

However, in another study, Welch (1982) concludes that contributions have little to no direct effect on votes regarding dairy price supports[8] and Chappell (1982) finds that contributions are not a statistically significant factor in the vote decision when controlling for other variables. Even in California, where the amount of contributions given is relatively unrestricted,[9] Dow and Endersby (1994) find no relationship between interest group money and votes. And, Wayman (1985) notes that PACs had only a "modest" effect on arms control and defense spending votes in the 1970s and 1980s. In perhaps the most comprehensive study, Wawro (2001) provides a panel analysis of contributions and finds that contributions have a minimal effect on voting. So, in these cases, contributions must have an access, electoral, or effort effect.

It is clear from this brief summary that even while our findings on the access, effort, and electoral effects are relatively consistent, our conclusions about the relationship between contributions and votes diverge greatly. This inconsistency in our findings is created by a misunderstanding of the true relationship between interest groups and legislators: that the exchange of contributions and votes is similar to a market relationship, where one is traded explicitly for the other. In turn, this affects our expectations regarding when and how votes will be affected and, therefore, drives the research designs we develop to study the question.

The expectations are, if money affects votes, then (1) a conscious *quid pro quo* takes place where (2) the money given is to influence a large number of votes. In addition, past research, by necessity, depends upon incomplete data, leading to a misunderstanding of the strategic nature of the relationship between legislators and lobbyists. With a few exceptions, these expectations and data limitations lead studies effectively to ignore the importance of political context and its impact on the relationship between donations and voting behavior. By failing to account for political context, the extent to which contributions directly affect votes is underestimated.

## 1.1 Assumption 1—PACs and the Congressional Supermarket

The first expectation is that for contributions to influence voting, there must be a *quid pro quo* relationship between donors and recipients. For example, one commonly sees references to the buying and selling of votes. The title of Grenzke's (1989) article "Shopping in the Congressional Supermarket" is indicative of this frame of thought, as is McCarty and Rothenberg's (1996) discussion of the "campaign contribution contract" and their emphasis on how both actors attempt to ensure long-term enforcement of those contracts. Wright (1996, 146) describes the most common model of contributions and legislative behavior:

> The legislative model assumes that candidates promise specific legisla-tive services if elected in exchange for campaign contributions and that they honor these agreements if elected. In this respect, there is an explicit quid pro quo between contributions and favors, making contributions essentially legal bribes, or what journalist Brooks Jackson has termed "honest graft."

Wright notes that the purpose of this model is not to argue that the *quid pro quo* actually exists, but helps to define what behaviors we should expect if it does (1996, 148). However, the types of behaviors we should detect if there is a *quid pro quo* are different than those we actually observe.

If the market analogy is appropriate, interest groups provide the necessary campaign dollars to candidates and legislators respond by changing their behavior (almost immediately) on those issues in which the group is interested. However, no matter how the relationship is studied, this behavior has not been found.

Our legal system supports this view as well. It is illegal for a legislator to accept money and then vote a particular way only if there is a direct and obvious connection made between contributions and behavior. Unless there is evidence of a direct trade, prosecutors cannot argue that a deal has been struck and a law has been violated. The Supreme Court decision on the McCain–Feingold campaign finance reform bill reflects this concern. Those in the majority (who upheld the reform) argue that the legislature has the responsi-bility to regulate contributions because of the perception of a *quid pro quo* where the dissenters argue that there is not sufficient evidence of such a relationship (*McConnell v. FEC* 2003). But, although this makes sense in the legal arena, in a theoretical context, it does not.

## 1.2 Assumption 2—Contributions Should Influence a Large Number of Votes

The second expectation is that if contributions successfully influence votes in a *quid pro quo* exchange, they will influence a large number of votes or at least influence voting more often than not. Although no individual specifically states that this is the case, the assumption becomes obvious when studying the language used in this literature.

> Overall, then, there is little basis for concluding that the car dealers "bought their way to happiness" on this issue or that the outcome of the voting in the House was determined by PAC contributions from the NADA [National Automobile Dealers Association].... Although campaign money may have changed a handful of voting decisions, and perhaps solidified a few others, the House would have voted overwhelmingly against the FTC's ruling even if the NADA had contributed no money whatsoever to representatives' election campaigns.
>
> (Wright 1996, 143)

Contributions probably did not change the outcome of the legislation in this one case (and, according to the theory to be presented below, probably did not affect votes either). What this quote illustrates, though, is a general belief that a large number or a majority of votes must change to determine that a relationship exists or for the correlation to be normatively problematic. Wright addresses a single bill that, admittedly, was deemed by observers to have been bought by the interested group. But, because the votes on that bill can be explained by other variables (e.g., ideology), he argues that contributions do not affect votes. This is common in this area of study; we consistently base our conclusions on analyses of few bills (often only one) or votes in a single issue area. Then, when we fail to find a relationship, we argue that contributions must not have an impact on policy making.

One of the reasons to focus on so few bills or votes is because, at the federal level, acquiring interest group positions on a large number of bills is problematic. Group testimony at committee hearings can be used as a measure of group interest in a piece of legislation, but testimony itself is determined partially by group power (Leyden 1995). To create independent measures of interest group positions, each bill and issue area must be studied to determine which groups are apt to be interested. Given limitations of time, this certainly reduces the number of bills that can be included in analyses and, therefore, leads to an overestimation of the access, electoral, or effort arguments and an underestimation of the extent to which contributions directly affect votes.

To avoid this problem and include a large number of votes, many use aggregate vote scores (Davis 1993; Dow and Endersby 1994; Neustadtl 1990; Wilhite and Theilmann 1987). However, when aggregate measures are used as the dependent variable, an inherent assumption is made. The assumption is that an interest group's contribution size will be positively correlated with a member's rate of support in roll call votes if contributions are ever an important factor in the members' decisions. In other words, a member must vote with a group on a regular basis or else he deserves no contributions. However, it may be that the member only votes with the contributing group when his vote is needed. Although he may vote with the group infrequently, his votes may be valuable to the group because of the nature of the environment within which those votes are taking place. In this case, high contributions may correspond to low support scores.

Similarly, Bronars and Lott (1997) argue that if contributions change behavior rather than follow ideology, then retiring legislators should alter their votes because their behavior is no longer shaped by the need for campaign donations. Finding that legislators' actions in their final terms were similar to their activities in their previous terms led these authors to conclude that contributions do not influence legislative action. But, once again, just because patterns of behavior do not change in the aggregate, does not mean that contributions do not influence individual instances of behavior.

Studying one or a few individual votes still misses this relationship. Relations between lobbyists and legislators are ongoing, crossing both issue areas and legislative sessions. Lobbyists interact with members numerous times over the course of a legislative session or over the course of a member's political career, so it is important to understand that the actions taken on a single bill may not be due to the group or member's short-run needs on that individual bill, but due to long-term goals regarding a legislative agenda and career needs. Lobbyists must please their employers (Berry 1997) (e.g., by appearing to accomplish something) and legislators are concerned about reelection and the development of their own power within the institution (Mayhew 1974). Given this understanding, it makes sense that "[o]rganized labor has perhaps twenty votes on their hit list every year, and voting against them two or three times is tolerated" (Senator Tom Eagleton [D-MO] as paraphrased in Smith [1988, 256]). An example of how current data limitations influence our conclusions helps clarify this point.

### 1.3 An Example of the Influence of Data Limitations

Imagine a committee with five members. For any bill to pass, it must be supported with an aye vote by any three of the members and only three of the members. Every member of the committee has a probabilistic understanding of the other members' votes, and even if they did not, they may ask each other what their votes will be. In any event, at some point (when the votes are actually counted) everyone's actions are known.

Consider a situation in this committee in which an interest group has contributed a large sum of money to all the committee members. Only three of them may vote in favor of the bill, and they may be the three most ideologically compatible with the group, but what is not known is important as well: what would the other two members have done if one of the supporting three had chosen to vote "no"?

Pattern A in Table 2.1 shows the relationship past studies were looking for. From this table, we see that although some money was contributed for access purposes, for the most part, campaign contributions bought aye votes. However, once we control for ideological compatibility between members and the contributing group, even that relationship fails to be supported by the data.[10]

Pattern B in Table 2.1, on the other hand, shows quite a different relationship. By examining only this one bill and the contributions made to members of the committee, one would have to agree that contributions do not make a difference. Members received similar amounts of money, but only three supported the group's bill: the same three who are ideologically compatible with the sponsoring group.

However, looking at Table 2.2, it becomes obvious that the contributions to M4 and M5 might indeed be having a significant effect on the policy outcomes relative to that group. Although M4 and M5 vote in support of the group only 33 percent of the time, they are responsible for the passage of the legislation each time they vote aye. When called upon, M4 and M5 cast the deciding vote in favor of the contributing group. Notice, too, that if the group did not contribute to M4 and M5, they would lose 67 percent of the time.

This is a critical point. When studying just one of these bills at a time and looking only at votes and not the outcomes of bills, there is no relationship between contributions and votes because, for any given bill, there is a contributions effect on only one of five votes once ideological compatibility is

**TABLE 2.1** Two Hypothetical Contribution Patterns on the Same Bill

| | Pattern A | |
| --- | --- | --- |
| Member | Vote | Money Contributed ($) |
| M1 (ic) | Y | 1,000 |
| M2 (ic) | Y | 500 |
| M3 (ic) | Y | 750 |
| M4 (nc) | N | 0 |
| M5 (nc) | N | 0 |
| | Pattern B | |
| Member | Vote | Money Contributed ($) |
| M1 (ic) | Y | 1,000 |
| M2 (ic) | Y | 500 |
| M3 (ic) | Y | 750 |
| M4 (nc) | N | 1,000 |
| M5 (nc) | N | 1,000 |

(ic) denotes that the member is ideologically compatible with the contributing group
(nc) denotes that the member is not ideologically compatible with the contributing group

**TABLE 2.2** Committee Votes on Six Bills

| Member | Contributions ($) | Bill 1 | Bill 2 | Bill 3 | Bill 4 | Bill 5 | Bill 6 | Total Support Score (%) |
|---|---|---|---|---|---|---|---|---|
| M1 (ic) | 1,000 | Y | Y | Y | N | Y | Y | 83 |
| M2 (ic) | 500 | Y | Y | N | Y | N | Y | 67 |
| M3 (ic) | 750 | Y | Y | Y | Y | Y | N | 83 |
| M4 (nc) | 1,000 | N | N | Y | N | N | Y | 33 |
| M5 (nc) | 1,000 | N | N | N | Y | Y | N | 33 |

considered. Even when studying all six bills, contributions change only four votes of a possible thirty. To understand the importance of the four votes, it is vital to understand why those four votes changed.

What this example shows is that although some contributions may affect votes and others buy access, the extent to which (1) voting behavior is affected by money and (2) this behavior affects policy outcomes is severely underestimated. By misjudging these relationships, we overestimate the access effect to the detriment of truly understanding the vote effect. This is illustrated by the fact that although contributions in the example only affect 13.3 percent of the votes cast on these six bills, they affect 67 percent of the outcomes. Using only the former statistic leads to a belief that contributions have little to no impact, however, using the latter illustrates the true influence of political donations.

## 1.4  Using California Data

Unfortunately, there is no way to access all group positions on bills at the federal level. Although obtaining data on interest group contributions to members of the U.S. Congress is quite straightforward,[11] finding group positions on a large number of bills is not. Interest group positions on bills are available in the records of testimony given in congressional committees, but those records do not provide the positions of those groups that have a position but were not allowed to testify. And, to the extent that testimony by groups is in and of itself a measure of group influence (Leyden 1995) and not solely of group interest in a particular piece of legislation, it is difficult to separate out the effect of contributions as an independent measure of group power. Therefore, federal information does not include data on group positions that is not already affected by relative group influence.

This problem is solved by using data from the California Senate rather than data from the U.S. Congress. Records kept by the California legislature are more conducive to studying the relationship between contributions and votes because each bill that receives a committee vote also gets a committee analysis that lists the groups that have taken a position on that bill prior to the vote, whether that position be support, oppose, or neutral. Having one's group position listed on the analysis is less likely to be related to group resources than is congressional testimony. All a group must do to be listed is send a letter stating their position to the committee prior to the day of the vote. Table 2.3

**TABLE 2.3** Total Amount of Money Contributed to Members of the Senate Committee on Governmental Organization and the Number of Members to Whom Money Was Contributed, by Group

| Name of Group | Senate Contributions ($) | Number of Members |
|---|---|---|
| Alliance of Latin Business Association | — | — |
| Amador Vintners Association | — | — |
| ARCO | 34,850 | 9 |
| Associated General Contractors of California | 8,125 | 10 |
| Bed and Breakfast Innkeepers of Northern California | — | — |
| California Agricultural Museum, Inc. | — | — |
| California Association of Homes for the Aging | — | — |
| California Beer Wholesalers Association | 62,550 | 11 |
| California Common Cause | — | — |
| California Council of Civil Engineers | 11,500 | 9 |
| California Council on Mental Health | — | — |
| California Homeless Coalition | — | — |
| California Professional Firefighters | 28,530 | 10 |
| California State Association of Electrical Workers | 700 | 2 |
| California State Firemen's Association | 8,700 | 8 |
| California Taxpayers Association | — | — |
| California Union of Safety Employees | 4,130 | 5 |
| Californians for Drug Free Youth | — | — |
| Committee on Moral Concerns | — | — |
| General Vineyard Services | — | — |
| Guild Wineries and Distributors | — | — |
| Hispanic Business Network | — | — |
| International Alliance of Theatrical Stage Employees | — | — |
| ISC Wines of California | — | — |
| Kenwood Vineyards | — | — |
| Los Angeles Turf Club | 35,200 | 11 |
| McDowell Valley Vineyards | — | — |
| NAACP | — | — |
| Orange County Employees Association | 1,500 | 1 |
| Pacific Merchant Shipping Association | 2,550 | 3 |
| Retired Officers Association (North Solano County) | — | — |
| San Bernardino Chamber of Commerce | — | — |
| Society of the Plastics Industry | — | — |
| State Alliance for Board of Equalization Reform | — | — |
| United Way of California | — | — |
| Western Center on Law and Poverty | — | — |
| YMCA of South Pasadena and San Moreno | — | — |

gives a short list of some of the groups used in this analysis and their contributions to members of the committees that I studied. Although this is not conclusive evidence, it seems reasonable to assume that group resources are unrelated to having one's position listed in the committee analysis. In fact, a full 70 percent of the 37 groups listed here, which took a position on at least one bill in the analysis, contributed no money at all to the members of the committee.[12]

California data have many other advantages as well. First, at the time of this study, California campaign laws did not set limits on the amount of campaign contributions given by a single group and, thus, allowed for more variance in the contributions variable. At the federal level, contributions are limited and many groups may give the maximum amount, which truncates the data at zero and at the upper limit.

Although the distributions of contributions at the federal and state level are quite similar, there are more extreme donations in the California data than in the federal data because of the federal contributions limits. Whether the impact of the largest of the California contributions are substantively different from the largest of the federal contributions is an empirical question that will not be addressed in this analysis. Meanwhile, if the relationship between level of campaign contributions and voting behavior does exist, the lack of a cap on contributions allows us an opportunity to see the full range of behaviors (Dow and Endersby 1994).

Second, there is a germaneness rule in the California legislature. The California Constitution requires that each bill introduced in the legislature concern a single subject.[13] This is generally referred to as the "single subject rule." In addition, California Senate rules require that all amendments to bills must be germane to that topic.[14] Unlike members of the U.S. House of Representatives, the members of the California legislature strictly adhere to this rule.

The U.S. Congress, on the other hand, often considers bills that concern more than one issue. Indeed, nongermane amendments are frequently added to "kill" or "save" a bill.[15] This causes two problems. If a bill covers more than one issue area, it conflates the issues on which any one legislator may be basing his vote, making it difficult to decide whether constituency, party, or contributions have had an effect. It also leads to the problems of strategic voting behaviors that I do not wish to address here (as outlined by Enelow 1981).

A third benefit of California as a case is that it has one of the most professionalized legislatures in the United States outside Washington, D.C. (Everson 1991). Although its institutional characteristics may make it much easier to model than the U.S. Congress, many of the attributes of the California legislature are as similar to the U.S. Congress as we can find in the United States. Because of the size and the economic and demographic diversity of the state, the California legislature and the U.S. Congress are similar in terms of

(1) the issues they address, (2) the groups that contribute and their contributions strategies, and (3) the professional goals of the legislators.[16]

In short, the problem of determining group positions on bills independent of group power can be addressed by using California data rather than U.S. congressional data. Although this means that the analysis is open to criticisms regarding the generalizability of California as a case, there is reason to believe that California is, in many key respects, similar to the federal case.

In the next section, I outline a relatively simple theory of contributions and committee votes that better explains the interest group and legislative behavior identified in this example. I argue that, given this new insight, it is clear that contributions influence votes, though not on a consistent basis. And, even though contributions only influence individual votes at the margins, the impact is great in regards to political outcomes.

## 2. A New Theory of Contributions and Voting Behavior

The theory presented here begins from an important theoretical contribution to the interest group literature advanced by Clawson et al. (1998). They argue that campaign contributions are not a legal form of bribery or part of a market relationship where one good (money) is explicitly traded for another (legislative behavior). Instead, they are similar to gifts (Clawson et al. 1998).

This is not to say that donations are altruistic—quite the opposite. Instead, contributions do not purchase votes per se, but they provide the basis for a relationship on which future behavior may be grounded. Gifts are given without some concrete understanding of what will be received in return, but they do engender a sense of obligation that something must be reciprocated (Mauss 1923 [1990]).

> In markets each exchange involves its own reciprocal: I give you $15.98 and you give me the last album by Ani DiFranco. Each accepts this as a fair and even trade; there is no expectation that one or the other of us will later do something additional in order to complete this exchange.... A gift, however, creates a more enduring relationship. From the moment I receive your gift we are bound to each other; me by the (implicit but very real) obligation to provide you with an object or service, you by the (unstated but nonetheless real) expectation of receiving an equivalent. Thus gifts create more dense and enduring social relationships than market exchanges.
>
> (Clawson et al. 1998, 34)

Clawson et al. argue that contributions from business interests are a form of gift giving in an attempt to create a relationship between their corporation and various legislators. This relationship should influence a legislator's thought process in two basic ways: it should make the legislator aware of the company and its interests and it should create a sense of obligation to reciprocate the gift or kindness received.[17]

It is quite probable that legislators view contributions this way. Former California State Senator Patrick Johnston (D-Stockton) noted that campaign contributions provide for a relationship between two political actors.

> All of a sudden, they appear to be your friends. They show up at your parties and they give you money. If a situation arises where their interests are at stake and you cannot decide which way to vote you have to decide somehow and you will probably give your friends the benefit of the doubt.
>
> (Johnston 2000)

Legislators, therefore, do not vote with their contributors because they give them money, but because they feel a connection with that group based on a relationship of which money is an important part.

Former Congressman Thomas Downey (D-NY) notes the following:

> I think there are members who might be more swayed by the friends who raised them some money. But you can't get away from the reality that ... in today's climate, almost everything you do is watched. So, it's going to be very difficult for you to have a voting record that takes you down one path that has nothing to do with your constituency.... But sure, if you are wondering about the benefit of the doubt, clearly the benefit of the doubt is going to go to somebody who has been helpful to you.
>
> (As quoted in Schram 1995)

### 3. The Relationship between Contributions and Votes as a Gift Exchange

The relationship between donors and recipients of campaign contributions resembles a gift relationship in three important ways. First, gift giving is a form of exchange that takes the place of a market where a market does not or cannot exist (Douglas in the foreword to Mauss 1990; Mauss 1923 [1990]). Because it is illegal to specifically exchange contributions for votes, the market, by law, cannot work in this circumstance. However, it is in the interest of both groups and legislators to maintain long-term relationships. Both achieve something of importance, besides money, from their interactions (e.g., information, access). The gift of contributions or the behavior that is reciprocated creates the bond between them that maintains this crucial relationship over time. It is a relationship that is impossible to preserve in any enforceable way.

Second, individuals give gifts to stabilize relationships (Simmel 1950), especially vulnerable relationships (Caplow 1982). They use gifts to reduce the uncertainty of the behavior of the other actor (Clawson et al. 1998). Because no market exists between contributions and votes, each participant is especially vulnerable to changes in the other's behavior. This bond is important even for those players in the political process who already have power, which explains why wealthy groups continue to participate in the process of contributions even when it does not provide a *quid pro quo* exchange.

> Until a system of mechanisms automatically ensuring the reproduction of the established order is constituted, the dominant agents cannot be content with letting the system that they dominate follow its own course in order to exercise durable domination; they have to work directly, daily, personally, to produce and reproduce conditions of domination which even then are never entirely uncertain…. They cannot appropriate the labor, services, goods, homage and respect of others without "winning" them personally, "tying" them, in short, creating a bond between persons.
>
> (Bourdieu 1997a)

The gift analogy also explains how contributions influence behavior when they are rarely large enough to use as a threat against legislators. They do so by creating a bond between the two actors who then desire to act in a particular way to maintain the friendship. In the words of Downey and Johnston in the examples above, legislators give the benefit of the doubt to their friends because of their relationship—not the money, although the relationship is likely built on the exchange of gifts. Perhaps this is why Bronars and Lott (1997) find no change in the behavior of legislators in their last term of office. These lawmakers continue to support donors' interests because they want to support their friends, but they would not have been friends had the money not been exchanged.

In addition, gifts are useful when developing new relationships with potential exchange partners (Carmichael and MacLeod 1997; Gouldner 1973). "[B]y imposing costs at the beginning of a relationship, [one] can support cooperation even in markets where cheaters never get caught" (Carmichael and MacLeod 1997, 485) or, in this case, where agreements are not enforceable. That campaign donors often provide new legislators with substantial contributions immediately after they are first elected to office would be consistent with this understanding of donations as gifts (Gordon 2003).

Third, the literature on gift giving emphasizes the conflicts created when a potential recipient refuses a gift. This is considered in many societies and circumstances to be unacceptable behavior. "To refuse to give, to fail to invite, just as to refuse to accept, is tantamount to declaring war; it is to reject the bond of alliance and commonality" (Mauss 1923 [1990]). Simply to give or to accept a gift is to admit that one is agreeing to participate in a relationship with the other. To refuse to do so is to state that the other is unworthy of friendship or alliance. This symbolism pertains to the giving and receiving of campaign contributions as well (Clawson et al. 1998). Sometimes legislators return campaign contributions to groups that are deemed unacceptable or illegitimate by their electoral constituency. This explains why some legislators will refuse to take or will give back contributions from tobacco companies or other "unworthy" groups. For example, during his presidential campaign, former U.S. Senator Robert Dole (R-KS) returned contributions to a gay Republican group—contributions that had been actively solicited by his campaign—as part of his strategy of shifting to the right of the ideological spectrum (*The Sacramento Bee* 1995, B6). Former Senate Majority Leader George Mitchell (D-ME) called the reaction to similar behavior "an interesting insight into human nature."

> Some of the most vigorous criticism I got and the worst chewing-out I got was from people whose contributions I returned. Very interesting. People really called me up and gave me hell: "What's the matter, isn't my money good enough for you? How come you accepted money from someone else?"
>
> (As quoted in Schram 1995)

The symbolism and obligation inherent in the gift itself, even if not recip-rocated, is taken quite seriously by political candidates, interest groups, and the electorate.

## 4. How the Gift Analogy Informs Our Understanding of Contributions and Legislative Behavior

The fact that the contribution relationship is similar to a gift relationship in a series of ways does not necessarily make the analogy useful for comprehending legislative and interest group behavior. However, understanding the types of behaviors and relationships that gift giving engenders provides important insights into the interactions between campaign donors and recipients and the impact they have on each other's behavior.

### 4.1 Lack of Visible Enforcement Does Not Mean Lack of Power

Clawson et al. (1998) note that power is viewed incorrectly in the context of donors and recipients of campaign dollars. They argue that power is not simply the ability to get someone to do something they would not do otherwise, as suggested by Weber, but the ability to change the nature of the political arena in a manner that provides incentives for other players to act in your interest. In other words, business interests are powerful not because they use their contributions to buy legislators or bribe them to vote a particular way, but because they can create situations and relationships that make legislators feel it is reasonable to support the goals of their organization.

Political scientists hold the view that if contributions do not force legislators to do something they would not do otherwise, they are not influential. For example, we question whether interest groups or legislators punish one another for violating conditions of their "contract" (Engel and Jackson 1998; McCarty and Rothenberg 1996). However, it is pretty clear that contributions are rarely large enough to be used as a "stick" with which to threaten legislators (Wilhite and Theilmann 1987, 267). If, with their contributions, they were forcing legislators to vote or behave counter to the legislator's own interests, it would take more than $5,000 to do so. Instead, what campaign contributions buy from interest groups are two products that are crucial to their influence in the political system: (1) a relationship based upon a sense of obligation or reciprocity and (2) legitimacy to take part in the policy making game.

However, I diverge from Clawson et al. in that I argue that this conceptualization of campaign contributions does not just apply to businesses because of their particular character and unique role in the legislative process. Nor does the gift relationship only influence the nondecisions, effort, and access that they address in their analysis. In fact, their conceptualization provides the basis for understanding why findings regarding contributions and voting behavior are so disjointed. In addition, and most critically, it furnishes the groundwork for a general theory of donations and behavior.

### 4.2  Look for Long-Term Relationships

The sociological literature on gift giving states that contributions are a part of a long-term and ongoing relationship between legislators and donors. Clawson et al. note that a market relationship consists of one exchange at a time where money is traded for a good and the exchange ends. Money is given to support a legislator during an election and the legislator's behavior should be affected during the next legislative session. However, relationships based on friendship and gifts are much more extensive. We may receive a gift from a friend and we are not expected to rush out immediately and purchase a gift of equal value in exchange. Instead, we receive a gift and it creates an obligation that we reciprocate at some point in the future when it is appropriate.

Bourdieu (1997b) argues that it is the lapse of time between gift and reciprocity that makes it appear as though gifts are altruistic, even when they are actually quite self-interested.

In other words, the interval that makes it possible to experience the objective exchange as a discontinuous series of free and generous acts is what makes gift exchange viable and acceptable by facilitating and favoring self-deception, a lie told to oneself, as the condition of the coexistence of recognition and misrecognition of the logic of the exchange.... But it is clear that individual self-deception is only possible because it is supported by collective self-deception.

(Bourdieu 1997b, 232)

This explains the general failure to recognize a relationship between contributions and legislative behavior. If the relationship between contributions and votes is conceptualized as market behavior and reciprocal behavior does not occur quickly and concretely after the first action, we determine that there is no relationship. However, when the behavior is put into the context of a gift, the timeline for the reciprocal behavior is extended. The vote given in return may occur much later than the original contribution.[18]

The gift analogy allows for behaviors to appear relatively unrelated primarily because of the inherent inefficiency of gift giving. A gift is given with some expectation, but the giver does not know when or how it will be reciprocated (although they may have a good idea) or even whether it will be reciprocated at all. Therefore, if a relationship between contributions and votes is to be found, we must determine those circumstances when reciprocity is likely to occur within some significant time period.

Therefore, although many scholars argue that they have found evidence to the contrary (e.g., Gopoian 1984), it is important to take account of the possibility that short-term losses may sometimes be taken by both legislators and lobbyists to ensure long-term policy success. Therefore, a member may vote against the group on the bill we study, but perhaps it is because their vote is not necessary for the group to achieve their goals or because there is a high potential for constituency anger on behalf of the vote. On another bill, where the group's goals rest on the member's actions or it is less costly for the legislator to support the group, it is possible that the member votes in support of the donor's interests. If votes are gifts, they will not necessarily be given by the legislator on an ongoing and regular basis. Instead, reciprocity can come at any point in the legislative process that is particularly important to the donor or less costly to the legislator. Those are reasonable circumstances for reciprocation to occur.

It should be noted that this does not mean that interest groups will not punish legislators for "bad" votes on important legislation. Research has shown that interest groups may use punishment as a strategy, but such punishment tends to be measured and short term (Jackson and Engel 2003) illustrating that interest groups take account of the long-term, reciprocal nature of their relationship with legislators.

### 4.3 The Value of the Behavior Matters

If a vote is given in an obligatory, rather than a market, exchange for contributions and the relationship between the donor and recipient is a potentially long one, it is vital to determine when reciprocity on the part of the legislator will occur. Therefore, the value of the vote becomes crucial. For example, contributing groups do not threaten their existence by their donations, so it is unrealistic to expect a legislator to provide services to the group that could endanger the future of his career. If any group is completely funding the election of a candidate, perhaps they could purchase every vote of importance made by that legislator. This may be what would happen if there were no contributions limits and the relationship took place in the context of a formal market. But, this is clearly not the case. At the federal level, contributions are limited at a relatively low amount compared to the total cost of campaigns. Even in California, where contributions were unlimited at the time of this analysis, the average contribution over a two-year period from any single group to any single legislator was less than $7,000. Therefore it is unrealistic to expect contributions to affect legislators' important votes or even their general voting patterns.

What aspects of a vote's value affect whether it will be influenced by contributions? Neither those votes that are of low value to the group nor those votes that are of high cost to the legislator should be affected. I discuss each below.

### 4.3.1 Votes with Low Cost to Legislators—Low Visibility Issues. One of the reasons there is such a strong and consistent relationship between contributions and behaviors like access and effort is because of the low visibility of these behaviors. They are relatively easy to give in exchange for the gift of a contribution because they are not as potentially costly as votes; they are not as visible or as concrete and therefore are more easily explained away if constituents are unhappy. Yet, they are quite valuable to interest groups.

It is also generally accepted that contributions affect voting behavior on less visible issues and at less visible stages in the policy process (Evans 1986 and 1996; Jones and Keiser 1987; Langbein and Lotwis 1990; Neustadtl 1990; Schroedel 1986). It is to control for issue visibility that so many studies of contributions take place at the committee level where constituents are less aware of the voting process (Evans 1996; Hall and Wayman 1990) or attempt to control for the media attention given to a particular bill (Jones and Keiser 1987; Neustadtl 1990).

If Mayhew (1974) is correct that the electoral incentive is the primary incentive for legislative behavior, constituent opinion on a salient and visible issue should be the primary concern of the legislator. Regardless of the number of contributions they might risk, members will vote with their constituencies because of the negative electoral effects of not doing so.

For example, rarely will any amount of contributions or television campaign advertising overcome a "wrong" vote on an issue such as abortion or gun control.[19] This point is made explicitly by Stern (1988) and is why many study votes at the least visible stage in the political process—the committee (Evans 1986 and 1996; Jones and Keiser 1987; Neustadtl 1990; Schroedel 1986).[20]

The impact of visibility on voting behavior has been so well documented because it is an important variable that affects the value that a legislator places on a vote by raising the potential costs paid for a wrong vote. Therefore, I study committee level behavior to analyze those votes that are least visible to the voting members' constituencies. Legislators feel less obligated to return a vote for contributions when an issue is highly visible, because personal interests will be stronger incentives than donor interests and no legal contribution will be large enough to overcome that calculus. In addition, although they may still lobby such members, successful group advocates will probably choose not to pressure legislators who are so conflicted.

*4.3.2 Votes with High Value to Donors—Critical Votes.* A member will not vote with a contributing group every time his constituents have no salient opinion on a bill or every time a vote is taken in committee. Although there is no reason to believe that specific votes, except a special few, have any salience with the general public at all (Abramowitz 1980; Stokes and Miller 1966), election outcomes may be dependent on legislator reputations (Fenno 1978), and reputation, in turn, may be dependent upon general voting behavior (Erikson 1990; Langbein and Lotwis 1990). Consequently, the vote context must be considered. The extent to which a member's vote is crucial to the outcome of a piece of legislation is one of the main determinants of the value that a lobbyist puts on that vote. Indeed, the formal literature has noted the importance and value of critical or swing votes. A legislator's ability or propensity to be a swing vote has been one of the ways in which scholars have measured relative power (Riker and Niemi 1962; Shapley and Shubik 1954), because of the ability of these votes to change the outcome of legislative policy making.[21]

How do legislators know when a critical vote is going to occur? There are three ways this information is made available to voting members. First, voting in committees is sequential, not simultaneous. The role is called and each member either casts a vote or abstains and at any time in the roll taking process can change that vote or add or remove that vote from the roll. As the votes come in on a bill, the potentially critical member can see whether or not that vote is necessary for passage. Second, prior to voting, members receive clues about the actions of others by the questions those legislators ask of witnesses during testimony on the bill. Although this information is fallible, it does provide some input as to how close the vote will probably be.

Third, the most important information that members receive about the critical nature of their vote is from the lobbyists themselves. One of the roles lobbyists play in the political process is to provide information to members regarding both the political and policy effects of legislation (Berry 1977; Milbrath 1963; Ornstein 1978). It makes sense that lobbyists also provide information about the probability of a bill's passage and the future votes of other members, especially if they know that members support them more readily when a vote is critical.

Whether this behavior actually occurs is an empirical question, but anecdotal evidence provides some support. An aide in the California State Assembly notes that lobbyists often provide members with information on the value and necessity of their vote. This behavior can occur during the vote process. "When lobbyists see a vote going against them they will send messages to the members to let them know their vote is critical—that the group needs their support on this one."[22]

Lobbyists often find it in their interest to pass this information on prior to a vote as well. They use this information in an attempt to consolidate their support. While waiting in a member's office immediately prior to a floor vote on state regulations regarding earthquake insurance, I witnessed a group of insurance lobbyists making the rounds of legislators who had yet to commit on the bill. The question that was being put to wavering members at that time was: "If we get within three votes of passage, can we count on your support to put us over?" In other words, if the bill only needs a few critical votes, are you willing to provide one of them?[23]

A California lobbyist explains why this is the case.

There are some members who want to support you but, for some reason, cannot do so all the time. Perhaps they want to be seen as independent or they don't want their constituents to think of them as a good vote on _____. There are other members that will only vote with you on your one important bill of the year. You need to let them know when those votes are coming up and when their vote is important.

In fact, some evidence has been provided that campaign contributions have a larger impact on the individual votes of moderate members when the outcome of a bill is decided by a small margin (Fleisher 1993). However, I believe that campaign contributions have a larger impact on critical votes (those that determine the outcome of legislation) regardless of the ideology of the voting member because the inherent power of these votes makes them so valuable (Riker 1962; Shapley and Shubik 1954). A single member's vote, when the outcome is unanimous, is less important to a lobbyist than that same member's vote when it means the difference between success and defeat and so this is when the effect of contributions should be the strongest.

## 4.4 Institutional Effects on the Relationship

If the value of a vote is important to understanding those circumstances when legislators feel obligated to provide a service to a donor, we should also look to potential institutional constraints on this behavior. Specifically, when studying committees in an attempt to control for the visibility of legislative behavior, one must also take account of the possibility that contributions have a different relationship with votes depending upon the jurisdiction of the committee being studied. The characteristics of various committee jurisdictions may have an impact on the willingness of legislators to support group interests and the expectation of interest groups regarding a return gift. Each of these important characteristics are discussed in more detail in Chapter 6, but the basic arguments are outlined here as well.

### 4.4.1 Committee Jurisdiction and Legislative Behavior. We have long been interested in how committee jurisdictions affect the relationship between legislators and their various constituencies. First, Cox and McCubbins (1993, 188–200) find that committees who face "a more heterogenous group of lobbyists on a regular basis" tend to be more representative of the house as a whole. On the other hand, committees with homogeneous clientele groups and whose decisions influence the districts of a small, select group of legislators are less representative of the house. We also know that committee jurisdictions influence the types of groups that characterize a committee's policy making environment. For example, committees with fragmented or broad jurisdictions have a larger number of diverse groups interested in their activities (Deering and Smith 1997).

In turn, the groups that define the constituency of a particular committee influence the types of behavior we observe from those legislators. Fenno (1973) notes that committees whose jurisdictions attract few, monopolistic, clientele groups are less influenced by partisanship, because the clientele groups work to avoid partisanship to maintain their own policy making power. Maltzman (1997) and Maltzman and Smith (1995) argue that the salience of the committee's agenda or jurisdiction is one factor that helps to determine to which "competing principal" a committee will be most responsive.[24] In fact, King (1997) maintains that jurisdictions can influence the power of interest groups in committee decision making.

### 4.4.2 Jurisdiction Size. Each of these authors identifies important characteristics of committee jurisdiction that influence the success of interest groups.

However, they fail to address how the size of a committee's jurisdiction influences a member's decision calculus by increasing or reducing the potential cost of a vote. This, in turn, affects the legislator's willingness to reciprocate for donor contributions.

Understanding how the sheer number of distinct issues that a committee addresses affects the responsiveness of legislators to financial supporters should bring new understandings of committee behavior to light.

I believe that the jurisdiction of the committee can also affect the relationship between contributions and votes, assuming that committee membership is, to some degree, self-selected.[25] In this case, in committees with limited jurisdictions—those who only hear bills on a very small number of issues—a member is more likely to have a substantive interest in any one bill that comes before the committee. This substantive interest increases the value of the vote to the legislator, which is why we find that contributions do not influence legislative voting behavior in cases where a member's predisposition on an issue is strong (Fleisher 1993). In other words, a member should be unwilling to be swayed by campaign contributions and act as a critical vote in cases where that member has a strong personal predisposition toward the legislation.

However, in a committee with a broad jurisdiction, a member may have a substantive interest in one or a few of the issues that come before the committee, but is probably relatively uninterested in many of the other bills on which he finds himself voting. To the extent that this is the case, campaign contributions given to legislators in broad jurisdiction committees are more likely to be reciprocated with critical votes, because it implies that more of the votes cast will not be of high value to the legislator.

### 4.4.3 Attraction of Ideologically Extreme Legislators to Certain

*Committees.* Some committee jurisdictions attract moderate members and others attract more ideologically extreme legislators. As already noted, Fleisher (1993) finds that ideology has a significant influence on the relationship between money and voting behavior, with moderate legislators being more easily influenced. This is consistent with the theory presented here, which focuses on the potential costs of votes. If moderate legislators do not hold a strong position on a specific political issue, it produces fewer psychic costs for them to choose to vote with a contributing group on a particular policy. Therefore, committees with extreme memberships should be less responsive to interest group gifts than those with more moderate memberships.

### 4.4.4 Attraction of Financially Well-Endowed Interests to Certain

*Committees.* Committee jurisdictions also determine the types of interest groups that are interested in the committee's activities. For example, committees that regulate the dealings of narrow, low visibility, but wealthy groups receive significant amounts of money from those groups. The issues that are directed to these so-called juice committees[26] have various characteristics that reduce the potential costs to the legislator deciding how to vote.

First, issues that affect the interests of narrow pressure groups (e.g., opticians, waste haulers) are not likely to raise the interest of a legislator's geographic constituency, nor do they tend to fall along partisan lines, so these votes have less potential cost to Congresspeople, giving them more leeway when deciding how to vote. Second, the more wealthy groups a committee attracts, the larger the pool of money available for campaigns. The higher the value of the first gift, the more valuable the reciprocal is likely to be.

Third, legislation with an impact on a narrow set of issues tends to have groups lobbying on only one side (Sabato 1984), eliminating the competition over the legislation. This gives those groups that do take a position significantly more power over the outcome because there are no opposition groups that the legislator must worry about angering. All three of these characteristics lead to a stronger impact of money on votes in these committees, because they reduce the potential cost of the vote to the legislator.

## 5. Conclusion

Contributions have become one of the most significant means by which interest groups attempt to gain power in the legislative arena. Groups use donations to affect electoral success, increase the amount of effort a member expends on their bills, and increase their access to members once those members are elected. Each of these relationships is empirically supported by the literature. A fourth theory has been proposed as well—that contributions directly change members' votes—but empirical support for this hypothesis is mixed.

Many find the contributions/vote hypothesis to be the most interesting. This is partially because of the inconsistent findings to date: why do so many who participate in the process think contributions influence voting behavior even though the findings of most scholarly studies would lead us to believe that is not the case at all? The issue is also crucial because of its implications for our normative theories of group representation.

Why are our conclusions regarding a relationship between contributions and votes so ambiguous? It is because we see the relationship as a market exchange where one commodity is traded for another. This view of the relationship implies that contributions must directly influence a large number of votes by forcing legislators to do something they would not otherwise do. Instead, the relationship between contributions and votes is similar to gift giving. We should not, therefore, expect to find a consistent and direct relationship between contributions and votes, but we should attempt to identify those situations when the probability of a vote (or gift) being exchanged for contributions is high. Traditionally, the literature does not take account of the way in which the political context affects the value of the behavior given in exchange for contributions.

Viewing contributions as gifts provides the basis for connecting the studies of contributions and effort or access to the analyses of contributions and votes. It provides an explanation as to why some studies of contributions and votes detect a relationship (e.g., those focusing on visibility and electoral vulnerability) and others do not.

Money is simply one strategy used by interest groups to achieve their goals in the political process. However, although contributions are a valuable tool used to help legislators gain reelection, they are not the end all and be all of a legislator's political career. And, given the practical and legal limitations on the amount of money that can be contributed, we should not expect contributions to affect so many votes as to be readily observable or to change a legislator's interest group support score. Instead, we should view contributions as gifts to legislators and determine which situations are appropriate for legislators to respond with an act in kind, whether that act is access, effort, or votes. What is of particular importance is determining the value of the behavior to be given in response to contributions: especially considering that, although contributions in the aggregate affect election outcomes, individual contributions are rarely large enough to be considered critical to electoral success.

This explains why our empirical results regarding the effort and access affects of contributions have so consistently identified a positive relationship. These behaviors are not as potentially costly to legislators because they are not readily observable by the general population and, perhaps, may be easily explained away in those rare circumstances that they are recognized. They are also valuable to interest groups because they provide those groups with services that they deem to be useful for affecting policy (Milbrath 1963). This makes them ideal reciprocal actions for the campaign donations received. Votes are more difficult because they lack the ambiguity of access and effort and because information regarding votes is readily available to both constituents and potential challengers for office. This makes each vote, and the impact that a large number of votes would have on general voting patterns, potentially costly to legislators, even among the inattentive public (Arnold 1990).

But this new understanding implies yet another important contextual influence that needs to be considered—the vote context. Research addresses the costs of votes to legislators when studying issue visibility and ideology, but does not question the extent to which some votes are more valuable to interest groups than others. That is, we need to ask the question: "On the bill we are studying, was the member's vote critical to the outcome of the legislation?" The value of a vote to the donating group or the potential cost to the legislator should be the primary determinants of the amount of pressure that a lobbyist places on that member and the likelihood of a positive response from the legislator to that pressure.

Political context has taken a back seat in studies, in part, because data limitations lead us to focus on only one vote, a small series of votes, or a small group of contributors when testing hypotheses. Because studies are so narrowly focused, we fail to see the true relationship between contributions and votes. By observing aggregate vote scores or a small number of votes, an implicit assumption is made that if donations do not affect many of the votes studied, their impact is relatively unimportant. However, although contributions affect relatively few votes because those votes are crucial to the outcome of legislation, contributions disproportionately affect policy.

There are four aspects of vote value/cost tested in the following chapters: (1) the amount of contributions given by groups on either side of a bill, (2) the visibility of the voting process to a member's constituency, (3) the relative importance of a single vote, and (4) the nature of the jurisdiction of the committee where the voting is taking place. Once we control for each of these aspects of the political context in a single model, it will become clear that what is important is not the number of votes that contributions change, but which votes are changed. Wealthier groups have a disproportionate impact on policy outcomes because their contributions affect those votes that change the outcome of legislation.

In the next chapter, the first steps are taken to provide support for this theory. Although a general empirical analysis is necessary to fully test the contextual nature of the relationship between contributions and votes, I first present a case study analysis of the relationship between one legislator and a single interest group—former California State Senator John Doolittle and the CTLA. This critical case outlines three important aspects of the relationship as conceptualized here. First, the association between these two actors illustrates how valuable critical votes can be to an interest group. The CTLA gave extremely large contributions to Doolittle even though he supported them relatively rarely. However, there is evidence that he was willing to provide critical votes for them when necessary. Second, it provides evidence that even the most ideologically extreme members may render such a service. Third, it depicts the extent to which the relationship of interest can be hidden from even the most astute observers.

# 3

# John Doolittle and the California Trial Lawyers Association

If campaign contributions have the same effect on the relationship between legislators and interest groups that gifts have on other social relationships, then donations are more likely to influence behavior on critical votes because those votes are most valuable to interest groups. If the vote on a piece of legislation is close, then a group will put more effort into lobbying on that bill. In addition, knowing how important the vote is to the group, a member to whom they have contributed will be more responsive to this pressure, because that member will identify the vote as a perfect reciprocal offering: it helps the group substantially, but will probably not impact that member's electoral security.

Do such activities occur in the real world of politics? Do interest groups give contributions to legislators who do not aid them a considerable percentage of the time? In this chapter, I present evidence that these types of relationships exist and that groups are willing to give large amounts of money to members who rarely support them to build a relationship with that member which may or may not pay off (e.g., result in a critical vote) in the long run.

In the 1987–88 election cycle, then California State Senator John Doolittle (currently a member of the U.S. House of Representatives), a Republican, received campaign contributions in the amount of $40,000 from the CTLA's PAC. Fifty-four percent of this amount or $21,750 came in the form of late contributions in the two weeks immediately prior to his reelection in November of 1988.

At that time, California law did not limit the amount of contributions that groups or individuals could donate to candidates for the state legislature, so, in and of itself, the amount of money is not unique. The CTLA gave $87,000 to Democratic Assembly Speaker Willie Brown and $224,000 to the Democratic leader of the California Senate during that same election cycle. However, it is unusual that Doolittle received such large contributions from the CTLA during that period. He is a conservative Republican who rarely supports the interests of any traditionally Democratic groups. The amount he received was unexpected, unless one understands that the CTLA was contributing to Doolittle to develop a relationship with him specifically to gain access to a member of the conservative wing of the Republican caucus. In addition, it appears as though Doolittle strategically abstained from at least one CTLA-opposed bill that would have passed had he not done so, perhaps due to his ongoing relationship with the CTLA based on their contributions.

In this chapter, I discuss the relationship between John Doolittle and the CTLA. First, I explain why Doolittle should receive little money from the trial lawyers given what we know about the contribution strategies of groups. Second, I conduct an analysis of the CTLA's contributions to members of the California State Senate and illustrate that Doolittle's contributions are extraordinary given his legislative behavior. Last, I argue that the reason Doolittle received so much money from the CTLA was not because he voted with them on a regular basis, because he certainly did not. To understand Doolittle's contributions from the CTLA, one must understand the nature of the committees to which the CTLA's bills were referred and on which Doolittle was a crucial member for the lawyers.

At the time to be discussed, the Senate Insurance and Judiciary Committees had large Democratic majorities. There were six Democrats and three Republicans on Insurance and eight Democrats and only three Republicans on Judiciary. However, there were only six Democrats who were consistent trial lawyer supporters in the Judiciary Committee and only five Democrats on the Insurance Committee. Therefore, having access to Doolittle in 1988 was important to the CTLA because they knew if they lost one more Democrat on a tort reform bill or insurance bill and the outcome of that bill came down to one vote, their interests would be threatened. Because Doolittle was an attorney prior to starting his political career, perhaps they also believed that he would provide support every once in a while if they desperately needed it. And, in fact, there is evidence that Doolittle did provide at least one critical nay vote for the trial lawyers and it is likely that the same type of behavior was occurring in the Judiciary Committee. Finally, I explain why isolating such activities more generally is so difficult and how this has influenced our understanding of contributions and votes.

## 1. John Doolittle and the CTLA

Past studies on the allocation strategies of interest groups focus on five variables that influence the amount of money groups contribute to individual legislators: (1) party, (2) member ideology, (3) leadership position, (4) committee assignment, and (5) electoral vulnerability. Using each of these variables, I predict CTLA contributions to each of the senate incumbents. From this, it is possible to determine whether Doolittle's contributions were unusually high. I discuss the expected impact of each variable in turn.

### 1.1 Party and Ideology

Party is an important variable when it comes to predicting how much money a legislator will receive from an interest group. Grier and Munger (1986, 354) suggest this is because "a legislator's party affiliation may carry information about his voters' preferences and his access to the leadership that affects legislative productivity."

Party is not always a successful predictor of contributions behavior, however (Fleisher 1993). Grier and Munger (1986) found that party affiliation was irrelevant when trying to predict corporate contributions to U.S. House of Representatives candidates. Even so, each of the two major political parties does have its compatible interest groups; Republicans tend to be supportive of the National Rifle Association's political position (Langbein and Lotwis 1990) and Democrats are more likely to support labor groups (Saltzman 1987). In addition, party is a significant predictor of union PAC contributions because "union PACs treat party affiliation as an important signal in distributing money" (Grier and Munger 1986, 357).

Party is also important to the CTLA. The trial lawyers traditionally support Democratic candidates. Only five members of the California Senate received more than $15,000 from the CTLA in 1987–88 and four of them were Democrats (the other was, of course, Doolittle). Democratic support for the CTLA makes sense considering the trial lawyers' political position on issues. Trial lawyers consider themselves to be consumers' only protection against corporate America[1] and are often found on the opposite side of business and corporate lobbies (Rosen and Nolan 1994; Schroeter 1992)[2]—the same businesses and corporations that tend to support Republican candidates.

Table 3.1 provides the correlation coefficients between political party and member ideology and CTLA contributions, both with and without Doolittle.

Member ideology correlates with contributions from the CTLA illustrating that the more liberal a member, the larger their contributions from the CTLA. When Doolittle is not included, the correlation rises, showing that Doolittle's ideology is not consistent with other recipients of the CTLA's largesse.

**TABLE 3.1** Correlations between Party and Ideology and CTLA Campaign Contributions

| Variables | Correlation with Doolittle | Correlation without Doolittle |
|---|---|---|
| Party/Contributions | .28* | .30* |
| Ideology/Contributions | .48† | .59† |

* Significant at .05
† Significant at .001

As expected, Democrats are more likely to receive contributions from the trial lawyers.

Doolittle's outlier status is especially surprising because Doolittle is not the average Republican; he is extremely conservative even compared to other senate Republicans. In 1989, Block wrote, "John Doolittle has emerged as the state Senate's keeper of the conservative flame, a combative black-belt conservative ..." (1989, 106). On almost all issues, he walks the conservative line. He is staunchly antigun control (Block 1989). In 1988, he scored a very low 44 out of a possible 100 points (100 is very supportive on environmental issues, 0 is not supportive) on the California League of Conservation Voters (CLCV) support score; his score was only 5 points higher than the lowest senate score for that year (CLCV 1988). In addition, he sponsored a series of acquired immunodeficiency syndrome (AIDS) bills in the late 1980s. Among the bills introduced was one that would have undercut individual privacy rights by allowing the testing and release of AIDS test results without consent of the persons being tested (Block 1989, 109). He was also a supporter of business interests during this time. His average Chamber of Commerce support score for 1987–88 was 73.7 out of 100, about 8 percentage points higher than the average senate Republican.

But Doolittle's differences with the Democratic Party are not just ideological, they have also been intensely personal. Doolittle has had an ongoing battle with Democrats since, in his first run for the senate, he ousted one of their most respected members, Al Rodda, in an extremely negative campaign (Block 1989). The Democrats responded in kind by redistricting Doolittle from an odd-numbered district (he beat Rodda in the 3rd District race) into an even-numbered district (the 6th District), which required him to run for the senate again in 1982. Because he lost the 1982 election to Democrat Leroy Greene, he again had to find a new district in which to run in 1984 in order to remain in the senate (Block 1989).[3]

In summary, everything about Doolittle suggests that he is a supporter of tort reform and an adversary of the CTLA. He is an extremely conservative member of the Grand Old Party (GOP). During this time period, he supported the interests of the California Chamber of Commerce on a regular basis. He felt extreme animosity toward the Democrats and went so far as to blame the Democratic Party for his Fair Political Practice Commission

(FPPC) violations in 1984 (Block 1989).[4] Finally, Doolittle is not known for his willingness to compromise on policy. In 1990, he was voted the least flexible member of the California Senate (Zeiger 1990). Based on this evidence, then, Doolittle should have received very little money in the form of campaign contributions from the CTLA.

## 1.2 Leadership

Legislative leadership positions bode well for fund-raising, if for no other reason than being in leadership is indicative of the power of a legislator (Chappell 1981). The more power a legislator has, the more a group will want his ear. The relationship between fund-raising and leadership positions should be even stronger in California than in the U.S. Congress. In the California legislature, leadership positions are often given out on the basis of fund-raising. If party leaders do not apply their fund-raising talents early and often, and dole that money out to party colleagues who need it, they may find themselves on the back benches once again (Clucas 1995; Richardson 1996).

During this time, Doolittle was a member of the Republican leadership. He held the number two Republican position in the senate as chairman of his party's caucus and was also a member of the powerful Senate Rules Committee.[5] However, even though the *Los Angeles Times* once identified Doolittle as a "heavyweight fund-raiser for GOP Senate candidates" (Ingram 1988) neither of these positions is necessarily related to substantial fund-raising. Table 3.2

**TABLE 3.2** CTLA Contributions to Members of the California State Senate Leadership, 1987–88

| Name | Party | Position | Contribution Amount ($) |
|------|-------|----------|------------------------|
| Roberti | Democrat | President Pro Tempore Chair: Rules | 224,000 |
| Maddy | Republican | Minority Leader | 14,500 |
| Lockyer | Democrat | Chair: Judiciary | 47,175 |
| Davis | Republican | Vice-Chair: Judiciary | 5,500 |
| Keene | Democrat | Majority Leader | 7,000 |
| Craven | Republican | Member: Rules | 2,000 |
| Ellis* | Republican | Member: Rules | — |
| Mello | Democrat | Member: Rules | 11,000 |
| Petris | Democrat | Member: Rules | 27,500 |
| Doolittle | Republican | Republican Caucus Chair Member: Rules | 40,000 |

* Senator Ellis was retiring from the senate and not running for any other elective office in 1988.

Note: Leadership positions are listed in order of importance to the CTLA. This order is somewhat arbitrary, but should represent the members of the senate who wield the most power over the trial lawyers' agenda.

shows the amount of money given by the CTLA to various members of the California Senate leadership.

The only two members of the California Senate who received more money than Doolittle were the President Pro Tempore of the Senate, David Roberti, and the Chair of the Judiciary Committee, Bill Lockyer. Doolittle received twice as much money as the Republican Minority Leader, the most powerful Republican member of the California State Senate and, next to then Governor Deukmejian, the most powerful Republican in California. He received $33,000 more than his counterpart in the Senate Democratic Caucus (the Democratic Majority Leader, Barry Keene) and $38,000 more than the ranking Republican on the Rules Committee.

Given the effect of his leadership status, we should expect Doolittle to be an above average recipient of the CTLA's largesse among Republicans. He certainly should receive more than the average CTLA contribution of $6,148.[6] However, he is far above the mean amount of money given to any members of the leadership. He received $22,000 more than the $18,000 leadership average. So, even though Doolittle should have received larger contributions because of his position, one would hardly expect a total of $40,000.

One might argue, on the other hand, that the combination of his two leadership positions could generate large contributions. If the Republican Caucus chair is a fund-raising position, that might be the case. However, I would argue that it was not a fund-raising position during the time it was held by Doolittle. Two methods may be used to measure whether a particular leadership position in the state legislature is used for fund-raising purposes. The first is to determine how much money was donated to Doolittle from other party members and subsequently transferred again to his Republican colleagues and compare that information to other legislators who are generally considered members of party leadership. If Doolittle raises and transfers as much money as other leaders, we can assume the that Republican Caucus chair is a fund-raising position. The second test is to ascertain whether Doolittle's 1988 contributions are unusual for a Republican Caucus chair. He was caucus chair for the Senate Republicans again in the 1989–90 session, but was not in a close race for his seat. Therefore, by comparing the two years, we can identify whether the money he received in 1988 was due to his election or his leadership position. If he raised as much money in 1990 as he did in 1988, then we can assume that he raised money as a member of leadership. If he raised more in 1988 than in 1990, he probably received the money because he was in a close race.

Table 3.3 presents the amounts received by leadership from other members and compares that to the average amount of transfers received by the legislature as a whole. It is obvious that Doolittle received far more money from his colleagues than the average legislator. He received even more than Barry

**TABLE 3.3** Average Contributions Received by Legislators from Their Colleagues

| Legislator | 1987–88 Session ($) | Amount Above/Below Average ($) |
|---|---|---|
| All Legislators | 100,673 | — |
| Maddy | 799,740 | 321,906 |
| Roberti | 523,252 | 422,579 |
| Keene | 100,000 | (673) |
| Doolittle | 253,097 | 152,424 |

Note: Amounts in parentheses are below average.

**TABLE 3.4** Average Contributions Transferred to Colleagues

| Legislator | 1987–88 Session ($) | Amount Above/Below Average ($) |
|---|---|---|
| All Legislators | 125,679 | — |
| Maddy | 675,000 | 549,321 |
| Roberti | 1,466,128 | 1,340,449 |
| Keene | 141,312 | 15,633 |
| Doolittle | 80,097 | (45,582) |

Note: Amounts in parentheses are below average.

Keene, his counterpart in the Democratic caucus. It appears that Doolittle is a member of the leadership who collects contributions for the purposes of supporting other, less well-endowed party members.

However, when one looks at Table 3.4 it is clear that Doolittle kept most of that money for his own campaign. He subsequently transferred only 32 percent of the money in Table 3.3 to his fellow Republicans, compared to the 84 percent retransferred by Maddy (the Republican leader), 280 percent by Roberti (the President Pro Tempore), and 141 percent by Keene (the Democratic Majority Leader). It is possible that Doolittle received that money not because he was a member of leadership, but because he was in a close race himself.

The second test is to compare the money transferred to and from Doolittle's campaign committee in 1989–90 to the amounts listed above. During the 1989–90 legislative session, Doolittle received no money from his Republican colleagues and transferred no money to party members other than approximately $10,000 to the Republican Leadership Fund. Given this data, it is probably not the case that Doolittle acted as a party fund-raiser for the Republican caucus.

In fact, Doolittle was not considered to be a heavyweight fund-raiser. It was not necessary that he raise money for the Republican caucus because the Republican leader of the senate, Ken Maddy, was well known as a successful fund-raiser. Instead, Doolittle was probably chosen by Maddy for his leadership position because of campaigning expertise, as illustrated by his ability to overthrow Al Rodda and maintain his seat even in the face of such vehement opposition by Democratic leadership. In addition, one of the reasons he may have been chosen was to balance the Republican leadership. Maddy was a moderate and Doolittle was a member of the conservative wing of the party. By including both of them in the leadership team, both wings of the party were represented.[7]

## 1.3 Committee Assignment

Committee assignments also play a crucial part in interest group contributions decisions (Fleisher 1993; Grier and Munger 1986). Committees hold a significant amount of power over the issues that fall under their jurisdiction (Grier and Munger 1986; Schroedel 1986; Shepsle and Weingast 1987) so, if a group is concerned about an issue being debated in a legislature, the first place they start is with the members of the committee to which the bill is to be referred (Gordon and Unmack 2003). How would committee membership affect Doolittle's contributions from the CTLA?

The types of issues found on the trial lawyers' legislative agenda include product liability, medical malpractice, attorney accountability, and no-fault auto insurance (Buchan 1996). All these issues hit trial lawyers in the pocketbook because attempts to reduce legal liability in any of these areas reduces the number of cases trial lawyers can take and the contingency fees they can collect. The CTLA's willingness to spend money to defeat tort reform measures was illustrated in California's March 1996 initiative campaigns. Three initiatives designed to reduce litigation were on the ballot. The lawyers planned to spend upward of $8 million to defeat them (Ferguson 1996).

Trial lawyers are willing to spend this money in legislative and executive campaigns at the state and local level as well. Between 1990 and 1994, trial lawyers spent about $20 million on local campaigns in Alabama, Texas, and California alone. This is "[m]ore than local candidates in all 50 states received from either the Democratic or Republican National Committees" (Eaton 1996, 20).

The committees in the California legislature that should receive most of this money are the Committee on Insurance, Claims, and Corporations and the Committee on the Judiciary. The senate committee that receives bills on most trial lawyer issues is the eleven-member Committee on the Judiciary. The Judiciary Committee is responsible for all bills that amend the Civil Code, which means that they hear bills having to do with civil liability (White 1987). In other words, they hear almost every bill the trial lawyers care about.

As noted above, the average amount of CTLA money given to legislators in the California Senate is $6,148. However, for Judiciary Committee members, the average is $12,722—over twice the amount as to the membership as a whole.[8] There is a significant correlation between amount of CTLA contributions and Judiciary Committee membership, so trial lawyer contributions are determined, at least to some degree, by committee membership.

Doolittle was a member of the Judiciary Committee during the 1987–88 session, therefore, we should expect Doolittle to receive more money simply because he is a member of the committee that has control of most of the CTLA's bills. However, even in that committee contributions vary from $5,000 to almost $50,000 (not including Roberti) and Doolittle is among the highest of those. He received nearly as much money as the chair of the committee, Bill Lockyer, a regular CTLA supporter on liability issues, and significantly more than the ranking Republican, Ed Davis, who voted in support of the trial lawyers more often than Doolittle. Those two members received only $47,175 and $5,500, respectively.

Doolittle was also a member of the Insurance Committee. Once again, any attempt to reduce the liability of insurance companies influences the financial well-being of the CTLA's members. However, membership on the Insurance Committee does not appear to have a relationship to contributions from the trial lawyers; there is no significant correlation between the two variables. Although insurance bills certainly could affect the CTLA, the Insurance Committee was generally known to be industry-friendly, if for no other reason than the chair of the committee was a supporter of the insurance industry.[9] In addition, the committee was chair-driven with most members of both parties willing to defer to his preferences (Johnston 2000). But, the Democrats on the committee were also more supportive of business interests than Democrats in the senate as a whole. The average ideology for Democrats on the Insurance Committee was 69.8 out of 100, just slightly more conservative (and, therefore, business-friendly) than the Democratic caucus as a whole (average ideology of 73) and much more conservative than the Judiciary Committee which had an average ideology of 77. This might explain the lack of a relationship between CTLA contributions and Insurance Committee membership. The trial lawyers knew that the Insurance Committee was not generally sympathetic to their position on issues and that any bills that affected tort reform would be double referred to Judiciary anyway (Johnston 2000; Kraus 2000).

### 1.4 Electoral Vulnerability

The impact of electoral vulnerability on contributions is unclear. Dow (1994) found that it was not a significant predictor of behavior while Fleisher (1993) and Grier and Munger (1986) found it was. However, in most cases, it is expected to have a positive impact on the amount of contributions that a member receives from a contributing group (Fleisher 1993). Grier and Munger (1986) explain this relationship best,

> The effort that a legislator will offer for a given contribution should depend on how badly money is needed to finance his campaign. That is, if a legislator expects a close race and needs extra money to defeat his

opponent, he will be motivated to solicit contributions by producing interest-group services simply because the money is more valuable to him than to an unopposed or secure incumbent.

(Grier and Munger 1986, 353)

Most scholars measure electoral vulnerability as the percentage of the vote the member received in the previous election, or some variant thereof. However, I measure electoral vulnerability here as the amount of money spent by the member's challenger during the election cycle. This has two benefits.

First, to the extent that ability to raise money shows candidate quality, challenger spending illustrates how threatened the member feels in the current election cycle rather than referring to a previous election. Just because a member was in danger in his previous election does not mean that he remains endangered in the current cycle as well. Second, this measure equals zero if the member is not up for election during the 1988 cycle, which takes account of the fact that only half of the senate is up for election during any two-year session.

The data are mixed on how vulnerable Doolittle was. Some might say that, in 1988, Doolittle was in a race for his political life. His challenger, Roy Whiteaker, was a well-liked local sheriff. Although the First Senate District has been known to support more conservative candidates, Whiteaker was a Democrat running in a district with a slight Democratic majority (Ingram 1988). In addition, he ultimately raised and spent over $650,000 for his campaign, all without the help of the Democratic leader of the Senate (Ingram 1988), so he showed himself to be an able fund-raiser and campaigner.[10]

However, some might argue that Doolittle was not in as much danger as one would think. Although Whiteaker was famous at one time—he was responsible for the capture of one of the most notorious mass murderers in American history, Juan Corona—not many knew him as more than a local law enforcement officer (Ingram 1988). Also, Doolittle had a lot of money to work with, eventually spending over $1 million for his reelection. He was also the incumbent with all the advantages that position implies.

Given what we know about interest groups' allocation patterns, Doolittle should have received more money from his supporters because he was facing a stiff reelection bid. However, because he was a Republican, the CTLA also could have taken this opportunity to unseat a powerful incumbent by funding his Democratic challenger. Given his party affiliation alone, we might expect he would secure little money from the CTLA, but if they viewed themselves as his supporters, they might take this opportunity to buy some goodwill.[11]

To test whether the CTLA gave larger contributions to the more electorally vulnerable of their supporters, I create a measure that combines political party with electoral vulnerability and correlate that measure with CTLA contributions. The correlation between contributions and the measure including vulnerability is 70 percent larger (.40) than the correlation between contributions and party affiliation alone (.28). This increase suggests that the trial lawyers give larger donations to those Democrats or supporters that are in particular need of money. Therefore, if they viewed Doolittle as an advocate, the CTLA probably gave him more money because he was vulnerable.

### 1.5 Summary

To conclude, expectations regarding Doolittle's contributions from the trial lawyers are mixed. Given party affiliation alone and the ideology that he has espoused over time, he most likely would get no money at all. Not only is he a conservative Republican, but he is extremely partisan and political. However, he was a member of the two committees in which the CTLA is most interested. Therefore, we should expect larger donations than party or ideology alone would allow. He was in a tight race during this particular election period but the impact of this is unclear as well. The CTLA could have chosen to show their support or attempted to elect a more ideologically compatible member. To know whether Doolittle's contributions were truly unusual, a more robust analysis must be conducted.

In the next section, I present evidence that Doolittle's contributions were substantially higher than standard theories would predict, thus providing the first piece of evidence for the gift theory that contributions help to create important and potentially valuable relationships for interest groups and legislators.

### 2. How Unique Are Doolittle's Contributions?

The results of the analyses of CTLA contributions to California senators are consistent with the theories posited in past research. Each of the variables discussed above successfully predict CTLA contributions to senate incumbents.[12] However, this does not answer the question about whether Doolittle's contributions were out of line with contributions to other members of the legislature. In Figure 3.1, I have taken the residuals from the statistical results and plotted them against predicted contributions. The further away an individual is from zero, the more unusual his contributions are. Doolittle is clearly an outlier in the analysis as he is the member who is the furthest above zero. This indicates that he received significantly more money from the CTLA than standard models suggest he should.[13]

What explains Doolittle's unexpectedly large contributions? Is it possible that he received more money than expected because he would vote in support of the CTLA, even given his ideology? To answer this question, I identified fourteen bills on which the trial lawyers took a position during the

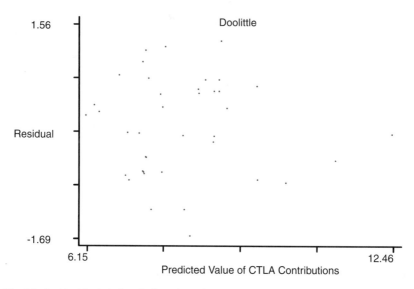

**Fig. 3.1** Residual Analysis from Ordinary Least Squares Regression
Note: Each point denotes a residual identifying an individual legislator. The residual from the Doolittle case is identified with his name instead of an asterisk.

1987–88 legislative session and on which the Judiciary Committee voted. Table 3.5 shows the breakdown of Doolittle's voting pattern on these bills.

On only three of these fourteen bills (identified with an asterisk) did Doolittle vote in support of the CTLA's position. In total, Doolittle voted with the trial lawyers only 21 percent of the time. This is not exactly a ringing endorsement of their position. It was the lowest support score in the entire Judiciary Committee and certainly does not appear to be a support score that would bring in extra campaign contributions.

In fact, when a CTLA support score for each Judiciary Committee member is created from these bills and included in the analysis (in lieu of a dummy variable for Judiciary Committee membership), and the same is done with ten bills from the Insurance Committee, Doolittle becomes a more significant outlier than in the previous analysis.[14] Figure 3.2 illustrates that Doolittle's support of the CTLA in these two committees should have earned him fewer contributions, not more.

To understand the paradox of the relationship between Doolittle's contributions and his support of the CTLA outlined above, we must understand the nature of the committees on which Doolittle served.

**TABLE 3.5** Votes by Senator Doolittle on CTLA Bills

| Bill Number | Vote CTLA Wanted | Doolittle's Vote | Outcome of Bill | Critical Vote |
|---|---|---|---|---|
| SB 48 | No | Yes | Passed (7–3) | No |
| SB 241 | No | Yes | Passed (9–2) | No |
| SB 282 | No | Yes | Failed (3–7) | No |
| SB 406 | No | Yes | Passed (9–0) | No |
| SB 773 | No | Yes | Failed (5–2) | No |
| SB 869 | No | Yes | Failed (5–5) | No |
| **SB 1662*** | No | Abstain (No) | Failed (3–5) | No |
| **SB 1663*** | No | Abstain (No) | Failed (1–6) | No |
| SB 2337 | No | Yes | Passed (8–1) | No |
| SB 2429 | No | Yes | Failed (3–4) | No |
| **AB 180** | No | Yes | Passed (6–2) | Yes |
| AB 643 | No | Yes | Failed (4–3) | No |
| **AB 2341*** | Yes | Yes | Passed (9–0) | No |
| AB 3935 | No | Yes | Failed (4–6) | No |

Note: The bills in bold typeface are either bills where Doolittle voted in support of the CTLA's position or he voted against them and was a critical vote.

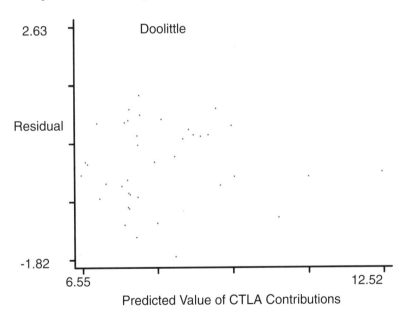

**Fig. 3.2** Residual Analysis, CTLA Support Score Instead of Judiciary and Insurance Dummies
Note: Each asterisk denotes a residual identifying an individual legislator. The residual from the Doolittle case is identified with his name instead of an asterisk.

## 2.1 The Judiciary Committee

The Judiciary Committee in the California State Senate in 1987 was a unique committee in many ways. First, many of most powerful members of the senate served on this committee. The President Pro Tempore, the Majority Leader, three members of the Rules Committee, and the Republican Caucus chair were all members. Of the eight members of the leadership listed in Table 3.2, a full five were members of the Judiciary Committee.

Second, and most importantly, the committee had a large Democratic majority. On the eleven-member committee, there were eight Democrats and only three Republicans. Given the CTLA's strong support of the Democratic Party, a majority of this size should bode well for the trial lawyers' agenda. But this was not always the case.

There were two Democratic members of the committee, Barry Keene and Robert Presley, who were not consistent CTLA supporters. The CTLA support scores discussed above illustrate this point. The rankings are shown in Table 3.6.

It is easy to see that both Presley and Keene were far below the mean Democratic support score. Clearly, these scores are not perfect, Lockyer and Torres were both below the mean as well and yet were generally considered to be strong supporters of the CTLA.[15] However, Presley was clearly a problem member for the trial lawyers, supporting their position less than 50 percent of the time.

Keene, on the other hand, did support the trial lawyers fairly regularly, but he and the CTLA had a less than harmonious relationship since Keene's tenure in the state assembly. During his service there, he was chair of the Assembly Health Committee and authored some of the most significant medical malpractice reform bills of the 1970s (LegiState 1989). The impact of those reforms affects the trial lawyers to this day and certainly influenced the level of trust that the CTLA had in Keene on bills that were important to their legislative agenda (Keene 1997). In other words, even though he voted with them fairly regularly, they knew they could not count on him on some of their most important issues. They were correct. When Keene retired from the senate, he

**TABLE 3.6** CTLA Support Scores for Members of the 1987–88 Senate Judiciary Committee, by Party

| Democrats | Avg. 69.4 | Republicans | Avg. 26.8 |
|---|---|---|---|
| Presley | 42.1 | Doolittle | 21.4 |
| Lockyer | 52.6 | Richardson | 27.3 |
| Keene | 58.8 | Davis | 31.6 |
| Torres | 64.3 | | |
| Roberti | 72.2 | | |
| Marks | 79.0 | | |
| Petris | 92.9 | | |
| Watson | 93.3 | | |

became President of the Association for California Tort Reform (ACTOR), an organization responsible for an initiative designed to reduce lawyers' contingency fees (Kushman 1993a).

In summary, although the committee had a significant Democratic majority, this did not guarantee smooth sailing for the CTLA. They could count on the consistent support of only six of the eight Democrats. Because of this smaller than expected coalition of support, the CTLA needed some insurance against losses on bills that affected them financially. They did not want to depend solely on those six Democrats. If one of those six had to switch their vote because of constituency interest, it could cause serious problems for the lawyers. The tort reform legislation was too dangerous to the interests of the trial lawyers to leave to such a small majority. The CTLA could not risk losing even one bill on this issue. They needed someone else they could count on, so developing a relationship with John Doolittle was very important, indeed potentially crucial, to their interests. To not attempt to create such a connection would have been irresponsible.

Of the three Republicans on the committee, Doolittle voted with the CTLA the least often, only 21 percent of the time. Notice, from Table 3.5, however, that on all the occasions that Doolittle voted against the CTLA in the 1987–88 session, his vote was critical to the outcome of legislation on only one bill, AB 180. On all other bills, his vote was irrelevant; changing his vote alone would not have changed the results of the bills.

In addition, on the one bill where his vote did matter, he was voting on an issue that was not of serious concern to the trial lawyers. They did oppose the bill, which reduced the number of preemptive challenges in death penalty cases from twenty-six to twenty, and Doolittle was one of the six aye votes that the bill needed to pass,[16] but this is not an issue over which the trial lawyers are willing to punish any members or risk relationships. It is not an issue that hits them where it hurts because it does not attempt to reform the tort system.

In fact, Doolittle's vote probably did not matter to the trial lawyers in most situations. They did not care how he voted when they were sure of winning or losing regardless of his vote. If the CTLA opposed a tort reform bill and it was clear it would pass eight to three, it did not matter to them whether Doolittle was on the winning or losing side. In addition, they did not care if he was the critical vote on a bill that did not have to do with one of the issues about which they felt strongly; the best example of this is AB 180.

Their relationship with Doolittle was simple. They contributed to him for the purposes of developing a relationship to gain the access necessary to make their argument when a tort issue came up. This potential relationship was especially crucial if the trial lawyers were in danger of losing: if only five Democrats would commit to the CTLA's position. Therefore, the most logical explanation for the CTLA's contributions behavior is that Doolittle was in a position to be the trial lawyer's critical vote in two important committees. Because of the power that this position as a swing vote implies (Shapley and Shubik 1954), developing that relationship through gift behavior (contributions) is a perfect strategy for the CTLA. And, evidence suggests that, because of the informal and potentially friendly relationship that they had developed over time, Doolittle was likely to feel it was appropriate to reciprocate in specific, though rare, circumstances.

## 2.2 The Insurance Committee

The second committee important to the CTLA is the Insurance Committee. The Senate Insurance, Claims, and Corporations Committee is responsible for "[b]ills relating to insurance, indemnity, surety, warranty agreements, liens, claims including retail credit, unclaimed property, collections, corporations, and franchises" (White 1989, 100). During the 1988 legislative session, its membership consisted of six Democrats and three Republicans.

The composition of this committee should have provided a relatively supportive environment for the trial lawyers. Unfortunately for the trial lawyers, both the Democrats and Republicans on the committee were slightly more conservative than their counterparts in the senate as a whole. Table 3.7 provides the ideology scores for the members of the Insurance Committee and compares them to the entire senate.

But, this ideological mix is not the only explanation for why the Insurance Committee was considered well disposed to the insurance industry. The chair of the committee, Alan Robbins (D-Van Nuys), was an industry champion and was close to one of the most powerful lobbyists in California (Clay Jackson of the lobbying firm of Jackson/Barrish), who also represented many in the insurance industry. The committee was controlled quite tightly by Robbins, with legislators from both political parties often deferring to him (Johnston 2000; Kraus 2000).

**TABLE 3.7** Ideology Scores for Members of the Senate Committee on Insurance, by Party

| Democrats | Avg 69.8 in Committee / Avg 74.0 rest of Senate Democrats | Republicans | Avg. 31.0 in Committee / Avg 34.9 rest of Senate Republicans |
|---|---|---|---|
| Deddeh | 71.52 | Davis | 42.18 |
| Green, C. | 76.33 | Doolittle | 25.43 |
| Keene | 77.93 | Nielsen | 25.27 |
| McCorquodale | 83.90 | | |
| Montoya | 39.23 | | |
| Robbins | 70.13 | | |

## 2.3 Identifying the Rare Critical Vote

Identifying the exact nature of the gift/critical vote relationship between former Senator Doolittle and the CTLA is extremely difficult. Some business lobbyists regarded Doolittle as a trial lawyer supporter in certain circumstances (Dunmoyer 1998; Krause 2000). However, many people close to the Judiciary and Insurance Committees during this period did not see a relationship. There is good reason for this conflict. First, the CTLA needed Doolittle's support so rarely that opposing groups or authors would seldom find themselves losing his vote on a CTLA bill. Therefore, a consistent relationship would not be obvious to them, especially given Doolittle's propensities.

Second, during this period, the CTLA almost always opposed legislation. In Table 3.5, only one of the fourteen bills listed was supported by the CTLA, the other thirteen they opposed. There is a straightforward explanation for this pattern. The CTLA was supported by the Democratic Party and the Democrats had controlled the California State Assembly and Senate since the early 1970s. By the 1980s, the CTLA had achieved most of its legislative goals, so the legal system was one that preserved the interests of the trial lawyers. And, because of their strong and consistent support for Democrats, the Judiciary Committees in both houses of the California legislature were set up to protect the interests of the CTLA (Johnston 2000). Therefore, most of their work was defensive: protecting themselves against tort reform attempts.

It is this consistent opposition to bills that makes Doolittle's behavior so difficult to identify. Most of the votes the trial lawyers hoped to gain from Doolittle were critical nay votes and because of the rules of the senate—a majority of the members of a committee are required to vote aye for a bill pass, regardless of the number present when the vote is taken—abstentions are as effective as nay votes. Doolittle would never have to actively vote against a bill for the CTLA to achieve their legislative objectives. If it appeared that a bill they opposed would pass with a bare majority of votes, Doolittle could simply be absent for the hearing or leave the room when the vote was taken. This makes critical abstentions in favor the CTLA's position relatively risk-free for Doolittle. If he wanted to provide a rare abstention for his friends, then he could do so and would probably never have to explain his behavior. Given his expected position on tort reform bills, it is unlikely that anyone would make a connection between the CTLA's position and Doolittle's absence.

The behavior of other members of the committee makes identifying this behavior problematic. When it is obvious that a bill will fail, other members who support the bill often abstain for strategic reasons (Cohen and Noll 1991; King and Zeckhauser 1997), leading the bill to fail one to five or two to three (in an eleven member committee) when, in fact, the vote was much closer. In other words, when members of the Judiciary or Insurance Committees see that a bill is going to fail by one vote, many of them choose to abstain rather than take a position, because taking a position on an irrelevant bill is more risky than abstaining, but leads to the same result. This should occur even more often when large contributors have an interest in legislation.

Identifying votes that provide evidence for the gift theory requires finding a lobbyist who observed the process from beginning to end. Although players not directly related to either Doolittle or the CTLA cannot say exactly what took place between the two on a particular bill, they do provide information supporting the theory. Evidence provided by one such lobbyist suggests that even though contributions were given to Doolittle for the purposes of gaining access to him when he was added to the Judiciary Committee, as the years passed, it became clear to the CTLA that Doolittle could sometimes be persuaded to provide critical votes. Once this happened, the relationship was cemented and their interest in his remaining in the senate grew. This explains the extraordinary contributions given by the CTLA during Doolittle's closest race.

### 3. SB 2662—Auto Insurance Reform[17]

Senate Bill (SB) 2662 by Senator Robert Presley (D-Riverside) was an auto insurance reform bill. It was sponsored by the Personal Insurance Federation (PIF) and, if passed, would have provided consumers with a low-cost auto insurance policy (approximately $180 per year). The policy was to provide limited personal injury coverage for medical, wage loss, and replacement services. It failed passage in the Senate Insurance, Claims, and Corporations Committee in 1990.

The bill was opposed by the trial lawyers on the basis that it would do the following:

1. Increase the cost of auto insurance for most consumers who pay for liability coverage because those who use the no-fault policy would drive up the cost of uninsured motorist coverage because they do not have liability.
2. Those with assets but fixed incomes would purchase the low-cost policy as other policies became too expensive and, therefore, risk everything if they caused injury.
3. Create a "liability gap" between those who have full insurance coverage and those who have no-fault.

Essentially, the CTLA believed that the option of a low-cost, no-fault policy would drive up the cost of uninsured motorist coverage without providing consumers of those policies with the right to sue those who have injured them.[18] The PIF, the sponsor of the bill, disagreed with this view of the bill and argued that, not only was it not a no-fault insurance policy, it did not deny anyone the right to sue for compensation for their injuries (Dunmoyer 1998). But, to the extent that the CTLA believed it reduced the right to sue, this bill was threatening to their interests.

The measure was authored by the chairman of the Senate Appropriations Committee, Robert Presley, a moderate Democrat. Because the bill was supported by the chair of the Insurance Committee, Alan Robbins (D-Van Nuys), the PIF needed the support of all the Republicans and only one additional Democrat for the bill to pass. This was not viewed as a problem, because two such powerful Democrats (Presley and Robbins) were authoring or supporting the bill and could pressure one of the other committee Democrats to assist in creating a successful majority (Dunmoyer 1998). Given the power of Robbins as the chair of this committee, this was likely to be a successful strategy (Johnston 2000).

While working the bill, Dunmoyer (the advocate for PIF) realized that he was having difficulty procuring Senator Doolittle's vote on the bill. He began from the assumption that he had Doolittle's support as he was a conservative Republican who tended to support business interests and had supported insurance interests in the past. But, Doolittle seemed uncommitted and, after meeting with him, Dunmoyer left the senator's office without a clear understanding of Doolittle's position on the bill (Dunmoyer 1998).

On the day on which SB 2662 was to be heard, June 28, 1990, Doolittle arrived at the committee hearing and listened to the testimony on the legislation. However, at some point during the hearing, Doolittle noted that he had a scheduling conflict and left. When it came time to vote on the legislation, it became clear to the insurance advocates that they were going to need his vote for the bill to pass. They began looking for the senator, but he was nowhere to be found. He was not in his office and no other committees on which he served had hearings that day. The insurance lobbyists even contacted the senate sergeants to ascertain whether he had left the building. He had not, but they were unable to find him before the end of the hearing and the bill failed for lack of support (Dunmoyer 1998).

Ultimately the vote on the bill was three ayes and five nays with one abstention. This outcome suggests that Doolittle's vote was not a critical one; if he had remained and voted aye, the bill would still have failed as it required five aye votes to pass. But, Dunmoyer argues that Presley and Robbins were willing to pressure another Democrat to support the legislation only if that Democratic vote would have led to passage of the bill. They were unwilling to do so, however, if the bill would fail with that additional vote. Therefore, all Democrats except Robbins either voted nay or abstained on the bill once they realized that it was failing. If Doolittle had remained at the hearing and voted aye on the bill, another Democrat would have voted aye as well and the bill would have passed. Dunmoyer believes that it was Doolittle's abstention that caused the bill to fail (Dunmoyer 1998).[19]

## 3.1 Summary

Because of the strategic nature of votes and abstentions, it is extraordinarily difficult to identify critical nay votes. This problem is compounded if the votes might appear to be influenced by contributions and the players want to avoid detection. Without Dunmoyer's narrative, the vote on SB 2662 itself does not illustrate how much the CTLA gained from Doolittle's absence.[20] PIF's lobbyist had a unique role in this legislation and the resulting contextual discussion he provides is necessary to fully understand this relationship. Indeed, the case illustrates quite strongly how widespread this behavior could be and, yet, still not be noticed by the casual, and not so casual, observer.

This case study acts as the first piece of evidence in support of the gift theory. However, even with an understanding of the context within which this behavior occurred, we do not know for certain whether it was the relationship and obligation engendered by the CTLA contributions that caused Doolittle's well-timed absence. But, the behavior found here certainly suggests that such a gift relationship existed.

It is important to note that the account chronicled above does not imply that either the CTLA or Doolittle was participating in an illegal *quid pro quo* exchange of money for votes. If contributions have the same impact as gifts by creating a sense of obligation to reciprocate, only four decisions must be made by the participants. It is probable that all four decisions were made by the CTLA and Doolittle.

First, the CTLA must contribute money to Doolittle if they have the resources to do so. The trial lawyers certainly have the money and they gave a large amount to Doolittle. Perhaps they gave the money for access purposes because he was a member of two important committees and because he was the Republican Caucus Chair in the senate. Perhaps they contributed the money because Doolittle had a solid relationship with the Democratic President Pro Tempore, David Roberti, a leader who actively and consistently defended the trial lawyers on virtually all their issues. Roberti has publicly identified his relationship with Doolittle as a good one (Ingram 1988).

Also, perhaps the trial lawyers believed that Doolittle could be swayed on some critical issues. Although he had a reputation as a conservative legislator, he was "more complicated than that" (Johnston 2000) and was sometimes willing to make deals on issues to develop relationships or further long-term goals. For example, one of Doolittle's most cherished goals is to build the Auburn Dam in his district. However, he was willing to put that off indefinitely in exchange for control of appropriations spending on energy and water (Whitney 2003).

Second, the trial lawyers must advocate more strongly on those issues where the outcome seems questionable. Were the trial lawyers heavily lobbying legislators on SB 2662? Most definitely. One of the most challenging issues for the trial lawyers during the late 1980s and early 1990s was auto insurance reform. Proposals to reduce the cost of automobile insurance in California either reduced the amount of litigation (usually through no-fault auto insurance) or reduced the amount of premiums to increase the number of insured motorists. The lawyers obviously opposed the former proposals and supported the latter. And, because they believed that SB 2662 was a form of no-fault auto insurance, they would have opposed it strenuously.

CTLA lobbying in the Insurance Committee would have been especially strong on this bill because the bill was not double referred to the Judiciary Committee, where it would have had an easier time creating a winning coalition against it. If it had been doubled referred, the CTLA probably would not have lobbied so hard in the Insurance Committee, knowing that lining up the votes against the bill in Judiciary would be relatively straightforward. However, defeating the bill in Insurance became crucial because there were to be no other policy committee votes in the senate.

Third, the interest group must lobby especially hard those members it believes can be moved to its side. While there is no evidence regarding who the CTLA lobbied on this bill, research on other legislation suggests that this is generally the case and the CTLA would likely do the same here.

Fourth, for Doolittle to use this abstention as an appropriate reciprocal gift, he must feel especially obligated to CTLA on this particular bill because it was so important to them. This is the stage of the process where information becomes thin, but it is probable that this decision process occurred. When the PIF lobbyist discussed the bill with Doolittle, it was not clear what the senator's position was. He stated neither clear support nor clear opposition for the bill (Dunmoyer 1998). It is may be that he was waiting to see how close the vote was before making his final decision.

## 4. Conclusion

In conclusion, there is reason to believe that interest groups invest in members who do not support them a large percentage of the time. All else being equal, it is difficult to understand why the trial lawyers' contributions to Doolittle were so large unless that were the case. He was a member of the Judiciary Committee, but he was a conservative Republican who voted with them rarely, even for a Republican. Yet, when he needed the money in a close race, the CTLA made large contributions. The CTLA's behavior is best explained by the characteristics of the rare votes that Doolittle appeared to be willing to cast in their favor.

This relationship between Doolittle and the CTLA did not exist, I believe, because they purchased his votes. Instead, the relationship probably developed over the ten years that Doolittle served in the California Senate. The CTLA provided the first gifts to him to build a relationship when he became a member of the senate and began serving on the committees in which they were most interested. Doolittle was placed on the Judiciary Committee during his first term and received $2,500 from the CTLA. That amount increased over the ensuing years as Doolittle received $15,750 in his second two years and $12,000 during the 1985–86 session. I believe that these contributions, and the relationships that developed through the access that the contributions provided, made Doolittle feel an obligation to provide a reciprocal gift when the group's interests were especially threatened and the risk to him was potentially quite low. In addition, when Doolittle was in a very close race, the CTLA contributed even more to Doolittle because of the beneficial friendship that had developed.

The Doolittle/CTLA relationship described here is, to some degree, unique, although the specific situation outlined is not. It is unlikely that each interest group has its own, individual critical votes on the committees that it lobbies most often. This is partially because there are not a lot of groups that command the financial resources of the trial lawyers. This situation is also different in that the nature of the Judiciary and Insurance Committees made Doolittle, in particular, the trial lawyers' one possible critical vote. Most interest groups should have a few members on their committees who could act as critical votes at different times. And, even this relationship may not have been apparent had Doolittle not found himself in such a precarious electoral situation where money was crucial.

However, this particular situation illustrates four important points. First, we cannot simply look at voting behavior in the aggregate if we want to understand the impact of contributions on voting behavior. Some votes are more important to groups than others and it is on those votes that we should see the largest impact of contributions as legislators reciprocate in response to contributions they have received.

Second, we cannot underestimate the value of the critical votes when they do occur. Those critical votes are important to the interest groups whose agendas they affect. The trial lawyers spent $40,000 on the one legislator who might end up supporting them once or twice per legislative session: when a tort reform bill would come up for a vote in the Judiciary or Insurance Committees and the Democrats in their coalition might vote against them. However, if SB 2662 had passed, it would have cost the trial lawyers millions. That one abstention by Doolittle alone was definitely an appropriate reciprocal gift for the $40,000 the CTLA contributed to him.

Third, it is not just moderate members who will be more likely to act as critical votes as Fleisher (1993) suggests. Although he is correct that more moderate members are not as ideologically tied to one position or another on issues such as national defense, it is possible that ideologically extreme members are also able and willing to act as critical votes if the circumstances require it. Even a very conservative member was willing to provide votes for his supporters, but not every time his vote was critical. Only on those bills that were particularly important to them and on those votes that did not threaten his electoral well-being.

Fourth, this case study illustrates why we have misunderstood this relationship so completely and for so long. Instances of this type of behavior are rare and difficult to identify. Because of this, we look at the wrong situations to study the relationship between contributions and votes and, when we fail to find a consistent relationship in these contexts, we conclude that there is no important connection at all.

However, because this situation is somewhat unusual, we need to determine whether this type of relationship occurs in other committees, with other members, and across a large number of bills. If my theory is correct, it should not just explain this one situation, but should hold up under additional contexts. In the next two chapters, I address this relationship between contributions and critical votes differently. In Chapter 4, I study four individual bills and determine whether contributions had an independent effect on voting behavior in various sets of circumstances. In Chapter 5, I extend the generalizability of the argument even further by studying a large number of bills in a single committee, the California Senate Committee on Governmental Organization to ascertain whether the relationship between contributions and critical votes occurs across a large number of members and groups.

# 4

# Bills on Which Contributions Did (and Did Not) Affect Critical Votes

In the last chapter, I provided evidence that interest groups are willing to contribute significant amounts of money to legislators who may support them only rarely. Usually these contributions are given to gain access. Those donations may then be the basis for a relationship between legislators and lobbyists: a cooperative relationship for which legislators are willing to act as critical votes when necessary. However, it remains to be determined whether the relationship between John Doolittle and the CTLA was unique. In this chapter, I present a series of cases that portray the relationship between contributions and critical votes in a more general setting. Although information regarding the connections created between legislators and lobbyists cannot be detailed here in the manner they were in the Doolittle case, these case studies will provide additional evidence regarding how contributions affect critical votes, but not noncritical votes, in various issue areas and contexts.

The first case illustrates the relationship between contributions and votes that develops when each vote is crucial to the outcome of the legislation even though contributions are not related to votes on the same bill when it passes by a larger majority. Although anecdotal evidence at the time suggested that money affected voting behavior on a beer distribution bill (AB 1500), objective analysis only supports such a relationship in the senate, where the bill passed on a bare majority, and not in the assembly, where it passed with much broader support.

The second case involves a public liability bill from the Senate Committee on Governmental Organization (SB 276) where groups in support gave significantly more money than groups in opposition and managed to win passage of the bill by the smallest of margins. Controlling for ideology and other factors, contributions are shown to be a significant factor in the voting decision on that bill.

In each of these cases, it is difficult to say conclusively what legislators were thinking at the time of the vote. It is also impossible to determine which legislator cast the critical vote. Unlike the Doolittle case, it is probable that no single legislator was. Instead, two or three members could possibly have voted either way and were being pressured by lobbyists for support. However, the behavior exhibited suggests that contributor preferences were an important piece of the puzzle. Lobbyists on both sides of each bill were lobbying quite heavily. Party, ideology, and other individual-level variables do not appear to be the deciding factor. Both bills passed by a minimum majority and empirical analysis suggests that the contributions were a crucial part of the decision making process for each of these bills.

Finally, I present two bills on which contributions did not influence voting behavior to reinforce the point that contributions cannot influence lawmakers in all circumstances—even when votes are crucial. Although we must study critical votes to examine how legislators respond when a vote is valuable to contributing groups, we must remember that the potential costs to legislators are still an issue. These two cases remind us of the conditional effect of contributions: how other variables influence the potential cost of a vote to a legislator. They suggest that the personal interests of legislators will overcome the interests of pressure groups, even on critical votes.

The first case concerns an issue that was both highly visible and salient to the California electorate in the late 1980s and large contributions by groups in opposition were unable to sway a single vote to defeat the measure. The second case addresses, once again, the influence of the trial lawyers in the California legislature. Analysis of this bill shows that although large contributions were given on both sides of an important insurance bill, and to different sets of legislators, contributions were not a deciding factor in the decision making processes of legislators, even though the bill passed by a minimum majority.

## 1. The Beer Barons versus the Grocers

In 1987, a bill affecting beer distribution in California was introduced. Assemblyman Jim Costa (D-Fresno) authored a bill that would have created effective beer wholesale monopolies in California by requiring those retailers that purchase beer to do so through beer distributors that would be solely responsible for distribution in their particular geographic area. The purpose of the bill was to codify the existing, geographically based system of beer distribution and restrict retailers' ability to buy beer directly from manufacturers.

Supporters argued that the bill would protect smaller retailers from being squeezed out of the beer market when the larger retailers struck independent deals with manufacturers. If these deals were made, smaller, mom-and-pop stores would have difficulty buying beer directly from manufacturers and, therefore, would have to pay the higher prices wholesalers would need to charge as a result of the declining number of customers (Reardon 1999).

Two studies conducted in 1987 to test the impact of geographic/territorial restraints on beer and wine prices supported the proponents' case. The first found that, among other things, (1) retail prices of beer were no higher in states with mandated wholesale territories, once other influences on prices were taken into account; (2) territorial mandates in two states actually resulted in lower prices; and (3) geographically based distribution systems did not affect consumer prices for other products (e.g., sodas) (Tollison and Ekelund 1987). A second study, focusing on the Alabama market, corroborated the first, citing that "no evidence can be found in these data that the territorial [beer distribution] bill has been harmful to the Alabama consumer" (Gregor-owicz et al. 1987, 32).

As expected, the bill was supported by the California Beer and Wine Wholesalers; the Alcoholic Beverage Merchants; and Barton Beers, Limited, each of whom wanted to avoid the wholesale competition that had been introduced in other states with negative results for wholesalers (Reardon 1999). Less obviously, perhaps, the bill was also supported by the Korean, Chinese-American, and Mexican-American Grocers' associations, the Rural Caucus of the California Assembly, and by Cal-Pac, the California State Package Store and Tavern Owners Association. The support of these groups suggests that some smaller grocers were concerned about higher wholesale prices. A June 9, 1987, letter to the editor of the *Riverside Press Enterprise* from the owner of a small liquor store stated the problem:

> Unlike large retailers ... I do not have the economic resources to buy trucks to pick up and deliver my beer, build facilities to warehouse my supply or buy beer in sufficient quantities to have a supplier extend me credit.... So who is going to deliver my beer if the distribution system breaks down and wholesalers [are] driven out of business?

Together, the groups in support of the legislation contributed over $450,000 to state assembly and senate candidates during the 1987–88 session with more than 95 percent of the money coming from the wholesalers.

Opponents to the bill focused on the monopolies that would have been created by its implementation. They argued that the bill would raise beer prices from 5 to 20 percent and cost consumers between $200 million and $400 million per year (Zelman 1988) by giving distributors sole control over the purchase price of beer and wine.

The Democratic Attorney General, John Van De Kamp, opposed the bill on the grounds that it would reduce or completely eliminate intrabrand competition and comparative shopping and thereby increase consumer beer prices. He argued, as did other opponents, that there was no compelling reason to give beer distributors such a broad-scale, antitrust exemption which would inevitably increase the wholesale cost of beer to large retailers.[1] The California Legislative Analyst agreed when reviewing an almost indistinguishable bill in the previous legislative session.[2]

The California Retailers Association, the California Grocers Association, California Common Cause, the Consumers' Union, and the Attorney General of the state of California all took positions in opposition to the bill. These groups, also noteworthy players in the policy process, contributed somewhat less money. They donated just less than $387,000 during the two-year session in which the bill was introduced. Their contributions amounted to approximately 15 percent less than those given by the bill's supporters.

The total amount of money given by each side is clearly not the only explanation for the relatively quick movement of AB 1500 through the legislative process. Other issues also came into play. First, the way in which the money was distributed was important. The issues important to the wholesalers do not tend to break down along ideological lines (Zelman 1988). Therefore, they donate money not to a particular party, but to incumbents more generally and to legislative leadership in particular. They also give during the primary period when many incumbents receive their greatest challenges and, most notably, when legislation is being actively addressed (Zelman 1988).

Second, the wholesalers' organization has a small membership with a limited economic scope of interest (Zelman 1988). This is not to say that they do not regularly have interest in legislation. In fact, one of the explanations for the wholesalers' history of large donations to legislative candidates is the fact that they participate in one of the most aggressively regulated sectors of the California economy (Reardon 1999). But, their interest is very specific—beer and wine distribution. On the other hand, although the retailers and grocers are interested in beer distribution they do not consider it to be their most important issue (Zelman 1988). They are affected by many different types of regulation including, but not restricted to, weights and measures, taxation, workers' compensation, and the California State Lottery. This distinction between the two groups is particularly meaningful when legislation like AB 1500 is before the legislature. The distributors viewed Costa's bill as critical to their economic well-being and, because of their limited legislative interest, when they contacted legislators about the bill, it was the only bill they discussed (Zelman 1988). This influenced legislators' responses to wholesaler lobbyists, legislators who wished to oppose AB 1500 could not find another issue around which to ease the wholesalers' disappointment. There was no other issue they cared much about. One was with them on AB 1500 or one was against them.

(Zelman 1988, 506)

In contrast, the retailers, grocers, and consumer groups had numerous issues on which they lobbied. Table 4.1 lists the number of bills lobbied by each of the groups during 1987 (when AB 1500 was passing through the process) and 1988, after the bill had passed and been vetoed by then Governor Deukmejian.

Third, even given their more narrow interest, this was clearly the most important bill to the beer distributors during the 1987 legislative session; almost all other legislation took a back seat to AB 1500 for the wholesalers. Their agenda included only ten bills while AB 1500 was being heard and increased threefold after its demise. The retailers' and grocers' agendas did not change dramatically between the two years. It was quite obvious to legislators to whom the bill was most important.

Given this background information, can an argument be made that contributions had an independent impact on legislative voting on the beer distribution bill? Editorials published in the major newspapers and magazines in California during the 1987–88 legislative session make it clear that most editors and columnists believed that voting on the bill was based on the large contributions given by the Beer and Wine Wholesalers Association. Papers as diverse as the *Los Angeles Times*, *The Sacramento Bee*, the *San Jose Mercury News*, *The Orange County Register*, the *Santa Barbara News-Press*, and the *Fresno Daily Legal Report* stated that AB 1500 allowed beer distributors to buy geographic monopolies which would eventually cost consumers millions of dollars in increased beer prices.[3] In addition, they argued that the legislation was successful only because of the money with which the wholesalers "greased the skids."

But, empirical evidence is mixed as to whether the "grease" affected AB 1500's legislative fate. The bill passed the assembly fifty-two to twenty (with six members abstaining and two members absent), a substantial majority. The bill passed the senate as well, but only twenty-one of the forty senators voted

**TABLE 4.1** Number of Bills Lobbied by Groups That Took a Position on AB 1500

| Group | Position on AB 1500 | Bills Lobbied in 1987 | Bills Lobbied in 1988 |
|---|---|---|---|
| Beer/Wine Wholesalers | Support | 10 | 35 |
| Grocers | Oppose | 63 | 65 |
| Retailers | Oppose | 35 | 34 |

aye. A more robust analysis is necessary before determining whether contributions had an independent effect in either of these two cases.

## 1.1  The Effect of Contributions on Voting on AB 1500

Party should have had an influence on this legislation. Legislators are more likely to vote aye on legislation authored by members of their party than not and, because Costa (D-Fresno) is a Democrat, as well as a key lieutenant in the Speaker of the Assembly's leadership team, Democrats should have been more likely to vote in favor of this legislation. On this bill, Democrats did vote in favor in higher numbers than did Republicans. All other things being equal, Democrats had a .72 probability of voting for AB 1500 and Republicans had a .65 probability.

Ideology should also have had an effect. More extreme legislators were in opposition to this legislation for various reasons. Conservatives opposed the bill because of the potential effect on the free market and liberals opposed it because it created effective monopolies (Zelman 1988, 509). Therefore, the majority coalition on the bill was primarily composed of ideologically moderate legislators from relatively moderate districts. As expected, more extreme members had a .52 probability of voting for the bill and moderate members had a .83 probability of supporting the legislation.[4]

The Assembly Rural Caucus took a support position on the legislation because of the potential effect on markets in rural districts. Members of the Rural Caucus were 25 percent more likely to support the legislation than non-caucus members.[5]

In summary, in the assembly, three legislator characteristics affected whether a lawmaker supported the legislation. As expected, Democrats and more moderate members supported the legislation and those on the extreme ends of the political spectrum opposed it. In addition, Rural Caucus members voted in support of the legislation in response to constituent interests.

The results in the senate are quite similar. In the senate, both party and ideology influenced votes. Democrats and moderates were each more than twice as likely to vote for the bill. However, being a member of the Rural Caucus did not affect votes in the senate, probably because the Rural Caucus was not as organized, nor as effective in that house.

Most interestingly, though, assembly contributions did not influence behavior. It does not matter which groups an individual received more money from, they were no more or less likely to vote in favor of the legislation. In stark contrast, in the senate, where each aye vote was critical to the outcome of the legislation, contributions were strongly related to voting. Controlling for the other variables, if a senator received more money from groups in support of AB 1500 than from groups in opposition, it resulted in a higher probability of an aye vote (see Figure 4.1).

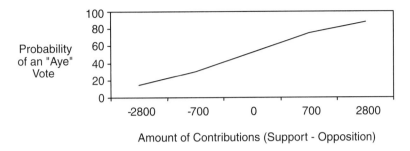

**Fig. 4.1** Effect of Contributions on Senate Voting on AB 1500

This does not necessarily mean that the numerous astute observers of the political process were wrong in their assessment that contributions influenced each stage of the process through which AB 1500 progressed. It is possible that the contributions given by each group led legislators to provide those groups with access to make their arguments. However, if contributions made to a legislator constituted a *quid pro quo* purchase of votes, those donations would have had an independent impact on voting in both houses in this analysis. That is not the case.

Instead, the results presented support the argument that contributions are used as the basis of an exchange relationship and legislators are more likely to reciprocate on votes that have more value to large contributors with the least amount of risk to themselves. Contributions create a sense of obligation or a relationship between the giver and the recipient and that obligation to reciprocate was stronger in the senate than in the assembly because the senate vote was so close.

Both groups gave contributions to legislative candidates because they have an ongoing interest in state legislation and because they require access to be successful. Both supporters and opponents lobbied quite aggressively on this legislation as it had implications for the economic future of each. However, it was obvious even to those who opposed the legislation that this bill was relatively more important to the wholesalers than to the grocers and retailers. Although the grocers provided significant contributions to legislators, they provided fewer than the wholesalers did. In addition, the opposition groups were lobbying on many different and equally important bills, but the wholesalers' interests were primarily directed toward this one bill. However, even given these characteristics of the opposing interests, contributions did not have a statistically significant impact on voting behavior in the California Assembly.

Only in the California Senate, where each individual vote was of more value to contributors, did money have an affect. It was the ideal opportunity for legislators to provide a reciprocal gift to their largest contributors. The bill was extremely important to those who contributed the most money, the issue was of very low salience among constituents, and each vote was critical to the outcome of the legislation. These results suggest that it is only on critical votes that contributions will influence legislative behavior.

## 2. SB 276—Public Liability

The second case is quite different from the first. SB 276 was not widely discussed and no one suggested that money influenced the outcome of the legislation. Partially because of this, the information surrounding the particularities of the bill is somewhat sparse. In addition, the legislation did have both supporters and opponents, but the supporters contributed significantly more money to committee members than did the opponents, who contributed nothing at all. However, the two bills are similar in that both passed by a minimum-sized coalition and it appears as though contributions by groups with positions on both bills had an independent impact on voting behavior.

SB 276 was a bill relating to public liability and was authored by Senator Leroy Greene (D-Sacramento) in 1987. The purpose of the bill was to allow the state to pay a punitive damages award that was levied against a state employee. The Department of Finance would be responsible for determining whether a damage award would be paid.

Two similar bills had been introduced on this issue previously. In 1985, SB 969 was passed by the legislature and signed by the governor. That bill allowed "local public entities to pay a punitive damages judgment against its employee when the governing body of that entity finds that the following conditions are met:

1. The conduct giving rise to the award was within the employee's course and scope of employment.
2. The employee's action was in good faith, without actual malice, and in the apparent best interests of the public entity.
3. Payment of the claim would be in the best interests of the public entity."

(Judiciary Committee Analysis of SB 276)

The second bill, SB 2459 (passed by the legislature in 1986, but vetoed by the governor) was identical to SB 276 with one exception: it gave the decision whether or not to pay the damages to the appointing power of the state employee instead of the Department of Finance. For example, if the employee worked for the Economic Development Department, the decision to pay would be made by that department.

SB 276 was supported by the Professional Engineers in California Government, the Association of California State Attorneys and Administrative Law Judges, the California Association of Professional Scientists, and the California Association of Highway Patrolmen. These groups supported the bill because they believed that state employees should be given the same protections from lawsuits as local employees when working within the scope of their employment. These groups contributed a total of $48,725 to members of the committee, almost $22,000 of which went to the President Pro Tempore of the Senate, David Roberti (D-Van Nuys).

The American Civil Liberties Union (ACLU) was the only group in opposition to the bill. They opposed the bill on two grounds. First, they felt that the provisions of the bill undermined the jury system by creating "a post-trial review and ratification of a state employee's conduct which had been found by a court to have been outside of that employee's duties and malicious and wrongful in its intent."[6] Second, they considered the terms in the legislation to be so vague as to allow the Department of Finance to find almost any reason to reverse the findings of a court in regards to punitive damages. The ACLU contributed no money to members of the Judiciary Committee.

A vote was taken on SB 276 in Judiciary Committee on March 10, 1987. The bill passed on a vote of six to four (one member was absent), a minimum majority. To what extent did contributions influence the outcome of this legislation?

An average of $4,095 was given to those members who voted aye on SB 276 (not including Roberti) and an average of $875 was given to those members who voted nay. The correlation between contributions and votes is important both substantively and statistically.[7] However, it is possible that this simple correlation is spurious and hides a relationship between either party or ideology and votes. Perhaps the groups in support of the bill tend to support liberal or conservative legislators and legislators vote on the basis of their ideological position. This is not the case. Contributions are not related to either party or ideology and neither party nor ideology is related to votes on this bill and the relationships (or lack thereof) remain when voting on this bill is analyzed controlling for other variables. The only variable that explains voting on this legislation is the amount of contributions given by groups in support of the bill. Figure 4.2 shows that as the amount of contributions increases, the probability of an aye vote increases as well.[8]

Whether the effect of contributions seen here is due to the fact that the bill passed by a minimum winning coalition remains to be addressed. One way to examine this issue is to study the impact of contributions on similar bills that passed on a larger majority. Fortunately, there is a bill that meets this requirement and which was acted upon by the same committee in the previous legislative session. SB 2459 was introduced during the 1985–86 legislative session and provided the same level of immunity to state employees as SB 276.

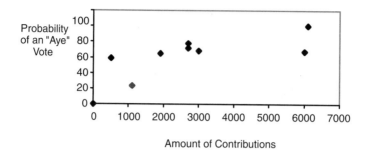

**Fig. 4.2** Effect of Contributions on Voting on SB 267

The only difference between the two bills was that the prior bill gave the appointing authority of the state employee the ability to decide whether the state government would cover the employee's liability instead of the Department of Finance. SB 2459 was supported by Professional Engineers in California Government and the California State Employees' Association and was opposed by the ACLU for the same reason that these and similar groups supported or opposed SB 276.

The bill first failed five votes to one (with four members abstaining and one absent) on April 16, 1986. It later passed nine votes to two when the absent member, two of those who had abstained previously, and one member who voted nay, changed their votes to aye. On the first vote, the average amount of contributions to those voting aye was $4,766 and the average amount contributed to those voting nay was $1,730.[9] On the second vote, the averages were $3,914 and $700, respectively. On neither vote are the interest group contributions significantly related to the probability of an aye vote either when bivariate or multivariate analysis is used.

Unlike AB 1500, whether contributions were the deciding factor in the different outcomes of these bills is less clear. The two bills analyzed here were slightly different and the small number of observations makes the conclusions somewhat suspect. However, the number of observations is the same in each analysis, the committee composition is the same, and the contributions were similar as well. In addition, the level of visibility of these two votes is identical. They were both low visibility votes that held little potential risk for legislators. Yet, contributions had an effect on SB 276 and did not on SB 2459. This suggests that contributions only affected those votes that were critical to the outcome of the legislation—those on SB 276. Although not conclusive, these findings, in combination with the other cases presented here, provide additional evidence that the critical nature of the vote may determine whether contributions will be a deciding factor in legislative voting decisions.

## 3. Exceptions to the Rule

If votes are given as reciprocals for contributions received, clearly we should not expect campaign contributions to affect every vote, not even every critical vote, cast by legislators. Another variable that influences the value or cost of a vote—and, therefore, the relationship between contributions and voting—is issue visibility. There are some issues that have special salience with the public. Votes on those issues are potentially risky for legislators and may not be affected by contributions even when votes are close and the outcome of legislation is in question.

Furthermore, there are interest groups with distinctive relationships with the majority party. Some groups contribute large amounts of money and are so consistently and actively supportive of the majority party that they need not worry about the passage of their bills. Even on critical votes, the outcome of their legislation usually is not in question because it is in the interest of the majority party leadership to make sure that the group's needs are met. The CTLA is one such group. Former Senator Frank Hill (R-Whittier) once called the CTLA, "the anchor tenant in the Democratic mall" (Johnston 2000). In other words, just as developers of shopping malls need a large tenant to bring in enough customers to attract tenants to the smaller retail spaces, the Democrats need the CTLA to contribute large amounts of money to Democratic campaigns so they can preserve their majority and serve other constituencies. Because of the role that the CTLA played in maintaining the Democratic majority in the 1980s, the party made it its business to provide support for trial lawyer bills. The cases below illustrate the unique attributes of these types of issues and groups.

### 3.1 Oil Drilling and the Governmental Organization Committee

Past studies have concluded that contributions will not influence voting behavior when an issue is particularly salient or visible to the voting member's constituency. This example shows how the outcome of a committee vote may be influenced by issue visibility. AB 284, an oil drilling bill, passed the Senate Governmental Organization Committee with a bare majority of aye votes even though it was supported by environmental groups that contributed less than $1,000 to members of the committee and was opposed by nine oil companies who contributed upward of $170,000 to those same legislators. A similar bill failed in the committee in 1984 with essentially the same groups in support and opposition. There are two possible explanations for this paradoxical behavior. First, the committee membership changed somewhat in the ensuing four years, with three environmentally sensitive legislators replacing three members who were more conservative in regards to environmental protection. In addition, the environment and oil drilling were much more visible and salient issues in the late 1980s.

In 1988, the Governmental Organization Committee passed AB 284. This bill would have added portions of the Humboldt and Mendocino coasts to the state oil and gas development sanctuaries.[10] Earlier legislation had designated most of the California coastline above San Luis Obispo County as development sanctuaries which forbids the State Lands Commission from leasing these tide and "submerged lands" for oil and gas development. The Humboldt and Mendocino Counties had not been included in these sanctuaries, even though a study conducted in 1976 by the State Lands Commission had predicted that the Humboldt County property could produce up to 91 million barrels of oil (California Senate Committee on Natural Resources and Wildlife 1988).

The passage of this bill is interesting for two reasons. First, the groups supporting and opposing this legislation (see Table 4.2) differed dramatically in their campaign financing capabilities. At the time of the bill's committee passage, two environmental groups, the Sierra Club and Campaign California, had taken support positions on the bill and the nine major oil companies (Exxon, Texaco, Shell, Phillip 66, Unocal, Chevron, Atlantic Richfield, British Petroleum, and Mobil) were listed as opposition. The supporting groups contributed $68,000 to all senate and assembly incumbents during the 1987–88 legislative session and the opposition oil companies contributed just short of $1 million during the same period. Notwithstanding, the bill passed against the objections of the oil companies with the minimum possible majority. Although contributions are significantly related to committee voting on this bill, they cannot explain why the bill passed, because opposition contributions were so much higher than support contributions. Neither can party affiliation alone explain the Governmental Organization Committee's voting behavior on this bill. The bill essentially passed on a party line vote on its way through the legislative process. In Assembly Natural Resources, all Democrats voted for the bill and all but one of the Republicans voted against it. The Republican voting for the bill was Bev Hansen, a legislator from the Napa Valley whose district would have been negatively affected by oil drilling off the coast of Mendocino. The bill passed the Assembly Ways and Means Committee, on a straight party vote and passed off the assembly floor with only two Republicans voting aye (both of whom abstained when voting to uphold the Republican governor's veto of the bill) and four Democrats voting nay. However, all of the votes that went against party can be explained by ideology or district interest (see Table 4.3). The Republicans who voted for the bill were either significantly more liberal than the average Republican or their districts would have been negatively impacted by the offshore oil drilling, and the Democrats were significantly more conservative than the average Democrat or were from an agricultural district that would be positively affected by increased oil drilling off the California coast, which would have produced lower gasoline prices.

**TABLE 4.2** Party and Ideology of Assembly Members Voting against Party on AB 284

| Member | Party | CLCV Score (Party Average) | District (Possible Interest) |
|---|---|---|---|
| Chacon | Democrat | 80 (88.55) | 79th District (interest unknown) |
| Costa | Democrat | 76.5 (88.55) | 30th District (agricultural district) |
| Duplissea | Republican | 47.5 (29.3) | 20th District (coastal district) |
| Filante | Republican | 83.75 (29.3) | 9th District (coastal district) |
| Hansen | Republican | 60.5 (29.3) | 8th District (coastal district) |
| Tucker | Democrat | 90 (88.55) | 50th District (oil presence in district) |
| Waters, N. | Democrat | 69.5 (88.55) | 7th District (agricultural district) |

Party, CLCV support score, and contributions are all strongly related to voting on AB 284 on the assembly floor. Yet, when these variables are included in an analysis together, only the environmental support measure of ideology is a significant predictor of votes.

The same behavior occurred in the senate. The bill passed on a straight party vote in both the Senate Natural Resources and Senate Appropriations committees. The only exception to the party line votes was when the bill passed the senate floor with only three negative Democratic votes, but with six out of fifteen Republicans voting aye. But, once again, the Republicans who voted aye were, on average, more liberal on the CLCV scale. The one exception was Republican Senator Campbell. He was running for a statewide constitutional office during this session and was probably not responding to his senatorial district, but to the state as a whole: a state with a strong opinion on oil drilling. The Democrats who voted in support of the bill came from districts with a solid manufacturing base and were strong union supporters (Breit 1999). Although the unions had not taken an official position on the bill, they tended to oppose any limitation on offshore oil drilling on principle (Breit 1999).

Just like in the assembly, there is no relationship between contributions and floor votes in the senate. And, when all the variables are included in an analysis together, ideology is the only predictor of votes on AB 284.

The same was not true in Senate Governmental Organization. Two Democrats voted against the bill—Senators Alquist (D-San Jose) and Dills (D-Gardena)—and the only Republican voting on the bill voted aye—Beverly (R-Redondo Beach). Neither party nor ideology are related to voting behavior in this committee.

**TABLE 4.3** Party and Ideology of Senators Voting against Party on AB 284

| Member | Party | CLCV Score (Party Average) | District (Possible Interest) |
|---|---|---|---|
| Ayala | Democrat | 71.5 (85.1) | 13th District (agricultural district) |
| Bergeson | Republican | 66.0 (48.1) | 37th District (coastal district) |
| Beverly | Republican | 62.0 (48.1) | 29th District (coastal district) |
| Campbell, W. | Republican | 47.0 (48.1) | 31st District (running statewide) |
| Davis | Republican | 61.5 (48.1) | 19th District (interest unknown) |
| Dills | Democrat | 73.5 (85.1) | 30th District (oil presence in district) |
| Greene, B. | Democrat | 82.0 (85.1) | 27th District (union supporter) |
| Morgan | Republican | 77.5 (48.1) | 11th District (coastal district) |
| Nielsen | Republican | 59.0 (48.1) | 4th District (interest unknown) |

The second reason that the 1987 passage of AB 284 is so interesting is that an almost identical bill failed in the Governmental Organization Committee during the 1983–84 legislative session. In 1983, Assemblyman Hauser (D-Santa Rosa) introduced the same bill as AB 221.[11] That bill failed in Senate Governmental Organization with three senators voting aye (two Democrats and one Republican) and the others abstaining as effective nay votes. The ideological make-up of the committee in which this bill failed was different from the committee in which it passed just four years later. Eight of the members who served on the committee in 1983 served again in 1987. Three members were replaced in the ensuing four years. Senators Carpenter (D-Cypress), Foran (D-Daly City), and Robbins (D-Van Nuys) were replaced by Senators Torres (D-Los Angeles), Garamendi (D-Stockton), and Lockyer (D-Hayward). All six were Democrats, but with the new members, the committee as a whole was more liberal environmentally. However, as already noted, ideology and party were not significant predictors of voting behavior on AB 284 in the Governmental Organization Committee.

But, there are two additional reasons why the bill failed in 1983 and passed in 1987. First, environmental issues in general and oil drilling more specifically had become increasingly salient by the late 1980s (see Table 4.4). And, second, the visibility of this particular issue was raised when the Reagan administration approved Lease Sale 91, which would have allowed for offshore oil drilling in the Humboldt/Mendocino area in 1989.

**TABLE 4.4** Percent of the California Public Concerned about the Environment

| Year | Environment Most Important Issue (%) | "Extremely Concerned" about the Environment (%) |
|---|---|---|
| 1983 | 5 | 58 |
| 1987 | 15 | 76 |

In 1983, the environment was not a particularly important issue to Californians. Even though 58 percent of those questioned by the Field Poll stated that they were "extremely concerned" about air and water pollution, only 5 percent named the environment as the most important issue facing California. But, by 1987, a series of events had brought the environment and oil drilling to the forefront of the political agenda. For example, a series of oil spills had fouled coastlines with grave results. The higher saliency of environmental policy is evidenced by the increase in the number of people who considered environmental issues to be important. In 1987, 15 percent of those polled stated that air and water pollution was the most critical issue facing Californians and 76 percent stated that they were "extremely concerned" about the environment.

The visibility of the oil drilling issue was enhanced again when the Reagan administration, through the actions of Secretary of the Interior Hodel, approved Outer Continental Lease Sale 91, which would have provided for oil drilling and exploration off the northern California coast in 1989. This had been an important local issue in the past[12] and by the late 1980s it was such an important issue that in 1988, all five Democratic candidates for U.S. president took a public position to oppose the Reagan administration policy. In addition, *Business Week* published a cover story on the leasing policy of the Reagan administration and even *The New York Times* printed an editorial on the problems surrounding the drilling for oil off of California, Alaska, and other coastal areas. Offshore drilling in California had risen to both the statewide and national agenda and had become a hot-button campaign issue.

Perhaps the best evidence of the visibility of the issue was the public's response to both Lease Sale 91 and AB 284. Field Poll results from 1987 reveal that 70 percent of Californians opposed additional offshore oil drilling in California. In addition, when given the opportunity, the public responded at Department of Interior hearings,

The scheduled one-day hearing [in Fort Bragg in Mendocino County] went past two in the morning, then into a second day. During 26 hours of testimony, fishermen, scientists, economists, loggers, elected officials, shopkeepers, doctors, waitresses, artists, educators, Native Americans, innkeepers and school children took their turn. Their unity and determination were awesome, deeply moving. They presented weighty volume of facts and analysis, they reasoned, they pleaded, they yelled, cried, sang and recited poetry. Some even threatened. All spoke from the heart.... The Department of the Interior had heard the people. Now it only remained to see how well they'd listened.[13]

The legislators also received numerous letters from individuals as the bill moved through the political process—a phenomenon not seen during the progress of AB 221. The bill file for AB 284 is filled with letters from various individuals, but the file for AB 221 in 1983 includes no such letters from concerned constituents. The lack of response to that bill suggests that the public was either unaware of its existence or was not concerned about its implications.

In summary, the explanation for the change in support for the bill appears to be threefold. First, the committee membership shifted to the left as three members left the committee and three new, more environmentally friendly legislators replaced them. If, however, contributions create the connection between legislators and lobbyists that I suggest, this alone should not explain why the oil companies failed to garner a single critical vote. Second, the Reagan administration's actions in regard to offshore oil drilling brought oil drilling to the top of the public agenda. Third, and perhaps most importantly, the public's opposition to oil drilling in California had both increased and solidified. In 1983, the legislators could respond to their contributors because the public was either unaware of or disinterested in the issue that the bill addressed. However, four years later, it was an issue no legislator could ignore without considering potential, negative repercussions. The environment and oil drilling were at the top of the public's agenda and a vote on that issue could have significant implications for a legislator's political future.

It is not only issues that can hold a special position in the policy making process. Some groups have unique advantages as well. I discuss the unusual role that the trial lawyers play in Democratic politics in the next section.

## 3.2  SB 3: The CTLA Fights the Insurance Companies

In 1988, California voters passed an auto insurance reform initiative, Proposition 103. This proposition, among other things, "allow[ed] any person to initiate or intervene in any insurance proceeding with the Insurance Commissioner or court awarding reasonable advocacy and witness fees and expenses" (California Senate Floor Analysis 1990). SB 3 created a specific position in the Attorney General's Office for this purpose. The Office of Consumer Advocate would reside in the Justice Department and would act as the consumer advocate allowed in Proposition 103 in any legal or administrative proceeding regarding insurance (California Senate Floor Analysis 1990).

The bill was supported by Common Cause, the Consumers' Union, the California Attorney General's Office, and the CTLA. These groups supported the bill on the grounds that consumers and consumer advocacy groups had difficulty representing group interests given the lack of financial resources and specific expertise. They believed that by creating a special advocacy position, it would provide a resource for consumers with cases against insurance companies: companies that already had the resources and expertise necessary for a successful court or administrative case.[14]

The Attorney General's office argued that positions such as these in the bureaucracy were not unique.

> This consumer advocate is similar in concept to the Division of Ratepayer Advocates which provides institutional representation of consumers before the Public Utilities Commission. The PUC regulates far fewer electric, gas and telephone companies than the insurance carriers that the Insurance Commissioner [also created by Proposition 103] will soon oversee. Nevertheless, the PUC found that public intervenors were not able to adequately represent consumer interests in large, complex rate cases. So too there is a need for an institutional advocate to represent consumers in insurance rate cases.
>
> (Letter from Attorney General Van De Kamp of Assemblyman Patrick Johnston, Chair of the Assembly Finance and Insurance Committee, June 27, 1990)

In opposition to the bill were the California State Personnel Board, the Association of California Insurance Companies, the National Association of Independent Insurers, State Farm Insurance Company, and the California Department of Insurance. Although the Personnel Board opposed the bill on the grounds that it unconstitutionally provided an additional exempt civil service position in the Attorney General's office,[15] most of the opposition to the bill stemmed from the belief by the regulated communities that it was redundant of the provisions of Proposition 103 as passed by the voters.

Specifically, the Association of California Insurance Companies opposed the bill for the following reasons (among others):

1. Proposition 103 already allowed for the reimbursement of those representing consumers for "substantial contributions" made on their behalf.
2. Proposition 103 already provided for a public representative, the newly created Insurance Commissioner (a new constitutional office).

In other words, they were concerned that there would be, in essence, two regulatory agencies overseeing insurance, one within the Attorney General's office and one within the newly created Office of the Insurance Commissioner.[16] In addition, the bill required a ten-cent assessment on each policy written as a means of funding the new office. Opposition groups believed that this assessment would be unable to meet the costs of the advocacy work required.[17] Supporters of the bill contributed just over $300,000 to California Senate incumbents; opponents contributed just over $88,000.

The trial lawyers had an interest in the maintenance of the Democratic majority because the majority party was primarily responsible for appointing committee memberships. In addition, the Democrats had been such strong supporters of trial lawyer interests to the point that, by the late 1980s, the California tort system was fundamentally reflective of the CTLA's preferred agenda.[18]

The trial lawyers have more recently begun supporting Republican candidates at both the federal and state levels, but during the 1970s and 1980s, they almost exclusively funded Democratic candidates, especially more liberal Democrats.[19] In addition, they contributed large sums to Democratic leadership. The Republican leader, Senator Ken Maddy, received only $6,500 during the 1989–90 legislative session, but the Democratic leader, Senator David Roberti received $166,000. Also, the CTLA was willing to spend considerable amounts of money in close races that the Democratic leadership identified as important. For example, they contributed over $28,000 to Senator Cecil Greene during his first campaign for the senate in 1988. Because of the potential impact that seat had on the future of reapportionment in California, it was considered one of the most important for the Democrats to win during that election and it was an extremely close race. Greene won by less than 2 percent of the vote.

The vote on SB 3 was as close as a vote on the senate floor can get. Twenty-one of the senators voted aye and eleven voted nay. But, was the CTLA able to achieve this minimum majority by significantly pressuring legislators to whom they contributed? The bill was quite controversial (Matthews 1990) and insurance issues during this period (especially auto insurance issues) were particularly politicized (Johnston 2000). So, it is probable that both sides were lobbying the bill quite aggressively.

Because insurance was such an important issue on the political landscape at that time, both sides in this battle contributed money, but to different legislators. Senate contributions by groups interested in the bill (measured as contributions by supporters minus contributions from opponents) indicate a strong and positive relationship with party, ideology, and membership on the Senate Judiciary Committee and a negative relationship to membership on the Senate Insurance Committee. In other words, the CTLA tends to donate to Democrats, liberal members, and Judiciary members, but the insurance companies donate to Republicans, conservative legislators, and Insurance Committee members.

Contributions were also positively related to voting on SB 3. Members who received more money from support groups tended to vote aye and those who received more money from opposition groups tended to vote nay. But, does this mean that contributions had an independent impact on voting on this bill? Not necessarily, especially because we know that supporters and opponents were contributing to very different sets of legislators. It is likely that it was not contributions that were influencing voting, but party and ideology were influencing both voting and contributions.

When senate floor voting on SB 3 is analyzed, the relationships between all these variables become clear. The only variable that has an independent influence on voting on this bill is member ideology, with liberal members more likely to vote aye and conservative members having a higher probability of voting nay (see Figure 4.3).

The fact that ideology is the only predictor of voting on SB 3 shows that contributions were not independently influencing voting on this bill. The bivariate relationship between money and votes is spurious with ideology driving both contributions and voting. Groups were contributing to legislators based on their ideology and it was their ideology, not the contributions, that were driving the votes. So, in this case, the CTLA did not have to pressure critical members to vote in support of its bill to ensure its passage, which is why we see no effect of contributions here. Instead, because the CTLA is a strong and consistent supporter of Democratic candidates (and of the Democratic Party more generally) and is a necessary part of the Democratic coalition, it can count on Democratic support whenever it is required.

For example, Democratic Senators Garamendi, B. Greene, and Robbins all voted for the bill even though none of these three members received any contributions from the CTLA during the 1989–90 legislative session. Although it is expected that Garamendi and Greene would support the bill—Garamendi ran for Insurance Commissioner in California on a reform platform and Bill Greene was among the most liberal members of the legislature—the same is not true for Robbins. Robbins was chair of the Insurance Committee and was

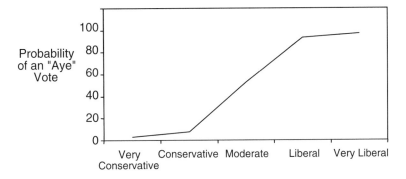

**Fig. 4.3** Effect of Ideology on Voting on SB 3

considered to be a strong supporter of industry interests. And, yet, Robbins supported the CTLA's position when his support was necessary for the bill to pass, likely in response to pressure by Democratic leadership.

Robbins had every incentive to go along with the desires of the party leadership. He held the chairmanship of the important and lucrative Senate Committee on Insurance and was one of just two members of the Budget Conference Committee; party leaders determine who will hold these positions. In addition, he was a crucial supporter within President Pro Tempore Roberti's leadership coalition. Roberti notes that he would not have been able to obtain his slim majority for leader of the senate without Robbins's support (Paddock 1991) and Robbins believed that his committee positions in the senate were obtained because of his loyal support of the President Pro Tempore (Gladstone 1993).[20] Under these conditions, Robbins would have been interested in supporting legislation that Roberti deemed necessary for continued majority rule.

This case also suggests that some idiosyncratic variables may affect the relationship between contributions and votes in an empirical analysis. SB 3 passed with a minimum winning coalition, but because the CTLA has large financial resources and is able to successfully utilize an electoral donation strategy, it did not need to pressure members to whom it has contributed when the outcome of its legislation is in question. Because it has have helped so many of its supporters gain reelection, there is no need to pressure any legislators to vote against personal ideology, party, or constituent interest. Instead, it can count on Democratic support regardless of contributions to individual party members because of the nature of its position in the Democratic coalition.

## 4. Conclusion

The circumstances surrounding each of the bills discussed above provide evidence that contributions may have an independent impact on the voting decisions of legislators when those legislators' votes are crucial to the outcome of policy. Particularly interesting are the results from AB 1500, the beer distribution bill. Clearly, those involved in the process, the executive director of Common Cause, Walter Zelman, and numerous political columnists and editors, believed evidence existed that contributions were influencing legislative behavior on this bill. This consensus is especially interesting because the groups in support and opposition did not contribute significantly different amounts of money. The distributors only contributed about 15 percent more to legislative incumbents than did the retailers and grocers. However, even given the consensus on the influence of money, a bias toward contributors can only be distinguished on those votes that are crucial to the outcome of the legislation, presumably because those are the votes that are most valuable to interest groups.

I have attempted to discuss alternative explanations for the conduct found, but others could (and probably would) provide additional explanations for the behaviors outlined above. Therefore, the next step in this process is to go beyond case study analysis and analyze numerous votes and contributions to determine whether the relationship found here is consistent across a large and diverse number of issues and groups.

# 5

# Campaign Contributions and Critical Votes in the Governmental Organization Committee

Campaign contributions are one of the most visible tools interest groups have to achieve their policy goals. Studies show that making donations can be a successful strategy for groups that want to (1) elect candidates supportive of their issue positions, (2) gain access to members of the legislature, or (3) increase the amount of effort that legislators put forth on their behalf. However, evidence connecting money and the voting behavior of members of legislatures has been more ambiguous. Some find that contributions have a significant impact, whereas others find no direct effects.

The primary reason our findings are so ambiguous is because we assume that all votes are created equal in the eyes of interest groups. But, if the theory developed here is correct, all votes are not equal. Therefore, we must account for the political context within which voting occurs, because only then will we find that some votes are worth more to interest groups than others and/or are less costly to legislators. It is on those votes that contributions will be given as an appropriate reciprocal exchange for contributions.

Four aspects of the political context affect the value of votes to donors and recipients and, therefore, are important to the success of political donations: (1) the amount of contributions given by groups either in support of or opposition to a bill, (2) the importance of a single vote to the contributing group, (3) the visibility of the voting process to a member's constituency, and (4) the nature of the committee where the vote occurs. The purpose of this chapter is to address the first two of these variables and control for the third, using data from the California State Senate Committee on Governmental Organization. Any conclusions regarding the influence of committee characteristics on this relationship are left to Chapter 6. I first discuss the characteristics of the committee to be studied and explain why it is an interesting and important case. After presenting the results from this committee, I further test whether the findings are consistent for all committees in the California Senate.

## 1. The Senate Committee on Governmental Organization

### 1.1 Why Study Committees?

Before outlining the details of the Governmental Organization Committee in particular, it is important to discuss the choice to study committee, rather than floor, behavior. Committee behavior is the focus here for three reasons. Schroedel (1986) states the first reason best:

> The committees function as gatekeepers by determining which legislative proposals are considered by the entire House. A crucial first step for lobbyists is to win support at the committee level. Much of the money an interest group gives to candidates is targeted at members of the committee considering legislation relevant to the giver. Therefore, if the money has an effect at all, it is most likely to appear in the behavior of members on committees dealing with the legislation affecting those interest groups (p. 371).

There is another, related argument regarding committees as gatekeepers. If lobbying is a strategic behavior, groups will center their attention on committee members because there are fewer of them to influence. This is particularly true if a group is trying to kill a bill rather than assist its passage. To kill a bill requires only that a majority of the members of a single committee vote against the bill. Therefore, the strongest relationship between votes and contributions will be found in committee, especially when groups are acting defensively, because this is the most efficient use of their time and effort. The allocation patterns of interest group contributions provide additional support for the significance of committees because committee assignments are important determinants of interest group campaign contribution patterns (Fleisher 1993; Gordon and Unmack 2003; Grier and Munger 1986).[1]

The third, and perhaps most important, reason for studying committee rather than floor votes harkens back to the contextual argument I have been making all along. One important aspect of political context is the visibility that a vote has among a legislator's constituency. Those votes a legislator makes during less visible stages of the political process have fewer potential electoral costs than actions of which constituents are aware. It is on these low-cost votes that legislators feel most compelled to provide a reciprocal gift to their contributors. Although this does not preclude the possibility that contributions can influence voting on the floor—the beer distribution bill discussed in Chapter 4 illustrates that they can—most agree that contributions have a stronger effect on voting behavior in committee (Evans 1986 and 1996; Hall and Wayman 1990; Jones and Keiser 1987; Langbein and Lotwis 1990; Neustadtl 1990; Schroedel 1986).[2]

## 1.2 The Senate Governmental Organization Committee

As in most legislatures, in California a few committees are considered to be prime appointments. Often seats or chairs of these committees are given to members of the legislature who have been particularly supportive of the party leadership or to members whose support the leadership is trying to woo. For example, former Speaker of the State Assembly Willie Brown gave seats on the Assembly Governmental Organization Committee to two of the more conservative members of his party. This assignment was an attempt to maintain their support by providing them with a basis for considerable campaign contributions (Clucas 1995, 137).

Seats on these so-called juice committees are highly regarded among the membership because they address issues that attract the most financially well-endowed interest groups (Block and Carniello 1987; Rios 1981). Membership on these committees makes fund-raising easier as wealthy interest groups try to gain influence over those members who will have the most opportunity to influence their legislative agenda.

Governmental Organization is one such committee. Legislating the organization of government sounds like a fairly mundane task, but it is one of the most sought after assignments in either house of the California legislature (Clucas 1995, 137). This committee is responsible for regulating such issues as horse racing, public gaming, and alcoholic beverages (White 1987). The jurisdiction attracts the attention of waste haulers, casinos, state contractors, alcoholic beverage distributors, agricultural interests, and many others. In recent years, this panel has determined how to spend tobacco settlement money and how extensively to regulate Indian gaming.

Most importantly, though, this and other juice committees address many "scope of practice" issues. These are issues that pit two or more well-financed interest groups against one another in narrow, low visibility legislative battles. Examples of scope issues include the licensing of interior designers (supported by the designers, but opposed by architects and engineers) and allowing psychologists—not just psychiatrists—to prescribe medication (Walters

2000). Much like the beer distribution bill, the outcome of these policy debates may have financial implications for consumers but, like that same bill, the possibility is remote that they will inflame the passions of constituents.

In 1981, anecdotal evidence suggested that the Governmental Organization Committee was the second most requested committee by members of both houses of the California legislature (Rios 1981), presumably because of the contributions received by members of that committee.[3] If committees are the stage in the process where campaign contributions affect voting behavior, then the Senate Committee on Governmental Organization is one of the committees where the relationship should be strongest because of the large amounts of money that change hands and the nature of the issues addressed.[4]

## 2. Restatement of the Theory

If contributions and votes are more analogous to a gift relationship than to a market relationship, political context is important to understanding the association. Exactly which contextual factors have an impact? The first is the most obvious. The amount of money a group contributes should influence the strength of the relationship. If those who give, receive more in return (Komter 1996), it is possible that the more one gives, the more one receives. Indeed, Mauss argues that to fail to accept a gift is to lose face because it indicates that the potential recipient is not capable of returning the favor in kind. The implication is, the larger the contribution, the greater the sense of obligation to reciprocate when possible. Therefore, as the amount of money a group gives increases, so does the probability that members will vote in accordance with the interests of that group.

Even if the first hypothesis is the most obvious, it is the second that motivates this analysis. It is not simply the amount of money groups give to members that affects what impact contributions will have, it is the relative importance of the vote that the member is casting. So which votes are most important to groups? Fenno (1978) notes that election outcomes are somewhat dependent upon a legislator's reputation with his constituents. In addition, Erikson (1990) found that a legislator's reputation is influenced by his general voting patterns. It is because of this electoral connection that legislators are concerned with how their voting patterns appear to the public.

> Will Medicare be fixed? Will education get more money and the military less? Those megamatters aren't manipulated by lobbyists. They're too big. Lawmakers side with their constituents or with their parties on subjects of that scope and size. Why? Because a misstep there can lead to defeat at the polls.
>
> (Birnbaum 2000, 171)

Consequently, we should not expect legislators to vote in accordance with group interests based only upon the amount of money those groups give. However, we also know that as long as general voting patterns remain consistent, specific votes have little impact on opinions of the general public (Abramowitz 1980; Stokes and Miller 1966). Therefore, legislators have some leeway in their behavior on individual pieces of legislation. To continue Birnbaum's (2000) point,

> [I]t's the obscure and relatively minor issues that produce the most frenetic lobbying. And it is there, on the lucrative edges of legislation, that lobbyists work their ways. Lobbyists constantly obtain special exceptions or extra giveaways for their clients, and few other people ever notice (p. 171).

Given that both interest groups and members know this to be the case, contributions only affect legislative voting behavior in situations where the legislation is narrow enough not to create a conflict for the legislator and the legislator can act as a critical vote for the group. It is in these situations that interest groups will lobby an individual member more aggressively and that a member will be more susceptible to the group's pressure.

### 3. Data

By addressing only a small number of bills or groups, previous studies cannot make generalizable statements about the circumstances that affect the efficacy of interest group contributions. To remedy this problem, I use most of the bills that came before the Senate Committee on Governmental Organization in the 1987–88 legislative session. The 1987–88 session is used because it is prior to the passage of California's legislative term limits initiative, which should change the nature of the relationships studied here (Gordon and Unmack 2003).

I use all bills that (1) came to a vote, (2) were voted on without amendments, (3) had at least one group that took a position on the bill, and (4) were not unanimous or on the committee's consent calendar.[5] Most of these decision rules are quite common in voting studies. However, only using bills that came to a vote and were voted on without amendments is problematic for two reasons. First, the bills that come to a vote are not a random subset of all the bills referred to committee. Bills that never receive a hearing probably would not have passed committee and thus not including them in the analysis artificially reduces the number of nay votes in the analysis. In fact, this is the case. In the analysis presented here, there are only 272 nay votes compared to 657 aye votes. Only 29 percent of the votes studied are nay votes.

Unfortunately, there are few committee analyses for the bills that are never voted upon. Those analyses that are created are often purged from the files if the bills die without a hearing at the end of the two-year session. Because the committee analyses provide the information about interest group positions on bills and because no actual voting takes place, these bills cannot be included in the analysis.

Second, bills passed with amendments may also be systematically different from the bills passed without amendments. However, amended bills must be dropped because it is not possible to know whether the groups that voiced opposition/support according to the analysis continued to do so after the amendments were taken. Once all these bills are excluded, 929 votes on 102 bills remain to be analyzed. The variables included in the previous analyses—political party affiliation, district ideology, and member ideology—are studied here as well.

## 4. Findings

### 4.1 Model 1—A Simple Model of Campaign Contributions and Voting Behavior

The first step is to identify a direct relationship between contributions and votes across a large number of bills, groups, and political issues. Past studies have produced inconsistent evidence on this point and the first order of business is to determine whether a relationship is observable when a large number of diverse bills are included in the analysis.[6]

**4.1.1 Party, Member Ideology, and District Ideology.** As found in previous chapters, political party influences voting because it is a good measure of legislators' policy positions in that members of the same party have similar positions on issues. Consistent with past theory, political party has a strong effect on votes in the Governmental Organization Committee as well. In this committee, the probability of an aye vote is .80 if the voting member is of the same party as the author of the bill and .61 otherwise.

District and member ideology may also affect voting as they, too, are measures of other pressures on a legislator's vote. However, in this committee, neither of these two control variables has the expected effect. If a member's district has an ideology similar to the author of the bill's district, he is less likely to support the legislation. In addition, a member's personal liberal or conservative disposition has no effect on votes whatsoever. These are curious results because measures of district ideology are almost always insufficient predictors—unless they are direct measures of constituent interest in the topic on which the members are voting (Grenzke 1989)—and member ideology is almost always a strong predictor of legislative behavior (Jackson and Kingdon 1992).

These unexpected relationships are caused by the relationships between the three control variables; they essentially all measure the same concept.

These three variables—personal preferences, district, and party—identify different pressures on a legislator's issue position. However, conservative districts will tend to elect candidates with conservative positions and those candidates are likely to be members of the Republican Party so, when we include all three of these in the analysis we cannot know which one is causing the behavior. Only the one with the most significant statistical impact will be identified as important. If this analysis is conducted with only the contributions variables and the personal ideology measure (both party and district ideology variables are dropped), ideology has the expected effect on votes—exactly as expected.[7]

*4.1.2 Contributions.* More interestingly, the findings on the contributions variables illustrate the inconsistency found in past research and already discussed in detail here. Once we control for the effects of party, district, and personal ideology on voting, the effect of support and opposition contributions variables conflict with one another (see Figure 5.1).

In the Governmental Organization Committee, donations given by groups in support of a bill do not influence voting behavior, but money given by groups in opposition to a bill does. Controlling for other pressures, the more money a member receives from groups that oppose a bill, the less likely that member is to vote in support of that bill. Figure 5.1 shows that with zero contributions from opposition groups, the legislator has a .64 probability of voting aye on the bill, but only a .47 probability if he received $10,000. A contribution of that size results in a full 25 percent reduction in the probability of vote support. However, larger donations from supporting groups do not mean a member is more likely to vote aye. The likelihood of voting aye is about 70 percent, regardless of the amount of contributions received. Why these conflicting results? It is possible that the effect of contributions is being dampened because we have not yet taken account of critical votes and, instead, are looking at all votes taken in the committee.

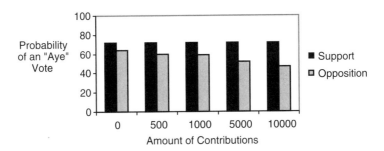

**Fig. 5.1** Support/Opposition Contributions on All Votes

### 4.1.3 Contributions and Critical Votes. To test this proposition, critical votes are separated from noncritical votes. A vote is deemed critical if a member's vote was any one of six aye votes (a simple majority of the eleven members of the committee) on a bill and that bill passed or if the member was any of the nay votes on a bill that failed. Otherwise, they are categorized as noncritical votes.

The reason all nay votes are critical votes on bills that fail is because bills rarely fail with a simple majority of nay votes (King and Zeckhauser 1997). Of the bills in this analysis that passed, 44 percent had a bare majority of aye votes, but none of the bills that failed were critical. This is because members who plan to vote for a bill often change their votes to abstentions (which count as nay votes here) when it becomes clear that a bill will not pass, because there is little incentive for a legislator to take a position on a bill that is not going to become policy. The tort reform bill, SB 2662, in Chapter 3 is an excellent example of this type of behavior.

However, there is reason to believe that outcomes on failed bills are more uncertain than they appear when only looking at final votes. Only 10 percent of the bills in this analysis failed, even after dropping all of the unanimous votes, suggesting that bills that will clearly fail are unlikely to receive a vote. It is probably the case that the outcomes of the failed bills must be somewhat uncertain for a vote to be taken at all. This is especially true in California where a bill can only receive two failing votes in committee before it is considered dead and becomes the property of the committee. Because of this, a member will tend to hold his bill over rather than have it voted on if it is clear that the bill will not pass.

A couple of examples are in order. In 1991, Assembly Speaker Brown (D-San Francisco) agreed not to ask for an Insurance Committee vote on his low-cost auto insurance bill when another low-cost plan failed and when "committee members, including Senate President Pro Tempore David Roberti, D-Los Angeles, said neither bill appeared to offer much savings to middle-income drivers" (Kushman 1991). Again, in 1998, a motorcycle helmet bill was referred to the California State Senate Transportation Committee and received a hearing. During the committee hearing, "the bill's author ... pulled it from the schedule after it did not appear to have enough support to advance to the full Senate" (Bee Capitol Bureau 1998).

Federal examples are available as well. On August 5, 1993, the U.S. House of Representatives voted on Clinton's economic plan. "On this vote the center of gravity seemed to be around 213. If they didn't get past that point, droves of Democrats could smell defeat and switch their votes. The whole thing could tumble back, and they could lose by 20 votes" (Woodward 1994, 301). In other words, there were two possible scenarios: the bill would pass with a simple majority or lose by 20. If the bill was going to fail anyway, the members would prefer not to take a position, especially if they were going to be on the wrong side.

The desire to claim credit may be another reason for this behavior. If a bill passes and voters feel positive impacts from the new policy, a member who voted aye can take credit for those results. For members who voted nay (or abstained), they can say that they had difficulties with some aspects of the bill but, because the bill passed anyway, their vote did not hurt it (i.e., they would have voted for it if it appeared as though it was going to fail). However, if one votes aye on a bill that fails, the member is taking a position on a bill that is irrelevant. If members are wary of constituent responses to the positions that they take on bills (Cohen and Noll 1991; Fiorina 1974; Thomas 1991), they are likely to abstain rather than vote, especially when that abstention does not change the outcome of the vote (Cohen and Noll 1991).

Note that there is no way to know, for sure, which of the members of the coalition of critical votes is the swing vote. It is possible that most of the votes that are coded as critical here are purely routine: members voting on the basis of their party affiliation or ideology, not because of contributions or interest group pressure. However, to the extent that these other pressures are included in the analysis they are being taken into account.[8]

So, once critical votes are separated from the noncritical, how much money does it take to influence a vote?[9] It depends. On noncritical votes, contributions do not influence votes regardless of the amount given. The only variable that has an influence on noncritical votes is political party: members of the same party as the author of the bill have a .76 probability of voting aye and opposition party members have a .56 probability of an aye vote.

However, on critical votes, contributions are the only variables affecting behavior. Although the probability of voting aye on a bill is relatively high even when support contributions are equal to zero (probability equals .87) that probability increases as contributions from supporting organizations increase. In fact, when a group contributes as much as $10,000, they can increase the probability of a critical yes vote by .08, making it almost certain that the member will vote aye if absolutely necessary (see Figure 5.2).

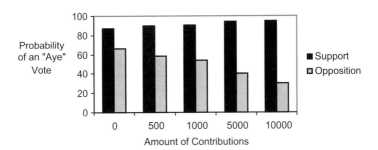

**Fig. 5.2** Support/Opposition Contributions on Critical Votes Only

The results are even more striking for critical nay votes. If a member receives no contributions from groups in opposition to a bill, the probability that he will cast an aye vote is .66. If he receives $5,000 in contributions, the probably that he will place a critical aye vote drops to .40. If he receives $10,000 from groups in opposition to that bill, the probability that he will cast that critical yes vote drops to .30. In essence, a group can reduce the probability of support by more than 50 percent simply by making political donations.

### 4.1.4 Why the Large Difference between Nay and Aye Votes? Figure 5.1 and Figure 5.2 demonstrate that although interest groups may improve the probability that a legislator will support their interests simply by donating to that member's political campaign, this relationship is particularly strong for critical votes, especially critical nay votes. This brings up an important question: why is the effect of contributions so much stronger on critical no votes than on critical yes votes? The answer has to do with the ratio of yes to no votes.

As mentioned in the discussion of how critical votes are categorized, the number of nay votes in this, or any, analysis is artificially low. If a bill comes to a vote, there is a greater likelihood that a legislator will support it than oppose it. There are two reasons for this. First, if a bill is coming to a vote, the author must either believe that it has enough support to pass or simply want to make other legislators take a position on the issue, so bills that fail are less likely to come to a vote. Second, because an abstention is the same as a vote against legislation, some members prefer not to take a position when their preference is for the bill to fail so, many no votes become abstentions.

This is especially true for critical nay votes when money enters the picture. A legislator might be more willing to respond to contributing interest groups if he can easily explain that behavior to his constituents. This is easy to do; if legislators want to vote nay but not take a position, they simply abstain. In 2002, a privacy bill in the California Assembly would have required financial institutions (e.g., banks and insurance companies) to get permission from consumers before selling their information to other vendors. This bill was strongly opposed by these wealthy, affected institutions that contributed a total of more than $5 million to every state lawmaker and the governor. On the last night of the legislative session, the bill failed (Yamamura 2002).

But, it is the patterns of contributions and voting on this bill that illustrate my point. Those who voted against the bill received $28,000 more from the banks and insurers than those who supported it. But, the seventeen Democrats who abstained from the vote—effectively voting nay and causing its defeat—received 60 percent more money than those who supported it. This Democratic opposition to the bill was unexpected because, not only was the bill authored by a Democrat, but Democrats are usually supportive of legislation that protects consumers against big business (Yamamura 2002). Because the Democrats who voted against the legislation were also voting against their own ideology (and potentially their district's ideology or preferences) they preferred to abstain rather than vote no, even though the two behaviors are functionally equivalent and have the same impact on the outcome of the legislation.

Each of these dynamics acts to reduce the number of no votes in the analysis and because of the artificially low number of negative votes, there is always a greater initial probability for an aye vote. This means there is less opportunity for that probability to increase. For example, if the initial probability for a nay vote is .56, it can drop from .56 all the way to 0 as contributions increase, a range of .56. But, if the initial probability for an aye vote is .70, it can only increase to 1.0, a smaller range of .30. Therefore, the measurable effect on supportive votes will always be somewhat constrained by the higher initial probabilities.

### 4.2  Contributions in All Senate Committees

In one of the committees in the California Senate where contributions are believed to have the strongest impact, contributions do influence members' votes across all issues and interest groups, but not across all votes. The votes that are crucial to a successful winning (or losing) coalition are more strongly affected by money from pressure groups than are votes in other contexts. The next task, however, is to replicate these results using votes from all senate committees. Although it is useful to know that contributions can dramatically affect legislative outcomes in this one case, if the results are limited to this one type of committee, the effect of contributions are still relatively limited as well.

**4.2.1  Party, District Ideology, and Member Ideology.** In this section, a random sample of all votes taken in all senate committees are included in the analysis and discussion. The results using these votes are much like those in the Governmental Organization Committee. First, if the author of the bill is of the same party as the member who is voting on the bill, the probability is higher that the voting member will support the bill (from .61 probability of support to .81 probability of support). However, in this case, ideology also plays an important role. A legislator whose personal ideology is below average (for the senate as a whole) is 10 percent less likely to vote aye than a legislator whose ideology is above average.[10]

**4.2.2  Contributions.** Most importantly, Figure 5.3 looks almost identical to Figure 5.1; the results on the contributions variables are exactly the same as those for the Governmental Organization Committee by itself. Contributions from groups in support of legislation appear to have no influence on voting behavior, but those from groups in opposition do. Figure 5.3 shows how the probability of an aye vote does not increase as the amount of support contributions grow, but decreases slightly as the amount of opposition contributions increase.

### 4.2.3 Contributions and Critical Votes.

Once again, the cause of these conflicting results becomes clear when critical votes are separated from noncritical votes in that both contributions variables became significant (see Figure 5.4). The larger the contributions from groups in support, the higher the probability a legislator will vote aye on a bill and the larger the contributions in opposition, the more likely the legislator is to vote nay.

On critical votes, party remains a significant predictor, but in the opposite direction expected. This suggests that contributions may even be able to override party considerations on critical votes. However, on noncritical votes, party is the only significant determinant of voting behavior. Members of the same party are almost twice as likely to support each others' bills as members of opposing parties. In conclusion, the contributions relationships found in the Governmental Organization Committee remain when all senate committees are included in the analysis.

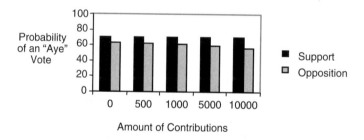

**Fig. 5.3**  Support/Opposition Contributions on All Votes, All Committees

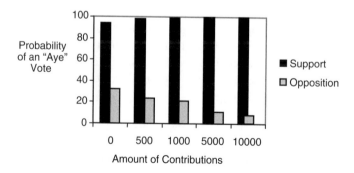

**Fig. 5.4**  Support/Opposition Contributions on Critical Votes, All Committees

## 5. Conclusion

If a relationship between campaign contributions and voting behavior is to be found anywhere, the California Senate Committee on Governmental Organization is where we should expect to observe it. Members of the California State Senate seek out membership on this committee to attract campaign contributions and they are rarely disappointed. Governmental Organization addresses issues that affect many well-endowed groups and its members raise large amounts of money from these interests.

However, even if large quantities of contributions change hands, and even if contributions do affect votes, a member will not respond to group pressure every time a contributor has a bill before the committee. First of all, legislators do not want their constituents to think they are owned by any given interest. And, second, a member's vote is not always needed. Often, indeed most of the time, a group has a natural majority that supports their bill based on other considerations, such as ideology or constituent interest. This is especially important to understand if contributions are not provided as a *quid pro quo* for votes. If, instead, those contributions are given for the purposes of gaining access, and the effect on votes is a by-product of the relationship that is created by that initial gift, we need to identify which circumstances are most likely to engender the obligation to respond with a reciprocal offering.

Sometimes an interest group needs a vote because a bill they support will not pass without it. It is at this point in the process where contributions have their greatest impact. If a bill is important to an interest group and the member's vote is necessary to the outcome of that legislation, lobbyists increase the amount of pressure they place on the members to whom they contribute and those members are more likely to support the group's position because of the implied obligation produced by the contributions given by that group. These are the situations that must be isolated if a relationship between campaign contributions and legislative voting behavior is to be observed. In fact, that is exactly what we find here.

Only by including a large number of bills that address many different issue areas and interest groups, can we determine whether campaign contributions affect votes in specific circumstances. In this case, the evidence supported both of the proposed hypotheses. In general, campaign contributions do appear to have an independent impact on voting behavior. The more money that a member receives from a group in opposition to a bill, the more likely that member is to vote in support of the group's interests. However, this relationship is driven by the impact of critical votes. Once critical and noncritical votes are identified, it becomes clear that campaign contributions only influence votes when those votes are necessary to the achievement of group goals.

Even though the relationships found in the Governmental Organization Committee, a juice committee, hold when votes from all committees are included, the question remains whether this relationship changes, even in minor ways, depending on various committee characteristics. In Chapter 2, I discussed how money might influence votes less dramatically in committees other than Governmental Organization. It is possible that the relationships found here for all committees is driven by votes held in committees more susceptible to the influence of interest group money. In the next chapter, I identify three important committee characteristics that might alter this relationship and test whether or not they do so. Only in this way can we establish whether the connection between critical votes and interest group donations is relatively common or whether it is even more complex and context-dependent than originally thought.

# 6

# Do Committee Characteristics Matter?

In this chapter, I further investigate the conditional influence of contributions. Specifically, I test whether various committee characteristics affect the strength of the relationship between interest group money and votes. The idea that committees differ and, therefore, have different decision making processes is not new. A committee's jurisdiction (Hinckley 1975; Maltzman 1997) and the nature of its clientele groups (Fenno 1973) have been shown to influence committee decision making. Based on anecdotal evidence and our understanding of the nature of committees, I identify three types of committees in which votes may be particularly appropriate as a reciprocal offering for contributions.

In narrow jurisdiction committees—committees that address relatively few distinct issues—the probability is higher that a member will have a strong position on any one bill that comes before the committee. On the other hand, in a committee that addresses a larger number of unrelated issues, a legislator is less likely to have a strong position regarding the individual policy on which he finds himself voting. This distinction is important because we know that a member's vote is less susceptible to the influence of contributions when that member's policy predisposition is strong (Fleisher 1993). Because members of broad jurisdiction committees have firm opinions on fewer of the bills referred to the committee, there is a higher probability that their votes are affected by the contributions they receive.

Second, contributions should influence behavior in committees where the membership is ideologically moderate as opposed to those committees where the membership is more extreme. This hypothesis, too, is based on Fleisher's (1993) research that moderate members are more easily influenced by contributions because their positions on issues are less concrete. For various reasons, to be discussed below, some committees attract moderate memberships and others attract legislators with stronger, more extreme issue positions. Those committees with extreme members are influenced by contributions less often.

Third, anecdotal evidence suggests that contributions might bias behavior more consistently in juice committees. As mentioned in previous chapters, juice committees are those committees whose issues affect interest groups with significant financial resources; examples include the Insurance Committee and the Governmental Organization Committee in the California Senate. If gifts in the form of campaign contributions create an unstated sense of obligation, larger gifts probably create a stronger bond than do smaller contributions.

In this chapter, I first discuss the effects of these various committee characteristics on legislative behavior. Then, I theorize why we should expect these same characteristics to be an important environmental factor in committee vote decisions. Finally, I test these three hypotheses using voting and contributions data on the same 104 bills from the California State Senate used at the conclusion of Chapter 5.

What I find is that the relationship between contributions and votes is extremely consistent. Contributions affect critical votes and not noncritical votes, regardless of the type of committee studied. However, the extent to which this relationship is hidden from view depends on committee characteristics. A consistent relationship between contributions and votes is not readily observable when looking at votes in narrow jurisdiction, juice, nonjuice, and extreme committees, until one separates critical from noncritical votes. This relationship is more obvious when looking at broad jurisdiction and extreme committees even when all votes are included in the analysis. However, it is clear even in these latter cases that the relationship found is being driven by the effect of the critical votes. The decision making dynamic in certain committees increases the probability that votes will be provided in response to contributions received.

## 1. Committee Characteristics and Legislative Decision Making

Various committee characteristics influence legislative behavior. First, Fenno (1973) notes that member goals are crucial to understanding the decision processes used by legislators in various committees. He states that members are attracted to different committees based upon their primary goals as legislators.

For example, members who primarily seek power within the U.S. House of Representatives request the Appropriations and Ways and Means committees. Those for whom reelection is the crucial issue seek constituency service committees such as the Interior Committee and the Post Office Committee. And, members interested in public policy seek membership on the Education and Labor and the Foreign Affairs committees (Fenno 1973).

Given these goals, different variables affect decision making once members secure a position on these committees. In particular, and within certain environmental constraints, those who seek power in the institution are influenced by other members in the house, those for whom reelection is a primary interest are responsive to their geographic constituencies, and those who want to make public policy respond to the groups that dominate the policy arena in which they operate (Fenno 1973).

Second, Fenno notes other factors that determine to which constituencies legislators are most responsive. These factors include both institutional and environmental constraints. He defines institutional constraints as limitations placed on the committee by the parent chamber (e.g., whether the chamber expects the committee to be representative of and responsive to party interests) and environmental constraints as the groups that dominate the committee's policy making environment. For instance, committees whose jurisdictions attract few, monopolistic, clientele groups are less swayed by partisanship, because the clientele groups work to avoid partisanship to maintain their own policy making power. On the other hand, committees whose jurisdictions involve competition between a larger number of groups are less affected by partisan behavior.

This may relate to committee jurisdiction as committee jurisdictions can alter the types of groups that characterize a committee's policy making environment. For example, committees with fragmented or broad jurisdictions have a larger number of diverse groups interested in their activities (Deering and Smith 1997) and, therefore, according to Fenno, may be more partisan in their decision making.

Hinckley (1975) identifies two aspects of committees' "policy content." She argues that both the stakes of committee jurisdiction (zero-sum versus positive-sum allocations) and the scope (how many Congresspeople are interested in the committee's agenda) affect legislative behavior in particular committees. She finds that broad scope committees are more attractive to legislators, have more stability in membership, and contain more senior members than narrow scope committees, but that the broadness or narrowness of the scope of jurisdiction has no affect on the cohesiveness of committee recommendations. However, she argues that the scope of a committee's jurisdiction does not alter behavior, but the competitive or noncompetitive nature of its policy domain does. Specifically, committees with competitive policy content tend to be less cohesive in their decision making than are non-competitive committees.

Maltzman (1997) and Maltzman and Smith (1995) note other aspects of jurisdiction that are important to understanding committee decision making. They argue that the salience of the committee's agenda or jurisdiction is one factor that helps to determine to which interest groups a committee will be most responsive.[1] The chamber as a whole and the majority party caucus are more willing to defer judgment to committees whose agendas are not of significant interest to a large segment of the population. In these situations, the committee is more responsive to narrow, outside constituencies with a strong interest in the issue at hand (e.g., district constituencies and interest groups) than to their colleagues within the U.S. Congress. In fact, this is exactly what is observed. As noted numerous times, campaign contributions have a stronger impact on voting behavior when issue salience is low (Evans 1986 and 1996; Jones and Keiser 1987; Langbein and Lotwis 1990; Neustadtl 1990; Schroedel 1986).

Finally, King (1997), too, maintains that differing jurisdictions influence the power interest groups wield in committee decision making. Drawing on research by Baumgartner and Jones (1993), he notes that fragmented committee agendas (caused by jurisdictional conflicts among legislators) have led to a decline in the power of interest groups in traditional iron triangle committees by "increasing the points at which interest groups can access Congress" (p. 144). Because groups must focus on more than one committee, close relationships that characterize iron triangles do not develop.

### 1.1 Size of Committee Jurisdictions, Contributions, and Votes

Although the impact of committee jurisdiction on various aspects of legislative and interest group behavior (Fenno 1973; King 1997; Maltzman 1997; Maltzman and Smith 1995) has been identified, how jurisdiction size directly affects the value or cost that a legislator places on a vote (and, therefore, influences the relationship) has not. The theory presented here suggests that legislators in narrow jurisdiction committees are influenced less by contributions than are those in broad jurisdiction committees.[2]

First, committee memberships are, at least to some degree, self-selected. Legislators request membership on certain committees because they come from districts with a strong interest in a particular committee's work product (Adler and Lapinski 1997). Others choose committees that will help them to achieve their legislative goals or because of a personal interest or expertise in a given policy area (Shepsle 1978; Sinclair 1988; Deering and Smith 1997). Some members request committees that are considered to be prime positions from which to raise needed campaign funds (Block and Carniello 1987; Rios 1981).

That is not to say that there are no restrictions on committee selection by individual members. For example, party interests (Cox and McCubbins 1993) and the limited number of seats available on the most requested committees (Shepsle 1978) each constrain access to committees that help members achieve their legislative goals. These restrictions explain why internal institutions have developed to ration committee assignments (Munger 1988). However, committees serve as a place from which legislators can claim credit for legislation important to their constituents for the purposes of reelection (Mayhew 1974), so parties have few incentives to keep their members off the committees they desire, if there is room. As Deering and Smith (1997) note, "[a]lthough there are opportunities to do so, current party leaders do not exercise special influence on the vast majority of assignment decisions. In general, steering committees attempt to grant the requests of members within the constraints of the number of vacancies" (p. 101).

Second, if members choose a particular committee because of their interest in an issue area, regardless of the reason for that interest, they usually have a well-developed and consistent position on the issue that led them to select that committee. On committees that address bills on only a few issue areas (narrow jurisdiction), there is a high probability that on any given vote a member has a strong position on the issue before him. However, on broad jurisdiction committees, members probably have a strong position on the one issue that led them to request the committee, but are ambivalent on the numerous other issues within the jurisdiction. If legislators have strong, personal feelings on an issue, the psychic costs of voting against that preference makes them less willing to use the vote as a reciprocal for contributions.

For example, in the California Senate, the Governmental Organization Committee has an extremely broad jurisdiction. This committee addresses horse racing, public gaming, alcoholic beverage control, use of state lands, the organization of state and local government, and veterans' affairs (White 1987). One of the members of the committee in the 1987–88 legislative session was the Republican leader, Senator Ken Maddy (R-Fresno). One of the reasons Maddy requested a seat on the committee was because of his interest in horse racing. In fact, Ken Maddy introduced six bills on horse racing during the legislative session. These six bills constituted 9 percent of Maddy's total bill load and over 50 percent of all senate bills introduced on horse racing. However, senate bills on horse racing made up only 7 percent of Governmental Organization's agenda. Even if Maddy's interest in horse racing extended to gaming, the bills on those two issues comprised only 13 percent of the senate bills referred to the Governmental Organization Committee in 1987–88.

Compare this to the Assembly Committee on Natural Resources, a narrow jurisdiction committee. The Natural Resources Committee is responsible for legislation affecting the resources of the state, for example, California

Environmental Quality Act legislation. Although this could be considered a broad jurisdiction, it is made narrow by the fact that in 1987–88 the committee shared much of its potential jurisdiction with three other committees—Agriculture; Environmental Safety and Toxic Materials; and Water, Parks, and Wildlife. In addition, even though the legislation referred to the committee could address clean water, air pollution, etc., each of these issues falls under the general policy area of environmental protection. Upward of 90 percent of the bills on which members voted addressed that type of issue. And, if members' committee requests are based on their positions on environmental quality, they will be unwilling to respond to constituent desires against their own preferences on a large number of those bills. This distinction between the strength of members' positions based on the nature of committee jurisdiction is critical, because the strength of a member's position on an issue is important to understanding how contributions will affect their votes.

*1.1.1 Measuring the Size of Committee Jurisdictions.* King (1997) notes that there two types of committee jurisdictions—formal and informal. In other words, for each committee there is the jurisdiction listed in the rules and then there are those issues that are actually referred to the committee over time as conflicts over turf arise. The first is not usually the most accurate measure of a committee's jurisdiction because it does not take account of the informal changes in referral behavior that are not reflected in the formal rules.

Committees are separated for this analysis based on a measure of their informal jurisdiction, using the number of unique bill topics (as listed in bill summaries) for each committee. The number of topics per committee is listed in column two of Table 6.1.[3]

A survey of fourteen long-term staff members of the California Senate was conducted to test the reliability of this measure.[4] Of these, eight surveys were returned. The respondents were asked to rank the jurisdictions of each of the senate's eighteen policy committees from the narrowest (1) to the broadest (18).[5] The lowest and the highest ranks for each committee were dropped and those remaining were averaged to create the final scores. The committees were ranked from one to eighteen on the basis of these scores. Those committee rankings are listed in column three of Table 6.1. Although the committees are ranked somewhat differently according to the two measures, for the most part, the broad versus narrow designation for each committee remains the same.[6] Because it is more objective, the number of bill topics is used to determine the narrow/broad committee designation.

*1.1.2 Findings: Broad versus Narrow Jurisdiction Committees.* In broad jurisdiction committees, where the relationship between contributions and votes should be the strongest, contributions do appear to affect votes regardless of whether the vote is critical or noncritical (see Figure 6.1). Support and opposition contributions have a slight positive and negative relationship, respectively, with the probability of supporting a bill. In addition, party has the expected effect on voting. A legislator of the same party as the author of the bill is 14 percent more likely to vote for the legislation; the probability increases from .62 to .76.

However, that does not mean that separating critical from noncritical votes has no effect. Figure 6.2 makes it clear that the relationship between donations and votes differs based on the vote context. The slope for support

**TABLE 6.1**  Size of Committee Jurisdiction

| Committee | Number of Topics | Survey Ranking (1 = Most Narrow) | Jurisdiction Size (on Survey if Differs) |
|---|---|---|---|
| Banking and Commerce | 26 | 4 | Narrow |
| Business and Professions | 81 | 15 | Broad |
| Education | 72 | 13 | Broad |
| Elections | 16 | 1 | Narrow |
| Energy and Public Utilities | 29 | 8 | Narrow |
| Governmental Organization | 197 | 17 | Broad |
| Health and Human Services | 109 | 16 | Broad |
| Housing and Urban Affairs | 40 | 3 | Narrow |
| Industrial Relations | 41 | 5 | Narrow |
| Insurance | 38 | 13 | Narrow (Broad) |
| Judiciary | 251 | 18 | Broad |
| Local Government | 98 | 9 | Broad (Narrow) |
| Natural Resources | 53 | 11 | Broad (Narrow) |
| Public Employees and Retirement | 31 | 2 | Narrow |
| Revenue and Taxation | 19 | 10 | Narrow |
| Toxics | 35 | 6 | Narrow |

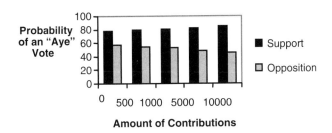

**Fig. 6.1**  Support/Opposition on All Votes for Broad Jurisdiction Committees

contributions is much steeper for critical votes than when all votes are included. On the other hand, no amount of support contributions affects noncritical votes. This pattern holds for opposition contributions as well.[7] Obviously the positive effect of donations on all votes is driven by the critical votes in the analysis. In broad jurisdiction committees, contributions only influence voting when votes are critical.

These findings are particularly interesting when compared to those for narrow jurisdiction committees. In those committees, the relationship between contributions and votes is completely hidden when all votes are included in the analysis: neither contributions variable is a significant predictor of voting behavior. This might lead us to believe that contributions do not influence votes in narrow jurisdiction committees. However, this hypothesis is not supported when critical votes are separated from the noncritical (see Figure 6.3A and Figure 6.3B).

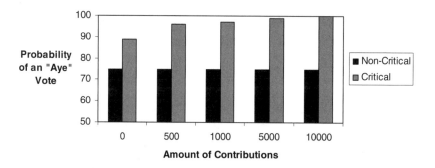

**Fig. 6.2**  Support Contributions to Broad Jurisdiction Committees

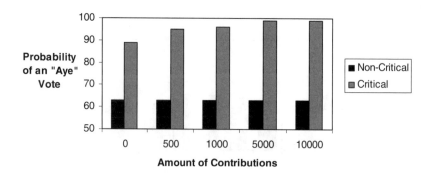

**Fig. 6.3A**  Support Contributions to Narrow Jurisdiction Committees

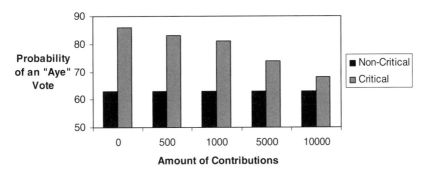

**Fig. 6.3B** Opposition Contributions to Narrow Jurisdiction Committees

Once again, consistent with previous analyses, both support and opposition contributions affect voting on critical votes, but not noncritical votes. Although it is not readily obvious from the graphs, it is important to note that the effects of the support and opposition contributions are much smaller than in the broad jurisdiction committees. So, although contributions do influence voting behavior in both contexts, the relationship is both clearer and stronger in broad jurisdiction committees. It is in broad jurisdiction committees that contributions have the most significant effect because the size of the jurisdiction means that legislators have less concrete opinions on any individual bill on which they are voting.

### 1.2 Campaign Contributions and Ideologically Moderate Committees

Another committee characteristic that may affect whether a legislator will feel obligated or be willing to provide a particular vote in response to contributions is the moderate versus extreme nature of the committee as a whole. Moderate members are more responsive to donor interests, presumably because their positions on the issues are less solidified (Fleisher 1993).[8]

But, which committees include more ideologically moderate members and which have more extreme memberships? Maltzman (1997) argues that committees whose jurisdictions encompass more salient issues are prone to have memberships that represent the interests of the majority party caucus so that the party can control directly the policy output of the committee. These committees are also likely to be more ideologically moderate. However, on constituency-related committees (e.g., the Agriculture and Interior committees) members are less representative of caucus interests, because it is in the party's interest to allow those members to respond to the constituencies who care about the legislation rather than the interests of the entire party. Potentially, these committees could be made up of more ideologically extreme members.

Fenno (1973) agrees and notes that the Appropriations Committee is given more leeway and power in making decisions, but is also expected to be more representative of house interests because it controls so many of the issues that are important to all house members. Therefore, the members of the Appropriations Committee are more ideologically moderate than other committees.

On the opposite end of the spectrum is the Judiciary Committee of the U.S. House of Representatives in the 1990s. In 1974, during the Nixon impeachment, the committee was quite moderate. However, in 1998, the Republicans on the committee were very conservative (more so than the Republican caucus as a whole) and the Democrats were much more liberal than their counterparts on the floor (Morgan 1998). The Republican contingent in 1998 was primarily (20 of 21 members) white, male, and Christian from suburban or rural districts; the Democratic side was composed of "six Jews, five blacks, three women and one declared homosexual" (Morgan 1998, A22).

The potential reasons for this political divide are twofold both related to jurisdictional issues. First, Representative Frank (D-MA) argues that the committee's jurisdiction encompasses new issues that have moved to the forefront of the American policy agenda and these issues (e.g., abortion, busing, gun control) incite and divide the American public. Therefore, the only legislators who feel safe serving on the Judiciary Committee have strong positions on these divisive issues and are from safe districts, so they can take overt positions on these issues without threatening their reelection chances (Morgan 1998). Second, others argue that "the Democratic and Republican leadership began applying their own political litmus tests for membership" (Morgan 1998, A23), only placing members on the committee who support the parties' generally accepted platform on these issues.

In conclusion, some committees are dominated by moderate members and others dominated by members biased in favor of particular policies (e.g., the Agriculture Committee) or with extreme members on either side of a policy (e.g., the Judiciary Committee). In the first case, contributions have a stronger influence and in the second and third, contributions are less efficacious.

*1.2.1 Identifying Extreme and Moderate Committees.* The average ideology for each committee is calculated by separating the members by party and averaging the ideology within each party. Then, the average Republican score is subtracted from the average Democratic score. A committee is designated as extreme if the absolute value of the difference between the party ideologies is greater than fifty. If the difference is less than fifty, the committee is coded as moderate.[9] The designation for each committee is listed in Table 6.2.

TABLE 6.2 Average Member Ideology, by Committee and Party

| Committee | Average Republican | Average Democrat | Extreme/ Moderate (Difference) |
|---|---|---|---|
| Banking and Commerce | 41 | 69 | Moderate (28) |
| Business and Professions | 32 | 75 | Moderate (43) |
| Education | 43 | 78 | Moderate (35) |
| Elections | 28 | 75 | Moderate (47) |
| Energy and Public Utilities | 41 | 70 | Moderate (29) |
| Governmental Organization | 45 | 74 | Moderate (29) |
| Health and Human Services | 35 | 72 | Moderate (37) |
| Housing and Urban Affairs | 20 | 76 | Extreme (56) |
| Industrial Relations | 35 | 70 | Moderate (35) |
| Insurance | 30 | 70 | Moderate (40) |
| Judiciary | 26 | 77 | Extreme (51) |
| Local Government | 40 | 68 | Moderate (28) |
| Natural Resources | 17 | 76 | Extreme (59) |
| Public Employees and Retirement | 20 | 80 | Extreme (60) |
| Revenue and Taxation | 38 | 71 | Moderate (33) |
| Toxics | 30 | 75 | Moderate (45) |

*1.2.2 Findings: Ideologically Moderate Versus Ideologically Extreme Committees.* Given that ideologically moderate members are more easily influenced by contributions because, theoretically, their positions are less concrete, it makes sense that the relationship between contributions and votes should be stronger in committees where moderate legislators are concentrated. Fleisher (1993) identified this relationship in regards to defense policy, but there is no reason to believe that the relationship will not apply regardless of the policy area, as long as positions on issues referred to the committee tend to be distributed along ideological lines.

The results for moderate committees are identical to those for broad jurisdiction committees, with three variables predicting voting behavior. Legislators of the same party are 21 percent more likely to vote for one another's bills than are members of opposing parties. Both of the contributions variables are significant as well. Figure 6.4 illustrates that as the amount of money from groups in support of legislation increases, so does the probability of an aye vote on that bill, although only slightly. As opposition group money increases, the probability of supporting a bill drops.

And, when critical and noncritical votes are separated, the relationship we have observed consistently is borne out again (see Figure 6.5A and Figure 6.5B).

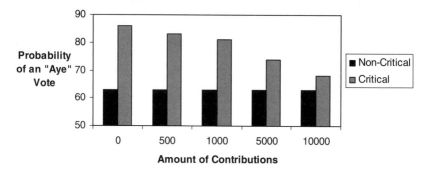

**Fig. 6.4**  Support/Opposition Contributions to Moderate Committees

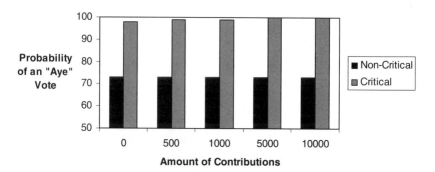

**Fig. 6.5A**  Support Contributions to Moderate Committees

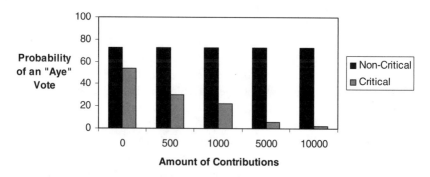

**Fig. 6.5B**  Opposition Contributions to Moderate Committees

On noncritical votes, party is the important variable, increasing the probability of providing support for legislation by 34 percent.

Once again, the slopes of the contributions variables in the critical votes analyses are substantially larger than in the analyses when all votes are included. The effect of support contributions is twenty-one times larger and the effect of opposition contributions is eight times larger. Substantively, this means that opposition money changes the probability of an aye vote from 52 percent with no contributions to 45 percent with $1,000 in contributions when all votes are included. That same $1,000 reduces the probability of an aye vote from 52 percent to less than 1 percent when only critical votes are included.

As predicted, the results for extreme committees are almost identical to those presented for narrow jurisdiction committees. Party is the only determinant of voting behavior for all votes in extreme committees. Members of the same party are slightly less likely to support legislation than those of opposite parties (.68 probability to .66). In addition, much like the analyses in Chapter 5, the contributions relationships are mixed when looking at critical votes only. Support contributions are not important to understanding votes, but opposition contributions are (see Figure 6.6).

In the noncritical votes analysis, party is the only predictor of voting behavior. Party members are almost twice as likely to support each other's bills as bills authored by members of the opposite party. Neither of the contributions variables even approaches statistical significance.

But, when critical votes are separated out and analyzed separately, the relationship, once again, becomes clear (see Figure 6.7A and Figure 6.7B). Both support and opposition contributions affect voting on critical votes, but not on any of the others.

Once again, contributions affect critical votes regardless of the committee type. However, the relationship is stronger and more obvious in the ideologically moderate committees, because it is in those committees that members are likely to have less solidified positions on legislation. But, even committees dominated by ideologically extreme members can have their policy outcomes affected by contributions; it is just less obvious to the casual observer when all votes (not just critical votes) are included in the analysis.

### 1.3 Juice Committees, Campaign Contributions, and Votes

It is also important to understand the influence of the committee's clientele groups on its decision making process. Juice committees (also known as money committees or cash cow committees) address issues that are of concern to groups with substantial financial resources. They tend to be the most popular among legislators because membership on those committees makes fund-raising, so necessary for modern campaigns, much easier.

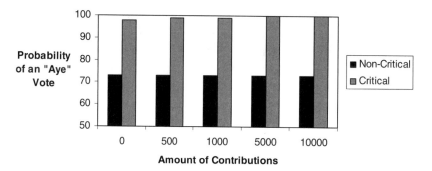

**Fig. 6.6**  Support/Opposition Contributions to Extreme Committees

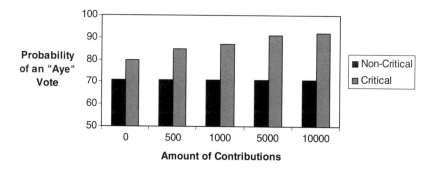

**Fig. 6.7A**  Opposition Contributions to Extreme Committees

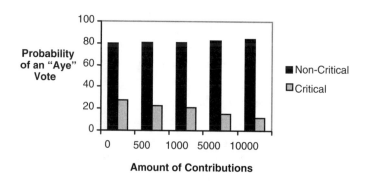

**Fig. 6.7B**  Opposition Contributions to Extreme Committees

> I remember when I got on Energy and Commerce [in the U.S. Congress], everybody jumped for the Telecommunications Subcommittee first.... There was a member sitting next to me, and every time another member bid for that subcommittee, he went "Ding!"—as if a cash register was going off.... There's a tremendous amount of money to be raised by members of that subcommittee from the telecommunications industry.
>
> (Kostmayer in Schram 1995, 2)

The same attraction to big money committees occurs in the California legislature. There are certain committees that invite more contributions and, therefore, are more popular among legislators.

> Why should [the Finance and Insurance Committee] be so popular? The committee has a huge bill load and its work affects insurance companies, banks, financial planners, mortgage bankers, savings-and-loans institutions.... Bills passing through the committee can sometimes cost (or save) businesses millions of dollars, and those industries tend to be generous givers. Also, titanic legislative battles over issues such as medical malpractice insurance can bring big spending lobbies into conflict, which also tends to generate campaign money for members.
>
> (Block and Carniello 1987, 179)

In the California State Legislature, committees such as Finance, Insurance, and Governmental Organization attract the most contributions (Block and Carniello 1987). In the U.S. Congress, committees such as Senate Finance and House Ways and Means are the cash cows (Schram 1995). Even legislators admit that the combination of large campaign contributions and the nature of committee jurisdictions for committees such as Finance are fodder for those who suggest that money alters voting behavior (Block and Carniello 1987). Part of the reason is that the issues that come before the money committees are not regularly covered by the press. Media coverage is only forthcoming when a major consumer bill is heard (Rios 1981). Therefore, members not only feel free to collect large amounts of money from interest groups, but can support their interests because their constituents are not paying close attention (Rios 1981).

The perception that juice committees are beholden to moneyed interests is further supported by the FBI sting in the California legislature in the early 1990s. Those legislators and lobbyists charged and convicted for illegal contributions practices tended to be involved in those issues addressed by the various money committees. For example, Clay Jackson was a lobbyist for many insurance companies (Richardson 1996), former Senator Alan Robbins was the chair of the Senate Insurance Committee (Walsh 1996), former Senator Joseph Montoya was chair of the Business and Professions Committee (White 1989), and former Assemblyman Frank Hill was a member of the Assembly Governmental Organization, Utilities and Commerce, and Ways and Means committees.

The combination of the large contributions available to members and the low salience of the issues addressed by big money committees produce a situation where the obligation and ability to reciprocate coincide.

*1.3.1 Identifying the Juice Committees.* Two measures are used to separate the money committees from the others. First, average contributions per member are calculated for each committee. This measure is problematic, however, because each member's contributions are determined by the combination of his committee memberships, no single assignment. Second, twenty staff members and lobbyists were surveyed to identify which committees they deemed to be juice committees.[10] The summary of these two measures is presented in Table 6.3.

It is obvious that the two measures are not strongly related.[11] For example, a few of the committees with the highest average contributions per member are clearly not large money committees as commonly understood by legislative staff and lobbyists. The Public Employees and Retirement Committee is not a money committee although its members received an average of $921,373

**TABLE 6.3** Average Contributions to Legislators, by Committee

| Committee | Average Contributions ($) | (Non)Juice Committee (% of Responses = Juice) |
|---|---|---|
| Banking and Commerce | 515,562 | Nonjuice (60) |
| Business and Professions | 451,671 | Nonjuice (50) |
| Education | 672,184 | Nonjuice (30) |
| Elections | 398,166 | Nonjuice (10) |
| Energy and Public Utilities | 513,123 | Nonjuice (60) |
| Governmental Organization | 692,437 | Juice (80) |
| Health and Human Services | 657,208 | Nonjuice (30) |
| Housing and Urban Affairs | 330,563 | Nonjuice (10) |
| Industrial Relations | 620,645 | Nonjuice (30) |
| Insurance | 972,912 | Juice (100) |
| Judiciary | 810,982 | Juice (70) |
| Local Government | 754,510 | Nonjuice (0) |
| Natural Resources | 397,021 | Nonjuice (20) |
| Public Employees and Retirement | 921,373 | Nonjuice (20) |
| Revenue and Taxation | 562,326 | Nonjuice (60) |
| Toxics | 452,103 | Nonjuice (30) |

in campaign donations. In addition, Local Government Committee members received $754,510 from contributors, but it is clearly not a committee that members request for the purposes of raising campaign funds.

Obviously the characteristics that define a juice committee are more than just the amount of money that is available from clientele groups. Rios (1981) notes that another important attribute is the lack of interest that the committees engender from the public and the press. The staff and lobbyists surveyed note that important attributes include the type of member who chairs the committee, the position of the majority party on the issues that come before the committee, and the lack of salience of the issues the committee addresses. Therefore, the staff surveys were used to determine which committees to code as juice committees and which committees to code as nonjuice committees. If a large majority of those surveyed considered the committee to be a money committee, it was identified as such here.[12]

In addition, a search for the term "juice committee" was conducted in *The Sacramento Bee's* archives. For the most part, the committees identified as the money committees in that context are consistent with those listed above. The two exceptions are the Business and Professions and the Banking and Commerce committees. Both of these panels are mentioned in almost every discussion of juice committees as among the most prominent because they deal with so many of the scope-of-practice issues discussed in Chapter 5. However, they are not identified by those surveyed as juice committees. For the purposes of the discussion below, I look at the effect of juice committees with those two committees included.[13]

### 1.3.2 Findings—Juice Committees versus Nonjuice Committees.

Party continues to be the most important variable explaining legislative voting. In juice committees, party affiliation increases the probability of support for a bill by almost 20 percent. Voting behavior in this context is affected by member ideology as well. However, the contributions results are mixed until we separate out the critical votes in the analysis. Figure 6.8 illustrates the different effects of support and opposition contributions. By now, this pattern should be quite familiar: although support contributions have no effect, support for legislation drops slightly as opposition contributions increase.

And, as in every other analysis, this relationship is driven by the effect of critical votes. Once the two types of votes are separated, the role of contributions becomes obvious again: they affect critical votes, but not noncritical votes.

Each of these results are the same for nonjuice committees. The only difference is that in nonjuice committees, party is negatively related to the probability of an aye vote on critical votes, suggesting that contributions can even overcome party pressures in some circumstances.

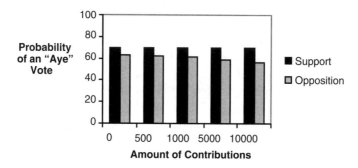

**Fig. 6.8**  Support/Opposition Contributions to Juice Committees

   These results on juice and nonjuice committees are somewhat different from those presented in the other types of committees and are quite unexpected. Unlike moderate and broad jurisdiction committees, the contributions variables have mixed results when all votes are included. There are three possible reasons for this. First, the measure of juice committees is quite subjective. It is possible that the true juice committees have not been identified with the measure presented here. The other possibility is that the money simply does not affect votes as strongly in these committees, regardless of the conventional wisdom. One of the characteristics of juice committees (noted by a respondent to the survey) is that moneyed groups are pitted against one another in these committees, leading both sides to give substantial contributions (Gladstone 1993). Although on critical votes legislators will probably still vote with the group that gave them the most money, large amounts of money almost always come from both sides, giving the impression that contributions do not have a significant impact. Third, and finally, legislators may be aware of the implication that money influences votes in these particular committees and may act in such a way as to defuse this preconception. Even though membership on these committees leads to large contributions, the results are no different than those presented for ideologically extreme committees, narrow jurisdiction committees, or nonjuice committees. The amount of money does not appear to affect the votes cast, unless those votes are critical to the outcome of legislation.

## 2. Discussion of the Results

The first thing to be noted about these results in their entirety is the consistency of the findings for the broad/narrow jurisdiction committees and the extreme/moderate committees, especially when compared to the Governmental Organization results presented in Chapter 5. The relationships found are consistent regardless of what type of committee is being studied. In narrow and extreme committees, contributions have no effect on voting behavior when all votes are included. In fact, no relationship is readily observable until critical votes are separated from noncritical, with contributions affecting critical votes, but not the others.

On the other hand, in broad and moderate committees, contributions have a discernible effect even when all votes are included. In each of the analyses on all votes, both of the contributions variables are significant predictors. When critical votes are separated from noncritical, however, the relationship between the variables becomes clear. On critical votes, the contributions variables remain significant and the coefficients are much larger than in the previous analyses. On noncritical votes, contributions do not have a detectable effect on voting.

These results provide meaningful information regarding the difference in the effect of contributions in varying committee situations. The most important point is that contributions affect voting on critical votes and not noncritical votes in all committee contexts. Legislators will respond to the interests of contributors when their vote is crucial to the outcome of legislation, but probably will choose not to do so when the results of the vote are more decisive. Contrary to expectations based on previous literature, this is true regardless of the type of committee and, therefore, the type of committee decision making process that is taking place.

Another important result is that the relationship between contributions and votes is much clearer, even when all votes are included, in the broad and moderate committees. The relationship between donations and critical votes is consistent across all committee situations, but the relationship between contributions and all votes is observable only in these two types of committees. This may explain why observers of the political process argue that money has such a significant effect in some committees and not in others. The relationship is simply more obvious in some committees.

It is possible that these incredibly consistent findings are a result of more critical votes occurring in moderate and broad jurisdiction committees. Perhaps in these committees, there are apt to be more critical votes due to the nature of the committee jurisdiction or committee makeup. For example, it is conceivable that committees with extreme memberships may have significantly more close votes than those made up of predominantly moderate members. This is not the case. Table 6.4 lists each type of committee and the percentage of the votes that are coded critical for each. The results are quite consistent. Approximately 20 to 30 percent of all votes are coded as critical, regardless of the type of committee. In fact, the only committees that have substantially more critical votes as a percentage of total votes are narrow jurisdiction committees (33 percent) and contributions have a weaker effect, not stronger, in those committees. So, the sheer number of critical votes is not what is driving the stronger results we find in some committee types.

Instead, the most logical answer is that the readily observable and consistent results are due to the stronger influence of contributions in some committees. Table 6.5 lists the coefficients on both contributions variables on critical votes in the different committee types. In every case, the size of the effect is consistent with the hypotheses proposed. Broad, juice, and moderate committees always have larger coefficients than their comparison committees (narrow, nonjuice, and extreme committees, respectively).

Finally, it is also possible that the consistent results are a consequence of the fact that the committees break down along the same lines regardless of the characteristics discussed. For example, committees with broad jurisdictions may also have extreme memberships and be juice committees. However, this is not the case. Table 6.6 contains the correlations between these three variables.

**TABLE 6.4** Percent of Votes that Are Coded Critical, by Type of Committee

| Type of Committee | Percent Critical |
| --- | --- |
| All Committees | 25 |
| Broad Jurisdiction Committees | 23 |
| Narrow Jurisdiction Committees | 33 |
| Juice Committees | 19 |
| Nonjuice Committees | 29 |
| Extreme Committees | 25 |
| Moderate Committees | 25 |

**TABLE 6.5** Contributions Coefficients on Critical Votes, by Type of Committee

| Type of Committee | Support Coefficient | Opposition Coefficient |
| --- | --- | --- |
| All Committees | .0304 | −.0114 |
| Broad Jurisdiction Committees | .0385 | −.0234 |
| Narrow Jurisdiction Committees | .0219 | −.0070 |
| Juice Committees | .0938 | −.0162 |
| Nonjuice Committees | .0260 | −.0161 |
| Moderate Committees | .0514 | −.0310 |
| Extreme Committees | .0138 | −.0071 |

**TABLE 6.6** Correlations between Committee Characteristics

| Committee Types | Correlations |
| --- | --- |
| Juice and Broad Jurisdiction Committees | .29* |
| Juice and Moderate Committees | −.40* |
| Moderate and Broad Jurisdiction Committees | −.16* |

*p .001

Although each of the correlation coefficients is statistically significant, none of them are large and two of the coefficients are negative. Broad jurisdiction committees may also be considered juice committees, but moderate membership committees are more likely to be both narrow jurisdiction committees and nonjuice committees. In Table 6.7, each of the committees used in the analysis is presented along with a note of how many of the characteristics they have that would lead to a stronger relationship between contributions and votes.

There is not a strong positive relationship between these characteristics that would lead to the surprisingly consistent findings demonstrated above. In addition, one committee provides almost one-third of the observations. The Judiciary Committee has by far the largest bill load in the senate as illustrated by the fact that it provides 333 of the 908 observations used in these analyses. The Judiciary Committee is a broad jurisdiction committee, an ideologically extreme committee, and a juice committee. However, when two-thirds of its observations are randomly selected and then dropped from the analyses, the relationships presented here do not change dramatically. The contributions results for broad jurisdiction committees become mixed.

**TABLE 6.7** Committees and Number of Characteristics Leading to Contribution Influences

| Committee | Broad | Moderate | Juice | Total |
|---|---|---|---|---|
| Agriculture | Yes | Yes | Yes | 3 |
| Banking and Commerce | No | Yes | No | 1 |
| Business and Professions | Yes | No | No | 1 |
| Education | Yes | Yes | No | 2 |
| Elections | No | No | No | 0 |
| Energy and Public Utilities | No | Yes | No | 1 |
| Governmental Organization | Yes | Yes | Yes | 3 |
| Health and Human Services | Yes | Yes | No | 2 |
| Housing and Urban Affairs | No | No | No | 0 |
| Industrial Relations | No | Yes | No | 1 |
| Insurance | No | Yes | Yes | 2 |
| Judiciary | Yes | No | Yes | 2 |
| Local Government | Yes | Yes | No | 2 |
| Natural Resources | Yes | No | No | 1 |
| Public Employees and Retirement | No | No | No | 0 |
| Revenue and Taxation | No | Yes | No | 1 |
| Toxics | No | No | No | 0 |

Support contributions become unimportant when explaining all votes and opposition contributions are significant predictors. However, the other results are not altered by the elimination of these observations. Even that one committee, a potential outlier, is not driving the results.

## 3. Conclusion

If the past is any indication, a clear understanding of the relationship between contributions and votes is dependent on an analysis that takes account of the conditional impact of donations. Issue or committee agenda visibility and salience (Evans 1986 and 1996; Jones and Keiser 1987; Langbein and Lotwis 1990; Maltzman 1997; Neustadtl 1990), whether a vote is taking place in committee or on the floor (Evans 1996; Hall and Wayman 1990), and whether a member's vote is critical to the outcome of legislation all influence the strength of the relationship between contributions and legislative voting behavior.

However, committee characteristics do not determine how successful an interest group's contribution strategy may be, except at the margins. Campaign contributions to broad jurisdiction and ideologically moderate committees appear more successful in achieving a group's legislative goals than the same amount given to committees with narrower jurisdictions or ideologically extreme membership, but that is only when all votes are included in the analysis.

Contributions influence critical votes and not noncritical votes in all committee types, but the relationship is less obvious in some committees than in others. Even though contributions influence voting on crucial votes in all types of committees, the coefficients on the contributions variables are much larger in broad jurisdiction and ideologically moderate committees than in their counterparts, illustrating that money buys more effect in those contexts.

What are the implications of these results? First, they suggest that legislative leadership may have significant control over a group's agenda, even without direct appeals to its legislative membership. For example, if committee jurisdictions are relatively flexible (King 1997), manipulation of a committee's jurisdiction or strategic referrals of particular bills may allow legislative leadership to manipulate not only a group's contribution strategies, but also the success or failure of a particular group's agenda in the policy making process.

Second, further attempts to clarify the relationship between campaign contributions and legislative behavior require that we address the complexity of the context within which this relationship exists. The goals and strategies of interest groups and legislators are complicated and the connection between the two will not be any less so.

# 7
## Conclusion

"I won't use the word corrupt, but I will use the word venal. Too often votes are cast for purposes which don't involve the merits or demerits of the bill. And contributions influence votes, there's no question about it."

Quentin Kopp (Independent)
*Former California State Senator* [1]

"There is absolutely no relationship between fund raising and votes, and I feel very strongly about that."

Antonio Villaraigosa (Democrat)
*Former Speaker of the California State Assembly* [2]

"We're all tainted by a system that the public believes—rightly—results in greater representation to moneyed interests than to average citizens."

John McCain (Republican)
*U.S. Senator, Arizona* [3]

"If, at the end of all this, the court determines it is unable to resolve this academic debate, that wouldn't shock you, would it?"

Judge Lawrence Karlton
*U.S. District Court Judge (asked of a political science professor during the Proposition 208 hearing)* [4]

In the1990s, an FBI sting operation netted numerous California legislators, lobbyists, and staffers who were eventually convicted of the buying and selling of votes and influence. In 2000, a major party candidate for the Republican nomination for president of the United States, John McCain (R-AZ), ran his campaign almost entirely on campaign finance reform. At this same time, the percentage of the citizenry who believed that government corruption is a problem increased dramatically. In a 2000 National Public Radio, Kaiser Family Foundation, and Kennedy School of Government poll, 65 percent of those questioned stated that they did not trust government because "special interests have too much influence on the federal government." Yet, professional opinion regarding whether contributions influence voting continues to be divided. The only common denominator in the arguments coming from politicians, lobbyists, journalists, and academics is the inconsistency in the conclusions and the vehemence with which those divergent beliefs are stated. The most basic idea offered in this effort is that both sides are correct. If we proceed with our current conceptualization of the relationship between contributions and voting, it will continue to appear as though moneyed interests have significant power, even while there is no consistent empirical evidence to support this contention.

If, on the other hand, contributions are seen as gifts that create an obligatory, reciprocal relationship between giver and recipient (Clawson et al. 1998), the complexity of the relationship becomes clearer. Interest groups or their lobbyists provide money to legislators, perhaps for the purpose of gaining access. But, that money has a secondary effect: it obliges the legislator to respond with some reciprocal at an appropriate future opportunity. Therefore, contributions do not affect all votes, only those votes that are perceived by both legislators and lobbyists as a suitable return gift.

We already know that contributions do not influence all votes equally, but we have tended to focus on the various costs of votes to legislators. For example, we recognize that moderate legislators are more easily influenced by contributions (Fleisher 1993) and almost all legislators will be more susceptible to the influence of money when votes are less visible (Evans 1986 and 1996; Jones and Keiser 1987; Langbein and Lotwis 1990; Neustadtl 1990; Schroedel 1986). In both of these circumstances, responding to contributor interests is less potentially costly to the lawmaker.

It is important to understand also that all votes are not equally important to interest groups. The obligation engendered by contributions will have a stronger influence on those behaviors that are more valuable to groups. Specifically, contributions influence legislative effort (Hall and Wayman 1990) and those votes that determine the outcome of legislation.

## 1. Contributions and Critical Votes

Other scholars have noted that issue visibility and electoral vulnerability affect the relationship between contributions and votes. But, understanding these characteristics of the political context is not enough to fully comprehend the influence of money. The relationship is even more complex. The results found here suggest two additional aspects of context that influence how much of an independent effect donations will have on voting behavior.

First, and most importantly, contributions have the strongest effect on voting behavior when a legislator's vote is critical to the outcome of legislation. If an interest group supports a bill and it is going to pass ten votes to one, the group does not care how each of the legislators votes on that particular bill. They will not even punish the one member who votes nay, because any one member's vote will not change the outcome of legislation—the bill will pass regardless. On the other hand, if the bill comes within only one or two votes of passing, the group will put more pressure on members to vote aye, and the contributions that group gives to a legislator are more likely to have an effect of his voting behavior. This is because the member knows that his aye vote on a bill that barely passes is more valuable to the group than his aye vote on a bill that is going to pass unanimously. And, yet, supporting the group on that one important bill will not change the lawmaker's voting pattern so significantly that his constituents will notice. These two characteristics make critical votes the perfect situation in which to respond to contributor interests. In fact, it is possible that this dynamic drives Fleisher's (1993) finding that contributions are even more effective on close votes.

In summary, the most important part of the findings presented here is that contributions have an effect on votes above and beyond the selection effects that have already been identified. Past research has shown that, for the most part, group donations follow ideology or power: money tends to flow to legislators who are supportive of or have influence on a group's agenda and those contributions help to create a legislature that is supportive of the interests of moneyed groups. That is why such a strong relationship exists between money and political party variables in these and all past analyses. However, even controlling for the variables that measure this selection effect (e.g., party, district, and member ideology), contributions have an independent influence on votes, if those votes determine the outcome of legislation. If nothing else, this effort has clarified our understanding of this aspect of the relationship.

## 2. Implications for Future Research

### 2.1 Contributions Can Influence even those Who Do Not Generally Agree with You—Personal Relationships Are Important

Research has shown that groups tend to lobby those members who are likely to support their interests (Bauer et al. 1963; Dexter 1969; Matthews 1960; Milbrath 1963; Wright 1990). In other words, contributions are used to access friends more than enemies. But, many interest groups, especially those with large coffers, contribute quite broadly to incumbents and those on their primary committees without regard for ideology or voting patterns (Austen-Smith 1995; Gordon and Unmack 2003; Grenzke 1989; Wright 1990). And, although those contributions may have a more significant impact on moderate legislators, they may also have a rare effect on members with more extreme policy positions.

Former Senator John Doolittle's contributions from the CTLA's PAC were extraordinarily high given his ideology, his position in the legislature, and his voting record on CTLA bills. The only variable to explain why Doolittle's contributions were so much higher than any other Republican's was his willingness to be the CTLA's critical vote on tort reform bills. Not only does this case study show that critical votes are more valuable to interest groups than votes that do not influence the outcome of legislation, it also illustrates just how much groups might be willing to spend to maintain important relationships, even with those legislators who support them rarely and, perhaps, reluctantly.

It is important to note again that this does not mean that the CTLA was purchasing Doolittle's vote. It is more likely that they first contributed to him because he was a member of the committees that were most important to them. Even though he was a conservative Republican, he was an incumbent and a former attorney and they wanted access to make their case to him. However, a relationship developed between these two political actors and over time it became clear to some that Doolittle could be counted as a supporter of trial lawyer legislation even though he actively defended their interests so rarely. Additional case studies of this type will help us to fully specify when these types of relationships are more likely to develop.

### 2.2 The Hidden Nature of the Relationship

I began this effort believing that if there is an observable relationship between contributions and votes, it would be most obvious in a committee like Governmental Organization, primarily because of its role as a juice committee in the California legislature (Clucas 1995). The empirical results on the obviousness of this relationship are mixed. In fact, there is reason to believe that at least two committee characteristics besides the affluence of clientele groups influence the relationship between money and votes: size of the committee's jurisdiction and the ideology of the legislators who make up its membership.

Although this new understanding gives insight into the types of behaviors we need to identify, it is also useful for comprehending a couple of disconcerting behaviors. Those who observe the policy making process on a regular basis have often and passionately disagreed as to the impact of money on votes. Are those who believe there is an effect unsophisticated or biased? Or, are those who argue there is no effect being disingenuous? Probably neither is the case. It appears that moneyed interests are benefited by legislation when one looks at aggregate policy outcomes, however, few legislators or lobbyists can identify situations where votes are bought for that purpose. If, on the other hand, votes are not bought but are given in response to the obligatory gift relationship created by contributions, they can influence legislative outcomes even while changing individual votes relatively rarely. Each legislator may respond to his contributors unconsciously on one vote per year because that vote is crucial to the group's goals, but this has an overall impact on the legislative product that is overwhelming. Moreover, neither observers nor participants need to notice this happening for policy outcomes to be highly responsive to the desires of moneyed interests.

### 2.3 Is It the Thought That Counts?

One potential implication of the gift theory is that "it is the thought that counts." In other words, just giving a gift, regardless of the size, may be enough to create the desired relationship. Although this is a well-known cliché, the literature suggests that this is not the case, even in personal relationships. For example, even though money is the most efficient gift (people can buy exactly what they want with it), individuals giving money to each other is frowned upon because it does not illustrate how well the giver knows the recipient or has thought about what that individual might like.

In the context of campaigns, money is not the only appropriate gift. In-kind contributions (such as travel expenses and catering services for fund-raisers) are gifts given from interest groups or individuals to political campaigns. In addition, interest groups can give independent expenditures by buying advertising supporting a particular candidate without consultation with that candidate's campaign. However, unlike most relationships where there are an infinite number of potential gifts, in campaigns, money is what recipients both want and need the most. Direct monetary contributions may even be preferred to independent expenditures under most circumstances, because controlling the message of advertising is so important to campaigns.

If just contributing something were enough, the relationship would look similar to that in Figure 7.1, with probability of an aye vote increasing with

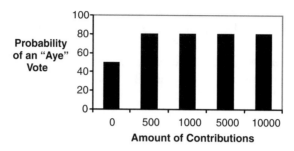

**Fig. 7.1** Hypothetical Relationship between Support Contributions and Votes

the minimum amount of contributions and staying at that level regardless of how the amount of the donation increases.

In fact, the graphs presented in Chapter 5 and Chapter 6 suggest that it is not the thought that counts, it is the amount given. In each case discussed in these two chapters, as the amount of contributions increases, the probability of legislators supporting that group's interest increases as well. And, this finding is consistent across all committees and in all contexts studied.

### 3. Implications for Reform

I will not do as others have done and suggest my particular formula for campaign finance reform, although it is clear that the conclusions presented here do have implications for the form that any change of the legislative or the campaign finance systems should take. First, disclosure and other information driven reforms of the process that require the public to recognize the connection between contributions and votes will not successfully alter the relationships found here. Second, legislative changes, too, are of dubious value for reforming the influence of money, except at the margins.

### 3.1 Campaign Finance Reform

Many reforms of the campaign finance system have been proposed. These suggestions tend to be of four classes. First, some suggest that we limit or increase the amount of money that can either be raised or spent on campaigns. This includes such reforms as doing away with any limits on contributions to candidates or substantially reducing the current federal contributions limits (Birnbaum 2000). Some states have attempted such reforms. For example, California voters established contributions limits with Proposition 34 in 2000. And, the U.S. Congress successfully outlawed soft money contributions to political parties with the Bipartisan Campaign Reform Act of 2002.

The second set of reforms involves changing the system so that less money is required for a successful campaign. This includes giving free television time to candidates (Birnbaum 2000; Broder 1999b), promoting debates (Birnbaum

2000), or providing free mail privileges to challengers, not just incumbents (Broder 1999a). Reforms of this type have not been successful at either the state or federal level.

Some suggest changing the source of the campaign contributions. Recommendations that fit into the third category have included outlawing fund-raising by lobbyists (Birnbaum 2000), requiring candidates to register their PACs in states where they live (West 2000), and public financing of campaigns. The states have been much more progressive about campaign finance reform of this sort than has the federal government. Six states have instituted some form of public financing. Maine has instituted a public financing system by initiative and Vermont passed a similar proposal by legislative mandate (Clawson et al. 1998).

A final class of proposals promotes increasing the amount of information available about where contributions are coming from and where they are going. This category incorporates strengthening advertising sponsorship rules, restructuring the FEC (West 2000), and, most commonly, immediate disclosure of campaign contributions. Representative Doolittle (D-CA) and Representative Tom DeLay (R-TX) have introduced just such legislation, but it has failed to pass beyond the committee stage of the process.

In fact, numerous and diverse proposals addressing almost all of these propositions have been introduced into the house or senate. Nevertheless, most of the reforms listed above are unlikely to receive a serious hearing in the U.S. Congress. Even the most widely understood and denigrated evil—soft money—took many years to outlaw and was probably only passed because of what the public deemed outrageous candidate behavior in the 1996 and 2000 presidential elections.

Even if they were to pass, how successful would each of these reforms be, given this new understanding of the process by which contributions can influence votes? If the relationship between money and policy outcomes is so subtle, can broad institutional changes of this type alter the incentive structure?

### 3.1.1 Why Raising Contributions/Spending Limits or Increasing the Amount of Information Will Not Improve Representation.

If immediate disclosure or raising the contribution or spending limits are to work, the public needs to be able to determine which legislators are being influenced by their contributions and which are not and respond accordingly. Doolittle (R-CA) explains, "If the tobacco companies want to give ... me $100,000, and that's OK with our constituents after it's disclosed, fine. What's the problem? Let the people decide."[5] In other words, if his constituents know who supports him financially and they do not care, why should anyone else care? And, if the public is willing and able to remove legislators who lack integrity (Mondak 1995)—such as being influenced by money—and contributions are unlimited but immediately disclosed, this provides new information that the public can use when deciding which candidates to support.

However, the findings here suggest that the relationship between money and legislative behavior is far too subtle and complex for this system to achieve the desired goals. Observers, participants, and academics disagree as to whether money has any influence in the current system; so how is the public expected to use this information to determine the influence of contributions on their representatives? Presumably, those interested in this type of behavior are more aware of contribution patterns than the public would be even if the information were readily available. Even so, two individuals participating in the same process cannot agree. During the campaign finance trial over Proposition 208 in California, former State Senator Art Torres (currently California Democratic Party Chairman) testified that "All I saw was money always followed ideology and ideology always follows a particular candidate."[6] This is in direct contrast to the testimony by his former Democratic colleague Keene who believed that money, in numerous and insidious ways, negatively influenced representation. Keene stated his position quite clearly, "I believe (campaign contributions) influence the judgment of individuals who have the understanding that money is security. I believe there is not a single legislator who doesn't weigh the effect."[7] If even those who so directly participate in policy making (who presumably have much more refined understanding of the process) cannot agree on the power of money, how is it possible for ordinary citizens to grasp that influence even with complete disclosure of both money and behavior?

### 3.1.2 Reducing the Amount of Money Needed to Run or Limiting

Contributions. It is possible that if we decrease the need for money by encouraging debates and providing candidates with free television time, politicians will not need to approach such a wide spectrum of interests to raise enough money to run. Or, in contrast, if we limit the total amount of money that groups give, legislators will not be beholden to any single interest, because they will have to collect such small amounts from so many different sources.

However, the results provided here suggest that, unless no money is collected from outside sources, financial considerations will continue to have an effect on policy. It does not appear to take extraordinarily large contributions to affect decision making on critical votes. In most analyses presented here, an effect was found with contributions as small as $500. To further address this issue, I dropped all contributions over $500 and ran the analyses for the Governmental Organization Committee again. The substantive relationships remained the same. These small contributions affected critical votes, but did not affect noncritical votes.

This makes sense in the context of the gift analogy. If contributions are given for the purpose of generating a relationship between legislators and interest groups and the critical votes impact is, in effect, a by-product of that association, then any size contribution will have some effect, even though larger contributions have a larger effect. Limits would have to be exceptionally low to reduce the power of this relationship (e.g., around $100): low enough to fail to make a distinction between those who give and those who do not. This does not contradict the previous discussion that larger gifts might engender larger reciprocals or that those who give are also those who receive (Komter 1996). Although those who contribute less might receive less, they are still more likely to gain something than groups who give nothing at all.

### 3.1.3 Changing the Source of Money.
If the public is unable to use increased amounts of information regarding campaign finance to achieve better representation, the only answer to solving the "money begets influence" problem is if we change the source of the money. This suggests that public financing is the most realistic solution. If the public is concerned about whether politicians are going to be more responsive to those who fund their campaigns, those citizens had better provide the money.

But, there is little support for public financing among the general public. In a 1999 Gallup poll, 81 percent of those surveyed supported limiting business contributions and 79 percent favored limiting the amount of money that candidates raise and spend, but only 43 percent supported public financing of campaigns (Sand 1999). These are similar to results garnered by a poll conducted for the Center for Responsive Politics (CRP). The CRP found that only 57 percent of those polled supported public financing (Center for Responsive Politics 1997). Even though some states have successfully instituted public financing systems, it appears questionable whether such programs can or will be instituted at the federal levels.

## 3.2 Legislative Reform

If fundamental changes in the campaign finance system are not politically feasible either because of a lack of support among the general public or lack of incentive among those in office, the next possibility is institutional reform of the U.S. Congress itself. Changes in the incentive structure created by various rules and organizational characteristics might have a similar effect.

### 3.2.1 Committee Reform.
It is clear from the results presented in Chapter 6 that even though the relationship between contributions and critical votes exists in all committee types, the relationship between money and votes is stronger in some committees than others. Figure 7.2A and Figure 7.2B show the differing effects of contributions in extreme/moderate committees.

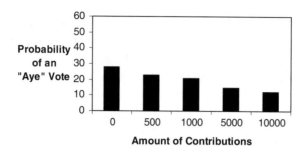

**Fig. 7.2A** Effect of Opposition Contributions on Critical Votes in Extreme Committees

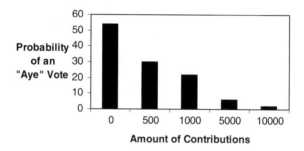

**Fig. 7.2B** Effect of Opposition Contributions on Critical Votes in Moderate Committees

In other words, contributions influence votes more strongly in some committees than in others.

This has implications for reform of the committee system if we want to reduce the effect of money on policy. The findings suggest two types of reforms, those based on the ideology of members and those based on the size of committee jurisdiction.

It would be impractical, if not impossible, for legislative leadership to allocate committee memberships based on political ideology. Not only would it be difficult to explain to the public why certain members are being placed on particular committees, but the incentives to allocate committee memberships are strong and fairly standard and are unlikely to change dramatically.

Legislators have electoral incentives to request membership on certain committees to meet constituent demands (Adler and Lapinski 1997; Mayhew 1974). Legislators from marginal districts might request committees that make fund-raising easier. Sometimes members request committees because they are personally interested in those issues or have expertise in the policy area (Deering and Smith 1997; Shepsle 1978; Sinclair 1988). And, although party leaders have both tools and external constraints that limit the extent to which they can respond to these interests (Cox and McCubbins 1993; Munger 1988; Shepsle

1978), they have countervailing incentives to place members on those committees: they too want their party colleagues to maintain their seats and committees help them to do so. Failure to provide party members with assignments that help them to achieve their goals not only threatens a party leader's coalition, but threatens the future of the party's majority (or hope thereof) in the legislature.

This analysis does suggest one type of committee reform that could change the relationship between money and votes, if only at the margins: create more committees with narrower jurisdictions. This, in combination with the incentives that already exist for committee allocation will result in committees with members who are more committed to a particular issue area and a certain position on that issue and, therefore, are less likely to be influenced by PAC money.

There are many limits to this as well. First, some may argue that there are already plenty of committees. In the spring of 2004, the U.S. Senate had 16 standing committees, 4 special or select committees, and 4 joint committees, as well as over 200 subcommittees. The U.S. House of Representatives had 19 standing committees and 5 joint or select committees in addition to the subcommittees. Although committee jurisdictions may be fairly broad, subcommittee jurisdictions may be narrow enough to solve this problem by creating the incentives discussed above. And, as the number of committees suggests, legislators already have too many demands on their time. So, either committees will have to have fewer members or legislators will have to fit in additional assignments.

Second, the incentive within the numerous congressional committees is not to decrease their jurisdiction, but to increase it (King 1997). There is no electoral or power incentive to decrease the jurisdiction of the committees that already exist. Third, limiting the breadth of committee jurisdictions will simply increase the overlapping of committee jurisdictions and increase the number of multiple referrals, complicating an already complex process.

Finally, there are still those "scope of practice" issues that do not fall along party or ideological lines and, therefore, altering committee jurisdictions will have no effect. For instance, it is doubtful that a legislator (unless that legislator is a doctor) has a strong position on whether podiatrists should be able to work on ankles and not just feet, regardless of political ideology. Those decisions will continue to be based on personal relationships or contributions from affected groups. No matter how narrow the jurisdiction of committees, these issues will probably still come down to the influence of money.

*3.2.2 Single Issue Legislation.* Another reform does suggest itself. One of the benefits of California data for studying the effects of money has to do with the single-subject rule regarding legislation. In the California legislature, bills can only affect a single area of policy and all amendments must be germane to that issue area. This precludes irrelevant or unrelated amendments being added to either kill or save legislation. One of the reasons this is so important is because it provides analysts with a reasonably good understanding of the issues on which legislators are voting.

In the U.S. Congress, on the other hand, the combination of omnibus legislation and riders often means that many, disparate policy areas are included in a single vote, giving legislators many reasons to support or oppose legislation. If one were more cynical, one could argue that this gives also legislators political cover when explaining a vote to constituents. It allows representatives to respond to the interests of contributors on one issue, but they can argue to constituents that they voted aye or nay based on another aspect of the legislation altogether.

It is important to note, though, that this may only change behavior at the margins. Although the germaneness rule has made statistical analysis of this relationship more accessible, Californians seem no more aware of the relationship between contributions and critical votes than do those who vote in congressional races.

## 4. Generalization to the U.S. Congress

In one way this study should be considered an attempt to provide a general test of our theories regarding voting behavior in legislatures. On another level, however, it raises the question of whether the findings here can be generalized to other contexts, particularly to the U.S. House of Representatives and Senate. I believe that while the institutions are clearly different in a series of important ways, the implications of this theory can be tested in various institutional circumstances.

The California data are preferable to the federal data because of the accessibility of large numbers of committee votes on final passage of bills and because of the availability of interest group positions on legislation. However, many will continue to wonder if the California legislature is so unique as to render this analysis useless in the application to other law making bodies. I argue that it is not. In the first place, the general understanding that this analysis provides is that contributions are more successful on those votes that are most important to interest groups. In California, that means critical votes in committee. This is observable in California because committees are relatively small, and committee votes are published regularly. Even though the same general understanding applies to the U.S. Congress, its observable implications may be different. In other words, where the difference lies is in the application of this understanding of contributions and votes to a particular institutional context. I turn next to how the California Senate differs from the U.S. Congress and how we might overcome these differences to further understand the effect of money. I will first discuss those differences that I do not believe have an influence on the relationship and explain how the other institutional variations can be overcome to extend this analysis to the federal level.

### 4.1 How are the California Senate and U.S. Congress Similar or Different?

**4.1.1 No Limits on California Contributions.** One way in which the California legislature and the U.S. Congress differ is that there are contribution limits at the federal level and, during the examined time period, California had no limits. Some might argue that $5,000 is simply not enough money to buy a vote in the U.S. Congress because of the significant cost of modern congressional campaigns.[8] However, there are few cases in this analysis where more than $5,000 was contributed to any individual by interest groups with a position on bills and, when those few cases are dropped, the results presented in the previous chapters do not change.

In addition, it takes slightly more money to run a state senate campaign than campaigns for the U.S. House of Representatives if not for the U.S. Senate. In 1998, the average cost of California State Senate campaigns was $509,000. The average amount spent on races for the U.S. House of Representatives during the same period was just under $364,000. So, if less than $5,000 was enough to influence critical votes in California in 1988, it should be enough money to do so in the U.S. House as well.

An example illustrates that even $2,000 might not be too little money to buy influence, even given the amount of money necessary to run modern campaigns. In 1993, former State Senator Alan Robbins testified that,

> he agreed to make a speech against the bill on the Senate floor at Jackson's [a lobbyist being tried, and eventually convicted, for racketeering, conspiracy, and mail fraud and against whom Robbins was testifying] behest even though they both knew it already had enough votes to pass.
>
> The speech was intended to provide then-Gov. Deukmejian with "political cover" to veto the legislation, which would have benefited a Riverside County development firm, according to Robbins. Jackson represented the Marriott Corp., which was a rival development in Indian Wells…. Five months later, Robbins received a two thousand dollar contribution from Marriott.
>
> (Walters 1993)

In summary, even though California candidates could accept an unlimited amount of money from contributors in the late 1980s, the data suggest that the difference between the actual money collected in those races was not significantly larger than the money raised in federal campaigns. Given the fact that it takes approximately the same amount of money to run a California State Senate Campaign as it does to run the average U.S. House campaign, the lack of contributions limits in California are not sufficient to undermine the generalization attempted here.

***4.1.2 The Germaneness Rule in California.*** Second, the germaneness rule in California makes the relationship between contributions and votes much easier to tease out. Because legislation can only concern a single issue and, therefore, riders cannot confuse the issues on which a legislator may be voting, testing the relationship between contributions and votes is a much more straightforward task. This raises two questions. First, do contributions have less of an effect when there are numerous interested groups because there are so many different pressures on a legislator? Or, a second possibility, do such complex pieces of legislation simply give legislators cover when attempting to explain their votes to constituents? We really cannot know. It makes sense that, if contributions are influencing critical votes, then we might see a smaller effect when large contributors are found on both sides of an issue. With whom will legislators side?

The analysis of juice committees in Chapter 6 suggests that contributions are not less effective when contributing groups take positions on both sides of an issue. In an example from Chapter 4, in Governmental Organization, the beer wholesalers were in conflict with the grocery stores and other retailers. Recently, Governmental Organization has been brokering disagreements between indian gaming groups and the Nevada casino interests. In the Insurance Committee, the trial lawyers are often up against the insurance companies or the insurance companies are competing with the medical doctors. In the Banking and Commerce Committee, the banks fight with the credit unions or the securities companies. However, even in these committees, contributions influenced critical votes. With groups on both sides of legislation contributing money, if a vote was crucial to the outcome of legislation, lawmakers still voted with the group that provided the largest donations. So, even though a germaneness rule might make the connection more accessible for those interested in whether a relationship exists, it does not appear to reduce the effect of contributions on votes.

The arguments stated above suggest that the differences between California and the federal legislature are not significant enough to affect the generalizability of this analysis; however, future analyses should address this issue more directly. It is to this issue that I turn next.

*4.2 How to Test the Critical Votes Hypothesis in the U.S. Congress*

Although there may be data deficiencies that make it difficult to evaluate these hypotheses in the context of the U.S. Congress, there are other observable implications that might be tested. And, when those results are taken as a whole, the combination of those findings would provide some evidence that the same relationships found here exist in the U.S. Congress.

First and most simply, additional committee case studies may be undertaken. We can study relationships between contributions and votes as we have done in the past, on a bill by bill or group by group basis, but while taking account of the critical nature of legislative votes. It would be particularly interesting to identify bills similar to AB 1500 that received a large majority of votes in one circumstance, but passed by a critical vote in another and determine whether the relationship between contributions and votes differs across these two contexts. There is nothing inherently wrong with studying the relationship in this manner. We must simply be aware of the limitations of our findings and not overemphasize the implications of our positive or null findings until a sufficient number of similar studies have been finished.

Second, we can extend our efforts to studying markup and amendment behavior at the federal level. This is a particularly hidden aspect of the policy making process in the U.S. Congress and, yet, studying voting on amendments would allow us to identify important, single issue, procedural, or legislative activity and we would be able to recognize the affected groups more readily. Most of those who argue that contributions influence legislative behavior at the federal level focus on the minor statutorial changes garnered by interest groups: changes that are of relatively little interest to constituents but have significant impacts on the affected groups (e.g., see Clawson et al. 1998; Birnbaum 2000). It is possible that in these circumstances the affect of contributions on voting behavior is much more apparent. Unfortunately, obtaining this type of data is significantly more time-consuming than accessing floor votes, so it must be left to future efforts.

## 5. Conclusion

Understanding every impact that interest groups have on the political process—positive or negative—is crucial to understanding how well or poorly our democracy functions. The extent to which groups are able to improve or weaken the link between representatives and the represented tells us how close we have come to the democratic ideal.

What this effort has shown is that past research has done well when it comes to theorizing about all of the possible impacts groups may have in the policy making process. For the most part, we have been successful at identifying and testing many of these hypothesized relationships with strong and consistent results. Unfortunately this success has not extended to our studies of the impact of contributions on legislative voting behavior. Although many have attempted to outline this complex relationship—leading to the evolution of strong theories regarding these behaviors and a large number of what are, in essence, case studies—developing generalizable studies has been more difficult, partially because of the difficulty of collecting the relevant data at the federal level.

I think the findings presented do suggest that we gain much from searching out data that will allow us to study both a large number of bills and groups. Without doing so, we will not be able to continue to test the contextual factors that influence the relationship between contributions and votes and that I believe will help us to understand the full influence of interest groups on democratic policy making.

What is particularly interesting about the findings here is that the relationship between contributions and votes is so subtle that even those participating in the process often do not see a direct effect. When legislators state that they do not believe that contributions affect votes, are they being insincere? Probably not. Even though various racketeering and bribery probes have found direct vote selling, for the most part, legislators do not take part in those practices. Instead, when they are deciding how to vote, they base their actions on many different variables (e.g., party and constituent pressure, personal beliefs). However, everyone who has received a gift knows that they make an unconscious calculation next time they are in a position to reciprocate; the obligation to reciprocate is particularly strong when it is the original giver's birthday or when the winter holiday season comes around and the appropriate time has come to return the favor.

This same sense of obligation is what develops in the relationship between the contributors and recipients of campaign contributions. Campaign contributors provide donations to candidates and those legislators do not respond immediately, nor are they expected to. Instead, they wait until the appropriate time. I believe that frequently the appropriate time is when the legislator has the opportunity to be a critical vote, because that vote determines the outcome of legislation, but does not affect the legislator's voting pattern.

Most importantly, we need to understand that the impact of contributions is considerable even if there is no direct trade, the relationship is uncertain, or a large percentage of votes are not affected. Certainly no one would argue that Hall and Wayman's (1990) or Clawson et al. is (1998) results on the effect of money on effort and other aspects of legislative behavior suggest that this association does not result in a significant impact on policy. Congressional scholars know that some of the most important decisions are made when Congresspeople pressure one another or choose to debate or not debate a bill. The Robbins example above illustrated how money affected his effort and led to a veto of important legislation by the governor. The effect of contributions is noteworthy partially because those donations influence critical votes and partially because even those who are affected are potentially unaware of their own decision making process. Even if they are aware of what they are doing, those participating in this process are able to deny the trading nature of this relationship (even to themselves) because of the lag time between the original gift and the response.

In the end, it is this inability of even the most sophisticated to identify numerous independent instances of control that will make any reform of the campaign finance system difficult. This may explain why the public does not place campaign finance reform at the top of the list of issues that they think the U.S. Congress and the president must address (Center for Responsive Politics 1997; Gallup 1999). It also explains why the U.S. Congress and other legislative bodies, with only a few exceptions, are unwilling to go out on a limb and make any fundamental changes in the system as it is currently designed.

# Appendix A
## Methodological Appendix

### 1. Two-Stage Limited Dependent Variable Model

The methodology used to study the relationship between contributions and legislative voting behavior must take account of both the nonrecursive nature of the relationship between donations and votes and the large number of zero dollar contributions in the contributions equations. This is done by using the Two-Stage Limited Dependent Variable (2LDV) model suggested by Nelson and Olson (1978). This procedure is similar to Two-Stage Least Squares (2SLS), except rather than using Ordinary Least Squares (OLS) for each stage of the analysis, Tobit is used in the first stages to predict the contributions instrumental variables and probit is used in the second stage.

Potentially, there are three techniques that could be used to deal with this joint endogeneity problem—a 2SLS analysis, a Simultaneous Probit-Tobit (SPT) procedure, or the Two-Stage Limited Dependent Variable (2SLDV) analysis. 2SLS solves the dilemma by creating an instrumental variable (in this case for contributions) that is purged of all of the effects of the dependent variable of interest (votes). Then, the instrumental variable is used as a fixed regressor in a second equation. Once this is done, any relationship between the instrumental variable and the dependent variable can then be assumed to be due purely to the effect of that independent variable (Chappell 1981; Pindyck and Rubinfeld 1981).

Even though it does take account of the joint endogeneity between contributions and votes, one of the main weaknesses of the 2SLS technique is the assumption that the error terms of the two equations are unrelated. Given the nature of the relationship between contributions and votes, this assumption is questionable (Chappell 1981). And, if the error terms are related, then any failure to take that correlation into account would erroneously lead us to believe a relationship existed between contributions and votes that, in fact, did not. Indeed, Chappell (1981) tested the relationship between money and votes using OLS, 2SLS, and SPT and found that the former two techniques overestimated the relationship between contributions and votes. The correlation coefficient between the error terms of the two equations (using SPT) was greater than zero, indicating that SPT, which takes into account the nonzero coefficient between the error terms, was a more appropriate technique than OLS or 2SLS.

Unfortunately, Chappell's SPT procedure cannot currently be extended to more than two equations and the analysis I present requires three equations: one to create an instrumental variable for support contributions, one to create an instrumental variable for opposition contributions, and one to predict votes. Therefore, I cannot use SPT here. However, Nelson and Olson (1978) have developed a procedure that provides unbiased estimates and that can be extended to a large number of equations.

The Nelson and Olson 2SLDV procedure is similar to the 2SLS procedure except that rather than using OLS for each stage of the analysis, it uses Tobit in the first stages to predict the contributions instrumental variables and probit in the second stage, just like the SPT analysis. What makes it different from the SPT procedure is that it does not take account of any correlation that might exist between the error terms of the equations.

This does create a potential problem if Chappell is correct and there is a correlation between the error terms. However, Nelson and Olson argue that their procedure provides unbiased estimates of the coefficients, if the model is correctly specified. In other words, the resulting coefficients should be unbiased as long as there are no variables omitted from either stage of the analysis that are related to the dependent variable in the other stage.

In addition, it is important to note that when Chappell compared his SPT-III model to the 2SLS, the substantive findings did not change.[1] Although the relationship between contributions and votes was stronger in the 2SLS analysis, the positive relationship between a group's propensity to contribute and votes was supported in both analyses. Therefore, by choosing to use the Nelson and Olson technique I need to be aware that I may be overestimating the impact of contributions on votes, but Chappell's own findings suggest that the bias may not be of an order of magnitude sufficient to alter my conclusions.

The second analysis issue is the distribution of the contributions variable. Because the contributions data form two of the dependent variables in this system of equations using 2SLDV, the distribution of the data is critical. The 2SLDV procedure solves the problem of the distribution of the dependent variables as well. OLS regression assumes a linear relationship between the variables of interest. To the extent that the contributions data are censored at zero, with a large number of observations that equal zero, the linearity assumption is violated causing the estimators to be biased. In these circumstances, Tobit is the preferred estimator (Amemiya 1984; Breen 1996). Not only does OLS result in biased estimators because of the distribution of the dependent variable, but it fails to use important information from the data that would allow us to estimate unbiased coefficients. We do have more information than the OLS technique allows us to use: (1) we know the value of the latent variable on those observations that do not fall below the zero threshold and (2) we know which cases fall at or below the threshold and which do not. We can use information both on the selection of cases (whether or not they fall below the threshold) and the outcome of cases (their true value if they do not fall below the threshold) to determine the expected value of the latent variable on those cases where it is not observed (Breen 1996). Using Tobit allows us to take account of this information on the latent variable to measure the relationship between the censored dependent variable and the independent variables of interest while minimizing bias. Therefore, I use OLS in the first stage in Chapter 4 because the contributions variable is normally distributed, but use Tobit in the first stage in Chapter 5 because of the truncated dependent variables.

In addition, the vote variable in the second stage of the analysis is dichotomous, only taking the value of zero or one, making OLS inappropriate as well. The 2SLDV model uses probit in that stage. Although uncommon, the 2SLDV model has been used in political science (Alvarez 1997; Caldeira and Wright 1998) and in studies of contributions and voting in the economics literature (Brooks et al. 1998).

## 2. Specification of the Models

The reduced-form first stage Tobit equations include all exogenous variables in the system of equations, with enough variables dropped to make the equations identified. The equations are as follows (the variables and Tobit results are presented and discussed in detail in Appendix B) for the analyses discussed in Chapter 5 and Chapter 6:

$$Y_1 = a_1 + b_{11}X_1 + b_{13}X_3 + b_{14}X_4 + b_{15}X_5 + b_{16}X_6 + b_{17}X_7 + b_{18}X_8 + e$$

$$Y_2 = a_2 + b_{22}X_2 + b_{23}X_3 + b_{24}X_4 + b_{25}X_5 + b_{26}X_6 + b_{27}X_7 + b_{28}X_8 + e$$

Where:

$Y_1$ = support contributions
$Y_2$ = opposition contributions
$X_1$ = amount available to give by groups in support of a bill
$X_2$ = amount available to give by groups in opposition to a bill
$X_3$ = leadership
$X_4$ = party
$X_5$ = district ideology
$X_6$ = member ideology
$X_7$ = challenger spending
$X_8$ = previous vote margin

The predicted values from each of these equations are used as fixed regressors in the second stage probit equation. The second stage equation is as follows:

$$Y_3 = a_3 + b_{34}X_4 + b_{35}X_5 + b_{36}X_6 + b_{310}X_{10} + b_{311}Y_1 + b_{312}Y_2 + e$$

Where:

$Y_1$ = predicted value from the first stage Tobit equation for support contributions
$Y_2$ = predicted value from the first stage Tobit equation for opposition contributions
$Y_3$ = vote dummy
$X_4$ = party
$X_5$ = district ideology
$X_6$ = member ideology
$X_{10}$ = ten dummy variables to control for member fixed effects

The models for the analyses in Chapter 4 differ slightly from those presented above. I use OLS in the first stage because of the distribution of the dependent variable. Moreover, additional exogenous variables must be included in the first stage equation because they are included in the second stage equation (e.g., the Rural Caucus Dummy in the analysis of AB 1500, the beer distribution bill) and, therefore, must be included in the first stage equation as well. Only the variables that are included in all the first stage equations are discussed in Appendix B. Those additional variables included in any analysis are discussed in the chapters in which they are included.

### 3. Testing for Errors in the Two-Stage Analysis: Bootstrapped Standard Errors

Nelson and Olson note that "the principal motivation of the 2SLDV estimation procedure is that it provides consistent estimates at a relatively low cost" (p. 702). However, the standard errors produced are incorrect. They are merely rough approximations of the true errors.

Amemiya (1979) and Newey (1984) have both created procedures to calculate more efficient standard errors, but these procedures are so difficult to employ that many political scientists have "settled for consistent estimates and possibly incorrect standard errors due to this problem" (Alvarez 1997, 87). Because of the complexity of the computation and the possibility of errors inherent in such a procedure, I use a bootstrap technique on the 2SLDV procedure, because bootstrapping has been shown to generate accurate tests of statistical significance even when the distribution of the dependent variable is nonnormal (Mooney 1996).

This is achieved by resampling the original data set (with replacement), rerunning the analyses, and calculating the standard deviation of the sampling distribution that is created. It is usually suggested that the number of observations in each resample equal the N of the original data set (in this case N = 929) and that, for significance testing, the number of replications equal 1,000 (Mooney 1996). I have followed each of these conventions here. For the purposes of the 2SLDV model presented here, the standard errors that result are asymptotically correct, but are much more easily computed.

In all analyses where it is possible, the corrected standard errors are used and noted as such. In analyses where the bootstrap method is not available for one reason or another (e.g., small number of observations makes it impractical), it is noted that the original standard error is used. It is important to note in the models where the corrected standard error is used, never is a contributions variable significant in the unbootstrapped case and insignificant with the corrected standard errors. Therefore, it is within reason to assume that in those cases where the original standard error is used the substantive results will not change from those presented.

# Appendix B
## Statistical Results

In this appendix, I present the results of the statistical analyses on which the discussions in the text are based. I discuss the analyses in Chapter 3 and Chapter 4 separately, because those models are slightly different than the ones presented in Chapter 5 and Chapter 6. In the third section, the independent variables used in Chapter 5 and Chapter 6 are discussed in detail and the second stage probit results are presented. Finally, I explain the variables included in the first stage contributions analyses and present all first stage results.

### 1. Chapter Three: John Doolittle and the CTLA

The dependent variable in the Doolittle and CTLA analysis is the log of the total number of contributions given to each member of the senate by the CTLA for the 1987–88 election cycle.

Democrat is a dichotomous variable that takes on the value of one (1) if the member was a Democrat or an Independent and zero (0) if the member was a Republican. Ideology is an average of the member support scores from three interest group rankings—the California Labor Federation, the California Chapter of the National Organization for Women, and the California Chamber of Commerce. The measure ranges from 0 (conservative) to 100 (liberal).

Leadership is a categorical variable that takes on the value of 1 if the member was President Pro Tempore, Minority Leader, or chair of the Judiciary Committee, 0 otherwise.

Two committee variables are included. Judiciary is a dummy variable that takes on the value of 1 if the legislator was a member of the Judiciary Committee, 0 otherwise.[1] Insurance is a dummy variable that takes on the value of 1 if the legislator was a member of the Insurance Committee, 0 otherwise.

Electoral Vulnerability is the log of the amount of money spent by the member's challenger in the 1988 election. It equals 0 if the senator was not up for election in 1988. Electoral Vulnerability is also included in an interaction with Democrat because Democratic members facing tough races are likely to receive even more money than other party members.

All of the independent variables are expected to be positively related to contributions from the CTLA for the reasons stated in the text. The results of the analysis are presented in Table B.1.

Ideology, Leadership, and the committee variables each have the expected, positive influence on the level of contributions from the CTLA and each are significant at (at least) the .05 level. In addition, the model as a whole is significant at the .001 level and explains 68 percent of the variance in CTLA contributions. The electoral vulnerability, party, and interaction variables are not significant, but this is due to multicollinearity with other variables in the model. Ideology correlates with Democrat at .87 (significant at .001) and when Ideology is dropped from the analysis, the party variable becomes a significant predictor. These results are consistent with the theories and findings of past empirical studies.

## 2. Chapter Four

### 2.1 AB 1500

The dependent variable, Contributions, is the predicted value of contributions from a first stage OLS regression equation (discussed in the last section of this appendix). The difference between this first stage model and those discussed in Appendix A is that, here, Contributions measures the difference between contributions from groups in support of the legislation and those from groups in opposition, therefore the variable may take on either positive or negative values. In most of the analyses support and opposition contributions are used as separate variables in the analyses. Unfortunately, for this analysis there are too few observations for such a complex model. The degrees of freedom become extremely low. Therefore, I calculate a single variable for contributions rather than two. In future analyses, using the difference in contributions rather than the two separate variables never changes the substantive results presented. This suggests that the findings here would stand if the two variables were included rather than just one. If contributions have an independent affect on voting behavior, this variable should be positively related to voting aye on the bill.

Party is the same dummy variable discussed above. Member Ideology is measured as the absolute value of a composite ideology score (based on three interest group ratings and discussed in detail in Chapter 5) minus 50. The ideology score is based on a 0 to 100 ranking with 0 the most conservative and 100 the most liberal. By taking the absolute value of the difference between this rating and 50, the more extreme legislators (regardless of liberalism or conservatism) will have the highest scores and the more moderate members will have the lowest scores. This variable is expected to be negatively related to the probability of an aye vote.

District Ideology measures the influence of electoral constituencies on legislative voting behavior. Assuming that more moderate districts are also more likely to support the bill, district influence is measured as the absolute value of the difference between the Democratic percentage of district registration and the Republican percentage of district registration. This variable is expected to be negatively related to the probability of an aye vote.

The Assembly Rural Caucus took a support position on the legislation because of the previously discussed effect on markets in rural districts. Rural is a dummy variable that takes on the value of 1 if the legislator was a member of the rural caucus in either house and 0 otherwise. It is expected to be positively related to an aye vote.

Results of the probit analyses predicting voting behavior in each of the legislative houses are presented in Table B.2.

It is clear from these analyses that contributions have a much different effect in the senate than in the assembly. Contributions only affected voting behavior in the senate, where the bill passed by the minimum number of votes.

## 2.2  SB 276

The second stage OLS results for SB 276 are presented in Table B.3. Unfortunately, the multivariate analytic technique appropriate for these data is not available because contributions over $1,900 perfectly predict success when a probit model is attempted. In the absence of a probit or logit model, I used OLS regression to analyze these votes. Party is a dummy variable that equals one if the member is a Democrat and 0 otherwise. The ideology measure used is the average of the member support scores from three interest group rankings discussed above.

Clearly, the results presented in Table B.3 must be taken within the context of all the analyses presented here. It is important to note, for instance, that the model as a whole is not significant (probability of F is greater than .23), probably due to the small number of observations in the analysis. Furthermore, this is only a single-stage analysis, which may be overestimating the impact of contributions (see Appendix A). That being said, it appears from these results as though contributions continue to have a significant effect on voting on this bill. Those who received more money from the groups in support of the bill are more likely to vote aye than those who received less money even controlling for Party and Member Ideology.

## 2.3 SB 3

The second stage probit results for SB 3 are presented in Table B.4. The variables are measured as discussed above.

## 3. Chapter 5 and Chapter 6

### 3.1 The Dependent Variable

The dependent variable in these analyses is an individual legislator's vote on a single bill. It is a dummy variable that takes on the value of 1 if the legislator voted aye and 0 if he voted nay. The variable is also coded 0 if the member abstained from the vote but was present at the committee hearing. I do this to take account of the possibility of strategic abstentions discussed in the main text.

Choosing not to vote may be as much of a choice as choosing which way to vote (Cohen and Noll 1991; Fiorina 1974; Thomas 1991). Members may choose to abstain when an issue is less salient to their constituents and the voting member is part of the majority coalition because the abstention does not change the outcome of legislation but allows the member to avoid taking a position that might anger constituents (Cohen and Noll 1991).

In the Cohen and Noll (1991) analysis, an abstention can either be an aye vote or a nay vote. However, this understanding is only appropriate under the voting rules of the U.S. Congress because a bill passes by a majority of those present and voting. However, in the California legislature, a bill must receive an absolute majority of votes in committee regardless of the number of members present at the hearing (in this committee, six votes are required because there are eleven members), consequently, an abstention is an effective no vote. Abstentions can still be strategic in the California legislature, but they can only be strategic nay votes.

Absences are not included as abstentions because a member is unlikely to miss an entire committee meeting for the purpose of abstaining on a single bill. Unlike the U.S. Congress, where hearings often are held on one bill at a time, California hearings almost always include a large number of bills. For example, the Governmental Organization Committee voted on an average of twelve bills per committee meeting during the 1987–88 session. A legislator would not want to be absent from an entire hearing simply to keep from taking a position on a single bill. Legislators are only considered absent in this analysis if they did not vote on any of the bills up for consideration on that day.[2]

## 3.2 The Contributions Instrumental Variable

The nonrecursive nature of the relationship between votes and contributions requires a system of three equations as discussed in Appendix A. Two of the equations (the first stage equations) in the system set up instrumental measures of contributions. There is one equation for contributions given by groups in support of a bill and another for contributions given by groups in opposition. The dependent variables in these equations are (1) the sum of the contributions to an individual committee member by all groups in support of the bill on which the member is voting and (2) the sum of the contributions to an individual committee member by all groups in opposition to the bill on which the member is voting. The square root is taken of each these sums to deal with the skewed nature of the data as discussed in some detail below. The predicted values from these equations are used as independent contributions variables in the second stage voting equation. An explanation of the independent variables used in these equations is listed in the second section of this appendix.[3]

Note that the contributions and votes data used are both from the 1987–88 session. One might argue that it is more appropriate to use contributions from the previous legislative session to predict votes from the current one because members will have information about the amount of contributions that they have received from a given group. This position would be supported by Box-Steffensmeier's view that war chests are important to legislators because they help to ward off potential challengers (1996). If this is the case, then contributions given earlier are of more value to members than contributions given later.

However, Stratmann (1995) studied the effects of the timing of contributions and found that contributions given near the time of the vote had a larger impact on voting behavior than did contributions received one or two years prior to the vote. Presumably, this relationship exists because members of the legislature are more aware of those contributions.

After Brooks et al. (1998), I argue that the decision to make contributions and the decision to vote in support or opposition to a group's position in any given legislative session occurs simultaneously. Often the timing of contributions is driven by when the legislator holds a fund-raiser or by the election calendar. For example, in the California legislature, many fund-raisers are held during the final week of the legislative session (Richardson 1996) and many legislators hold fund-raisers for their birthdays. However, important votes occur in between these times. It is probable that, if contributions influence votes, members' voting decisions are dependent upon their expectation of contributions, not simply those contributions they have already received. This expectation is based not only on past contributions and the relationship that has developed between the legislator and the lobbyist over time, but is also dependent upon session-specific characteristics, e.g., based upon the legislators' need for contributions during a particular election cycle. The latter information only becomes clear as the election cycle progresses.

Using contributions and votes from the same legislative session solves another problem as well. Legislators use their committee membership to predict which groups will donate to them and how much they expect to receive (Block and Carniello 1987; Rios 1981). Although a legislator may have been receiving $500 from the California Medical Association, thus developing a relationship with that group, the legislator will certainly expect larger contributions if that legislator is placed on the Health Committee. Because committee membership changes across legislative sessions, we must take account of these changes in expectations. For example, in the 1985–86 legislative session, Senators Garamendi, Lockyer, and Torres were not members of the Governmental Organization Committee. Therefore using the previous session's contributions for those members that are new to the committee would be an inappropriate measure of the members' expectation of contributions for the current session. Although the legislator may have had a relationship with the group previously, to the extent that that legislator will now have a larger impact on their policy objectives, that legislator will expect more support.

### 3.3 Party

As in the above analyses, Party is a dummy variable that takes on the value of 1 if the voting member is of the same party as the author of the bill and 0 if she is not. Party is included in almost every analysis of legislative voting behavior because it has been such a successful predictor of behavior (Truman 1959; Turner and Schneier 1970): Democrats tend to vote with Democrats and Republicans tend to vote with Republicans. As noted by Cox and McCubbins (1993), why this is the case is the cause of much debate. For example, one reason party members vote together may be "that they have entangled themselves in various logrolls or policy alliances" (p. 156). The consistency could also be due to similar constituency pressures (Kingdon 1989). It could be that party members vote together because if members of the public do, in fact, vote retrospectively (Arnold 1990; Fiorina 1981), party members could believe that they share a collective fate (Arnold 1990).

Whether it is because of party pressure or similar ideologies or constituencies, we should expect that members of a committee are more likely to vote aye on a bill that is authored by a member of their party than they are on a bill authored by a member of the opposite party. Therefore, the dummy variable Party should be positively related to the probability of an aye vote.[4]

### 3.4 District Ideology

Even though party members are ideologically similar, they are not identical. Individual members have diverse districts. For example, Clinton's key Democratic vote on his 1993 economic package was Representative Marjorie Margolies-Mezvinsky from the very conservative 13th District of Pennsylvania (Woodward 1994). Convincing Representative Margolies-Mezvinsky to vote consistent with the wishes of her party leaders was difficult for the president because of the pressure she felt from her constituency. The pressure was real: she lost her seat in the next election, primarily because of this one vote.

Legislative leaders in California have found themselves facing similar dilemmas. The one true threat to former Speaker Willie Brown's leadership during his fourteen-year tenure was when he could not appease five of the more conservative members of his own caucus (Clucas 1995) and Senate Pro Tempore David Roberti had the same problem in 1986 (Shuit 1986), illustrating that, often, appeals to party loyalty are not enough to keep members in line because of the differing constituent pressures each member feels.

Therefore, controlling for party alone is not sufficient to explain the voting behavior of members of the legislature. We must take account of the differences in constituent preferences as well. Whether constituents are placing pressure on members, as in the example above, or different types of districts simply choose different types of representatives (Bernstein 1989), members' behavior varies even within each of the parties. District Ideology is the percentage of two-party registration in the voting member's district that registered in the author of the bill's party (i.e., if the bill has a Republican author, the variable will be percentage registered Republican/(percentage Democratic registration + percentage Republican registration)). Given its construction, District Ideology is expected to be positively related to the probability of voting aye on a bill.[5]

### 3.5 Member Ideology

Member Ideology is another measure of a member's initial position on a bill that takes account of differences across party members. I took member support scores from three interest groups—the California Labor Federation, the California Chapter of the National Organization for Women, and the California Chamber of Commerce. Each was on a 100-point scale with 100 being the most liberal and 0 the most conservative.[6] To create the measure, I added the three scores together for each member of the California State Senate and Assembly and divided by three.

The Member Ideology variable should measure the degree to which the member, based on his ideology, would prefer the new bill to the status quo and, because, the status quo is different for each bill included in these analyses, the calculation of the ideology measure is somewhat complex. I define the status quo as the average of all bill authors' ideology scores, assuming that any status quo legislation should be representative of the average ideology of the house as a whole. I subtract the status quo from the committee member's basic ideology score. Finally, I subtract the absolute value of the individual bill author's ideology minus the voting member's ideology. Given its construction, Member Ideology should be positively related to the probability of an aye vote.

Jackson and Kingdon (1992) have illustrated that there are significant problems with legislator ideology scores based on interest group rating schemes. In particular, because these measures conflate many variables other than member ideology, they often overestimate the relationship between member ideology and votes and underestimate the relationship between voting and other variables. Caldeira and Wright (1998) note that this actually makes it more difficult to reject the null hypothesis of interest. Therefore this issue, though real, should not affect any substantive evidence I find in support of my hypotheses regarding contributions.

Three separate models were run for each analysis. The first included all votes from the given set of bills, the second included critical votes only, and the third included noncritical votes only. The results for each of these models are presented in the tables below.

### 3.6 First Stage Instrumental Contributions Variables

**3.6.1 Dependent Variable.** To create the dependent variable for the support contributions equation, I summed the contributions to an individual committee member from all groups in support of the bill on which the member is voting and took the square root of that sum. For the opposition contributions dependent variable, I summed the contributions to an individual committee member from all groups in opposition to the bill on which the member is voting and took the square root of that sum.

The square root was taken to deal with the skewed nature of the contribution data. The usual transformation of a skewed variable is to log the values. Unfortunately, logging contributions does not create a distribution that is consistent with the assumptions of the Tobit model. The Tobit model requires that the dependent variable be normally distributed, but truncated at some value (usually 0). Logging the contributions variable creates a distribution that is normally distributed with a large number of 0 contributions as shown in Figure B.1.

The distribution of the square root of the contributions variable is presented in Figure B.2.

Clearly, the distribution created by taking the square root of the contributions variable is consistent with the assumptions of the Tobit model, but the distribution created by logging is not.

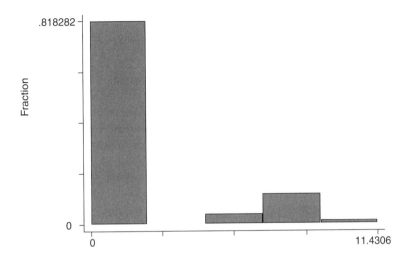

**Fig. B.1** Distribution of Logged Contributions

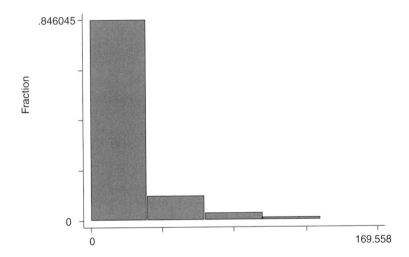

**Fig. B.2** Distribution of the Square Root of Contributions

*3.6.2 Independent Variables.* There are seven independent variables used to predict the propensity of an interest group to contribute to an individual member. First, it seems logical that the size of the contribution that a group gives to a legislator is largely a function of the amount of money the group has to give. Amount Available to Give is measured as the square root of the total amount of money contributed to campaigns of all state legislative incumbents by all the groups that took a support (or opposition for the Opposition equation) position on the bill.

The second variable that should affect the amount of contributions that a member receives from a group is whether that member is part of legislative leadership. Leadership is not only a measure of the power of that legislator over an interest group's legislative agenda (Chappell 1981), but is especially important in California because party leaders are expected to raise and distribute money to membership for elections (Richardson 1996). Leadership is a dummy variable that takes on the value of 1 if the committee member is President Pro Tempore of the Senate, Majority Leader, Minority Leader, a member of the Rules Committee, or chair of the Governmental Organization Committee and 0 otherwise.[7]

Party is often included in these analyses because it is one measure of a member's initial position on a bill (Chappell 1981; Grenzke 1989) and groups often contribute to members of the legislature who agree with their positions to help them gain office. In addition, each of the parties is ideologically compatible with particular interest groups (Langbein and Lotwis 1990; Saltzman 1987). However, there are too many bills (102 bills) and groups included in this analysis to calculate ideological compatibility for each issue. Therefore, the Party variable will equal 1 if the voting member and the author of the bill are of the same party and 0 otherwise, under the assumption that members author bills that are similar in position to their ideologically compatible interest groups and that groups tend to give more money to members of that same party.[8]

The fourth variable is the District Ideology of the voting member. Like Party, this is an approximate measure of the member's initial position on a bill. This variable, District Ideology, is measured as the percentage of two-party registration in the voting member's district that registered in the author of the bill's party (i.e., if the bill has a Republican author, the variable will be percentage registered Republican/[percentage Democratic registration + percentage Republican registration]).[9]

Another measure of a member's initial position is Member Ideology. Member Ideology is measured as the absolute value of the committee member's ideology minus the status quo and subtract the absolute value of the author's ideology minus the voting member's ideology. Calculation of the status quo and of the individual members' ideology scores are discussed in the text.

Some scholars have found a relationship between electoral vulnerability and campaign contributions (Fleisher 1993; Grier and Munger 1986). I measure Electoral Vulnerability as the amount of money spent by the member's challenger during the 1987–88 election cycle. Some might argue that using challenger spending in the 1988 election cycle to predict 1987–88 contributions behavior creates an *ex post* measure. I disagree. This analysis takes the

1987–88 legislative session as a single point in time, not a time series. If that is the case, then the contributions, voting, and challenger spending behavior are all taking place simultaneously in this single time period. Although challenger spending does not actually end until the election in November of 1988, neither does the contributions behavior in which I am interested. In addition, there are other indicators during this time period (i.e., challenger fund-raising) that give both contributors and members information about the potential amount of challenger spending.[10]

Another measure of members' electoral vulnerability is the margin by which they won their last election. Incumbents' electoral margin in their previous election has been shown to be a significant predictor of the amount of campaign contributions they receive from interest groups (Grier and Munger 1991). Previous Vote is the difference between the voting members' percentage of the vote and the next highest competitor in their last general election. The last election may have taken place in 1984 or 1986.[11]

Note that I do not include the ten member dummies (discussed earlier) in any of the first stage Tobit equations. If I include these dummy variables in the first stage of the model, the substantive results do not change from those presented in the text. However, they do cause a problem when I attempt the bootstrap. The reason for this is the small number of nonzero observations in the opposition contributions Tobit equations for all models. When I attempt to bootstrap the model with 1,000 replications, eventually the Tobit will not converge because the program randomly selects too few nonzero observations given the number of dummy variables. The only way I could determine to reduce the dimensionality of the model was to eliminate the member dummies. This being said, I was able to bootstrap the analysis for all votes with the ten dummies in the first stage for 100, rather than 1,000, replications. The substantive results were no different than the corrected standard errors for all votes.

The purpose of the first stage Tobit analyses is to predict the latent propensity of groups to contribute, while purging the measure of the impact of votes. These models meet that objective quite well. The models as a whole are significant at the .001 level and the predicted values of the support and opposition contributions correlate with the actual contributions at .84 and .87, respectively, for all votes, and .87 and .84, respectively, for critical votes only in Chapter 5. Finally, each of the dependent variables is predicted quite well by exogenous variables not included in the vote equations.

The results of the Tobit analyses for each of the chapters are presented in Table B.13 through Table B.22.

**TABLE B.1** OLS Results for CTLA Campaign Contributions in the California Senate, 1987–88

| Variable | Coefficient |
|---|---|
| Democrat | .07 (.70) |
| Ideology | .02* (.01) |
| Electoral Vulnerability | .05 (.05) |
| Member of Leadership | 2.35‡ (.55) |
| Judiciary Committee | 1.34‡ (.32) |
| Insurance Committee | .69* (.34) |
| Democrat X Electoral Vulnerability | .05 .06 |
| Constant | 5.78‡ (.51) |
| Number of Observations | 40 |
| Adjusted R-Squared | .68 |
| F | 12.61‡ |

*p <= .05
†p <= .01
‡p <= .001
Note: Coefficients are the result of OLS regression. Standard errors are in parentheses.

**TABLE B.2** Probit Results of Voting Models, Voting on AB 1500

| Independent Variables | Assembly Floor (Vote Not Critical) Correct S.E. | Senate Floor (Vote Critical) Correct S.E. |
|---|---|---|
| Party | .21 (.58) | 1.03*a (1.46) |
| District Ideology | .42 (1.57) | −1.04 (8.80) |
| Member Ideology | −.06* (.04) | −.05* (.07)a |
| Rural Caucus Member | .79* (.49)a | −.11 (1.06) |
| Contributions | .01 (.02) | .03* (.15) |
| Constant | 1.73† (.73) | .79 (.78) |
| Number of Cases | 78 | 40 |
| X² | 16.58† | 10.07* |
| Goodman/Kruskal Tau | .36 | .30 |

*p <= .10
†p <= .05
‡p <= .01
a Significant with percentile confidence interval only.
Note: The coefficients are the result of the second stage probit analysis. The standard errors are in parentheses (one-tailed tests of significance). Only 250 repetitions are used in the bootstrap in these analyses rather than the standard 1,000 because of the Rural Caucus dummy variable. Because so few of the legislators are members of the Rural Caucus, the bootstrap often selects sets of observations that include no Rural Caucus members and the model fails to converge.

**TABLE B.3** OLS Results of Voting Model for SB 276

| Independent Variables | OLS Coefficient |
|---|---|
| Party | 1.24 (1.23) |
| Member Ideology | −.03 (.03) |
| Contributions (square root) | .19* (.10) |
| Constant | .04 (.52) |
| Number of Cases | 10 |
| F | 1.91 |
| Adjusted R-Square | .23 |

*p <= .05

Note: Standard errors are in parentheses (one-tailed tests of significance).

**TABLE B.4** Probit Results for Voting Model, SB 3

| Independent Variables | Coefficient (Original S.E.) |
|---|---|
| Party | −1.07 (1.37) |
| District Ideology | .06 (.04) |
| Member Ideology | .10† (.04) |
| Contributions | −.01 (.01) |
| Constant | −8.11† (3.03) |
| Number of Cases | 40 |
| $X^2$ | 31.40‡ |
| Goodman/Kruskal Tau | .75 |

*p <= .10

†p <= .05

‡p <= .01

Note: The coefficients are the result of the second stage probit analysis. The standard errors are in parentheses (one-tailed tests of significance).

**TABLE B.5** Probit Results for the Governmental Organization Committee

| Independent Variables | All Votes | Critical Votes Only | Noncritical Votes Only |
|---|---|---|---|
| Party | .5417† | .3719 | .5568* |
| | (.2132) | (1.7969) | (.2546) |
| District Ideology | −.8904 | −1.6546 | −.4827 |
| | (.4925) | (3.6421) | (.6082) |
| Member Ideology | −.0002 | .0095 | −.0062 |
| | (.0044) | (.0405) | (.0055) |
| Support Contributions | .0017 | .0067† | −.0009 |
| | (.0012) | (.1284) | (.0016) |
| Opposition Contributions | −.0045† | −.0096‡ | .0002 |
| | (.0016) | (.0066) | (.0034) |

**TABLE B.5**  (continued)

| Independent Variables | All Votes | Critical Votes Only | Noncritical Votes Only |
|---|---|---|---|
| Constant | .4348 | 1.5732[†] | .0570 |
|  | (.2993) | (.6254) | (.3618) |
| Number of Cases | 929 | 311 | 618 |
| $X^2$ | 98.54 | 50.55 | 82.48 |
| Probability of $X^2$ | .0000 | .0000 | .0000 |
| Goodman/Kruskal Tau | .33 | .39 | .35 |

*p <= .05
[†]p <= .01
[‡]p <= .001

Note: The standard errors on the independent variables are produced with a bootstrap procedure discussed in Appendix A. By necessity, the $X^2$ and the standard error on the constant are produced from the original (nonbootstrapped) probit analysis.

**TABLE B.6**  Probit Results for All Senate Committees

| Independent Variables | All Votes | Critical Votes Only | Noncritical Votes Only |
|---|---|---|---|
| Party | .5884* | −1.2231* | 1.0816* |
|  | (.1653) | (.7127) | (.1971) |
| District Ideology | −.1877 | 1.5566 | −.8767 |
|  | (.4811) | (1.9057) | (.5876) |
| Member Ideology | .0073* | .0439* | −.0027 |
|  | (.0037) | (.0152) | (.0044) |
| Support Contributions | .0017 | .0304* | −.0020 |
|  | (.0012) | (.0130) | (.0013) |
| Opposition Contributions | −.0021* | −.0114* | .0005 |
|  | (.0008) | (.0048) | (.0009) |
| Constant | .2084 | .6724 | .3413 |
|  | (.2481) | (.6305) | (.2878) |
| Number of Cases | 908 | 223 | 685 |
| $X^2$ | 82.42[‡] | 109.19[‡] | 59.35[‡] |
| Goodman/Kruskal Tau | .31 | .60 | .34 |

*p <= .05
[†]p <= .01
[‡]p <= .001

Note: The coefficients are the result of the second stage probit analysis. The standard errors are in parentheses (one-tailed tests of significance). The significance levels are based on percentile and bias-corrected confidence intervals.

**TABLE B.7** Probit Results for Broad Jurisdiction Committees

| Independent Variables | All Votes | Critical Votes Only | Noncritical Votes Only |
|---|---|---|---|
| Party | .4059* | 1.8210† | .8760* |
| | (.2017) | (.6421) | (.2324) |
| District Ideology | .2810 | 3.3686* | −.1160 |
| | (.5631) | (1.8827) | (.6453) |
| Member Ideology | .0058 | .0457‡ | −.0039 |
| | (.0046) | (.0112) | (.0056) |
| Support Contributions | .0028* | .0385‡ | −.0012 |
| | (.0016) | (.0127) | (.0018) |
| Opposition | −.0029* | −.0234‡ | .0005 |
| Contributions | (.0011) | (.0066) | (.0012) |
| Constant | .0125 | −1.9013 | .1648 |
| | (.3157) | (1.4561) | (.3619) |
| Number of Cases | 725 | 163 | 562 |
| X² | 64.67‡ | 93.67‡ | 38.13‡ |
| Goodman/Kruskal Tau | .30 | .62 | .32 |

*p <= .05
†p <= .01
‡p <= .001

Note: The coefficients are the result of the second stage probit analysis. The standard errors are in parentheses (one-tailed tests of significance). In the models including all votes or noncritical votes, the significance levels are based on percentile and bias-corrected confidence intervals. In the critical votes analysis, significance levels are based on the original standard errors.

**TABLE B.8** Probit Results for Narrow Jurisdiction Committees

| Independent Variables | All Votes | Critical Votes Only | Noncritical Votes Only |
|---|---|---|---|
| Party | 1.0953† | −1.9525 | 2.1311‡ |
| | (.3774) | (1.4181) | (.4809) |
| District Ideology | −1.2149 | 5.4346* | −5.9637‡ |
| | (1.0894) | (2.5712) | (1.8178) |
| Member Ideology | .0074 | .0481 | .0085 |
| | (.0100) | (.0410) | (.0106) |
| Support Contributions | .0029 | .0219† | .0012 |
| | (.0023) | (.0077) | (.0027) |
| Opposition | −.0014 | −.0070† | .0007 |
| Contributions | (.0015) | (.0031) | (.0019) |

**TABLE B.8** (continued)

| Independent Variables | All Votes | Critical Votes Only | Noncritical Votes Only |
|---|---|---|---|
| Constant | .5292 | .9788 | 2.4114† |
| | (.5123) | (1.0917) | (.8162) |
| Number of Cases | 183 | 60 | 123 |
| X² | 28.76‡ | 22.23‡ | 30.93‡ |
| Goodman/Kruskal Tau | .37 | .46 | .42 |

*p <= .05
†p <= .01
‡p <= .001

Note: The coefficients are the result of the second stage probit analysis. The standard errors are in parentheses (one-tailed tests of significance). In the analysis including all votes, the significance levels are based on percentile and bias-corrected confidence intervals. In the other two analyses, they are based on the original standard errors.

**TABLE B.9** Probit Results for Moderate Committees

| Independent Variables | All Votes | Critical Votes Only | Noncritical Votes Only |
|---|---|---|---|
| Party | .6201* | −2.6527* | 1.0284* |
| | (.2245) | (1.5312) | (.2702) |
| District Ideology | −.0115 | 3.7413 | −.9088 |
| | (.6564) | (3.1162) | (.7900) |
| Member Ideology | .0044 | .0458* | .0005 |
| | (.0050) | (.0273) | (.0063) |
| Support Contributions | .0024* | .0514* | −.0015 |
| | (.0015) | (.0259) | (.0016) |
| Opposition Contributions | −.0037* | −.0310* | −.0007 |
| | (.0014) | (.0135) | (.0017) |
| Constant | .2165 | 1.4730 | .4271 |
| | (.3138) | (1.1005) | (.3714) |
| Number of Cases | 491 | 128 | 363 |
| X² | 44.08‡ | 52.44‡ | 32.70‡ |
| Goodman/Kruskal Tau | .34 | .49 | .35 |

*p <= .05
†p <= .01
‡p <= .001

Note: The coefficients are the result of the second stage probit analysis. The standard errors are in parentheses (one-tailed tests of significance). The significance levels are based on percentile and bias-corrected confidence intervals.

**TABLE B.10** Probit Results for Ideologically Extreme Committees

| Independent Variables | All Votes | Critical Votes Only | Noncritical Votes Only |
|---|---|---|---|
| Party | .5614* | −.0675 | 1.0648* |
| | (.2714) | (.6230) | (.3560) |
| District Ideology | −.6914 | −.4341 | −.5364 |
| | (.8352) | (2.0374) | (1.0053) |
| Member Ideology | .0107 | .0654‡ | −.0020 |
| | (.0062) | (.0147) | (.0079) |
| Support Contributions | .0016 | .0138ᵗ | −.0022 |
| | (.0019) | (.0088) | (.0025) |
| Opposition Contributions | −.0012 | −.0071‡ | .0017 |
| | (.0009) | (.0019) | (.0013) |
| Constant | .5292 | .6613 | .2966 |
| | (.3394) | (1.2174) | (.4808) |
| Number of Cases | 417 | 95 | 322 |
| X² | 40.66‡ | 63.58‡ | 29.17‡ |
| Goodman/Kruskal Tau | .27 | .83 | .39 |

ᵗp <= .10
*p <= .05
†p <= .01
‡p <= .001
Note: The coefficients are the result of the second stage probit analysis. The standard errors are in parentheses (one-tailed tests of significance). In the models including all votes or noncritical votes, the significance levels are based on percentile and bias-corrected confidence intervals. In the critical votes analysis, significance levels are based on the original standard errors.

**TABLE B.11** Probit Results for Juice Committees

| Independent Variables | All Votes | | Critical Votes Only | | Noncritical Votes Only | |
|---|---|---|---|---|---|---|
| | With BP & BC | Without BP & BC | With BP & BC | Without BP & BC | With BP & BC | Without BP & BC |
| Party | .5699* | .6483* | −.8609 | −.3282 | 1.0587* | 1.1625* |
| | (.2331) | (.2515) | (.7701) | (.7626) | (.2746) | (.3079) |
| District Ideology | −.7477 | −.8083 | 2.7367 | 1.6510 | −.9550 | −.7426 |
| | (.6987) | (.7138) | (2.8942) | (2.7727) | (.8292) | (.8831) |
| Member Ideology | .0091* | .0103* | −.0148 | −.0927* | −.0031 | −.0047 |
| | (.0050) | (.0053) | (.0274) | (.0482) | (.0056) | (.0062) |
| Support Contributions | .0014 | .0005 | .1401‡ | .0938‡ | −.0022 | −.0024 |
| | (.0015) | (.0015) | (.0462) | (.0305) | (.0016) | (.0017) |
| Opposition Contributions | −.0016* | −.0011 | −.0449† | −.0162† | .0005 | .0004 |
| | (.0008) | (.0008) | (.0154) | (.0058) | (.0011) | (.0011) |

**TABLE B.11** (continued)

| Independent Variables | All Votes | | Critical Votes Only | | Noncritical Votes Only | |
|---|---|---|---|---|---|---|
| | With BP & BC | Without BP & BC | With BP & BC | Without BP & BC | With BP & BC | Without BP & BC |
| Constant | .6107* | .6226* | −3.5364 | −4.5903* | .4579 | .2799 |
| | (.3321) | (.3440) | (2.2283) | (2.4396) | (.3815) | (.3959) |
| Number of Cases | 516 | 480 | 96 | 83 | 420 | 397 |
| X² | 39.07‡ | 42.19‡ | 88.78‡ | 72.74‡ | 29.06‡ | 33.75‡ |
| Goodman/ Kruskal Tau | .25 | .26 | .75 | .78 | .32 | .33 |

*p <= .05
†p <= .01
‡p <= .001
BP=Business and Professions Committee
BC=Banking and commerce Committee
Note: The coefficients are the result of the second stage probit analysis. The standard errors are in parentheses (one-tailed tests of significance). In the models including all votes or noncritical votes, the significance levels are based on percentile and bias-corrected confidence intervals. In the critical votes analysis, significance levels are based on the original standard errors.

**TABLE B.12** Probit Results for Nonjuice Committees

| Independent Variables | All Votes | | Critical Votes Only | | Noncritical Votes Only | |
|---|---|---|---|---|---|---|
| | With BP & BC | Without BP & BC | With BP & BC | Without BP & BC | With BP & BC | Without BP & BC |
| Party | .4799* | .3220 | −2.2119† | −1.8768* | .8453† | .7939† |
| | (.2614) | (.2612) | (.9800) | (1.7238) | (.2912) | (.2795) |
| District Ideology | .6968 | .8880 | .0397 | .9405 | .1498 | −.1007 |
| | (.7386) | (.8104) | (1.3384) | (2.5888) | (.8941) | (.8832) |
| Member Ideology | .0095 | .0092 | .0721‡ | .0616* | .0006 | .0010 |
| | (.0068) | (.0069) | (.0218) | (.0353) | (.0082) | (.0081) |
| Support Contributions | .0017 | .0023 | .0240* | .0260* | −.0008 | −.0004 |
| | (.0020) | (.0018) | (.0121) | (.0223) | (.0020) | (.0018) |
| Opposition Contributions | −.0046* | −.0071* | −.0114† | −.0161* | −.0029 | −.0021 |
| | (.0028) | (.0029) | (.0038) | (.0118) | (.0031) | (.0030) |
| Constant | −.3710 | −.4980 | 2.8178* | 1.9367* | −.4278 | −.1786 |
| | (.3810) | (.3692) | (1.4447) | (1.1992) | (.5221) | (.5054) |

**TABLE B.12** (continued)

| Independent Variables | All Votes | | Critical Votes Only | | Noncritical Votes Only | |
|---|---|---|---|---|---|---|
| | With BP & BC | Without BP & BC | With BP & BC | Without BP & BC | With BP & BC | Without BP & BC |
| Number of Cases | 392 | 428 | 127 | 140 | 265 | 288 |
| X² | 49.48‡ | 50.91‡ | 32.31‡ | 45.81‡ | 31.68‡ | 27.17‡ |
| Goodman/ Kruskal Tau | .32 | .31 | .41 | .53 | .33 | .26 |

*p <= .05
†p <= .01
‡p <= .001

Note: The coefficients are the result of the second stage probit analysis. The standard errors are in parentheses (one-tailed tests of significance). The significance levels are based on percentile and bias-corrected confidence intervals for all votes and critical votes. The original standard error is used when the Business and Professions and Banking and Commerce Committees are included and in both noncritical votes analyses.

**TABLE B.13** First Stage OLS Results, AB 1500 Contributions

| Independent Variables | Assembly Floor | Senate Floor |
|---|---|---|
| Leader | 30.39‡ | 48.24‡ |
| | (8.51) | (9.53) |
| Party | −42.51* | −34.87 |
| | 22.58) | (23.04) |
| District Ideology | −40.70 | 122.92 |
| | (54.86) | (77.45) |
| District Ideology Minus 100 (extreme) | 25.73 | 14.48 |
| | (34.50) | (53.30) |
| Member Ideology | .98† | .38 |
| | (.40) | (.39) |
| Member Ideology Minus 100 (extreme) | .32 | 1.13† |
| | (.38) | (.48) |
| Challenger Spending | −1.09* | 1.66* |
| | (.63) | (.76) |
| Previous Vote Margin | −.80* | .52* |
| | (.43) | (.31) |
| Seniority | 1.31* | −.88 |
| | (.65) | (.65) |

**TABLE B.13** (continued)

| Independent Variables | Assembly Floor | Senate Floor |
|---|---|---|
| Rural Caucus Dummy | 2.87 | −.92 |
| | (6.24) | (9.92) |
| Governmental | 10.91 | 1.44 |
| Organization Dummy | (6.87) | (8.90) |
| Constant | 24.17 | −124.58$^\dagger$ |
| | (43.83) | (48.42) |
| Number of Cases | 78 | 40 |
| $X^2$ | 36.75$^\ddagger$ | 40.44$^\ddagger$ |

$^*$p <= .05
$^\dagger$p <= .01
$^\ddagger$p <= .001

Note: The coefficients are the result of the first stage OLS analysis. The standard errors are in parentheses (one-tailed tests of significance).

**TABLE B.14** First Stage OLS Results, SB 3 Senate Floor Contributions

| Independent Variables | Coefficients |
|---|---|
| Leader | −25.96$^*$ (13.98) |
| Party | 28.18 (30.51) |
| District Ideology | −.09 (.69) |
| Member Ideology | .58 (.59) |
| Challenger Spending | .89 (1.36) |
| Previous Vote Margin | −.32 (.31) |
| Seniority | .05 (.89) |
| Judiciary Committee Dummy | 34.71$^\dagger$(12.80) |
| Insurance Committee Dummy | −46.39$^\ddagger$(13.94) |
| Constant | −19.34(41.46) |
| Number of Cases | 40 |
| F | 4.89$^\ddagger$ |
| Adjusted R-Square | .47 |

$^*$p <= .05
$^\dagger$p <= .01
$^\ddagger$p <= .001

Note: The coefficients are the result of the first stage OLS analysis. The standard errors are in parentheses (one-tailed tests of significance).

**TABLE B.15** First Stage Tobit Results, Senate Governmental Organization Contributions

| Independent Variables | All Votes | | Critical Votes | | Noncritical Votes | |
|---|---|---|---|---|---|---|
| | Support | Oppose | Support | Oppose | Support | Oppose |
| Amount Available | .19$^\ddagger$ | .20$^\ddagger$ | .19$^\ddagger$ | .20$^\ddagger$ | .20$^\ddagger$ | .21$^\ddagger$ |
| to Give | (.01) | (.01) | (.01) | (.02) | (.01) | (.02) |
| Leader | 10.01$^\dagger$ | 7.62 | 5.94 | 15.26* | 12.49$^\dagger$ | 1.10 |
| | (3.31) | (4.89) | (5.22) | (8.78) | (4.21) | (5.74) |
| Party | −.88 | −.45 | 20.58* | −6.72 | −11.58* | −1.76 |
| | (5.78) | (8.16) | (10.17) | (13.97) | (7.25) | (10.32) |
| District Ideology | .48 | 1.07 | −23.20 | −1.79 | 9.89 | −1.35 |
| | (16.69) | (22.39) | (28.78) | (50.76) | (20.55) | (24.31) |
| Member Ideology | .18 | −.24 | −.10 | −.43 | .39* | .02 |
| | (.13) | (.18) | (.21) | (.30) | (.17) | (.23) |
| Challenger | .83$^\dagger$ | −.13 | .17 | .41 | 1.28$^\dagger$ | −.06 |
| Spending | (.37) | (.50) | (.58) | (.89) | (.47) | (.63) |
| Previous Vote | −.53$^\ddagger$ | −.16 | −.43* | −.33 | −.56$^\ddagger$ | −.16 |
| Margin | (.14) | (.18) | (.22) | (.38) | (.18) | (.21) |
| Constant | −38.67$^\ddagger$ | −61.93$^\ddagger$ | −36.35* | −65.49* | −40.70$^\ddagger$ | −48.32$^\dagger$ |
| | (10.58) | (16.15) | (17.99) | (35.13) | (13.16) | (17.37) |
| Number of Cases | 929 | 929 | 311 | 311 | 618 | 618 |
| X$^2$ | 740.28$^\ddagger$ | 417.56$^\ddagger$ | 277.74$^\ddagger$ | 170.88$^\ddagger$ | 473.52$^\ddagger$ | 257.68$^\ddagger$ |

*p <= .05
$^\dagger$p <= .01
$^\ddagger$p <= .001

Note: The coefficients are the result of the first stage Tobit analysis. The standard errors are in parentheses (one-tailed tests of significance).

**TABLE B.16** First Stage Tobit Results, All Senate Committees

| Independent Variables | All Votes | | Critical Votes | | Noncritical Votes | |
|---|---|---|---|---|---|---|
| | Support | Oppose | Support | Oppose | Support | Oppose |
| Amount Available | .05$^\ddagger$ | .26$^\ddagger$ | .17$^\ddagger$ | .29$^\ddagger$ | .15$^\ddagger$ | .25$^\ddagger$ |
| to Give | (.01) | (.01) | (.02) | (.03) | (.01) | (.02) |
| Leader | 12.59* | 20.54$^\dagger$ | 8.93 | 20.49 | 15.01* | 21.98$^\dagger$ |
| | (5.97) | (8.30) | (7.30) | (17.37) | (7.66) | (9.56) |
| Party | 20.12* | −4.92 | 18.02 | −21.56 | 22.56 | −.27 |
| | (11.38) | (14.37) | (14.14) | (29.44) | (14.45) | (16.27) |
| District Ideology | −26.67 | 91.49* | −5.97 | 105.16 | −48.83 | 85.12 |
| | (32.00) | (47.03) | (36.72) | (90.73) | (42.46) | (55.07) |
| Member Ideology | .10 | −.66* | −.06 | .26 | .00 | −.89$^\dagger$ |
| | (.25) | (.31) | (.31) | (.69) | (.32) | (.35) |

**TABLE B.16** (continued)

| Independent Variables | All Votes | | Critical Votes | | Noncritical Votes | |
|---|---|---|---|---|---|---|
| | Support | Oppose | Support | Oppose | Support | Oppose |
| Challenger | .47 | 1.69* | 1.60* | 2.12 | .14 | 1.81* |
| Spending | (.59) | (.82) | (.75) | (1.77) | (.76) | (.93) |
| Previous Vote | .16 | .21 | .20 | .15 | .09 | .26 |
| Margin | (.16) | (.22) | (.18) | (.44) | (.21) | (.25) |
| Constant | −92.95‡ | −193.21‡ | −76.34‡ | −190.22‡ | −89.44‡ | −192.63 |
| | (17.13) | (27.04) | (20.32) | (49.40) | (22.49) | ‡(32.52) |
| Number of Cases | 908 | 908 | 223 | 223 | 685 | 685 |
| X² | 357.30‡ | 511.88‡ | 151.51‡ | 142.91‡ | 243.80‡ | 374.68‡ |

*p <= .05
†p <= .01
‡p <= .001

Note: The coefficients are the result of the first stage Tobit analysis. The standard errors are in parentheses (one-tailed tests of significance).

**TABLE B.17** First Stage Tobit Results, Broad Jurisdiction Committees

| Independent Variables | All Votes | | Critical Votes | | Noncritical Votes | |
|---|---|---|---|---|---|---|
| | Support | Oppose | Support | Oppose | Support | Oppose |
| Amount Available to | .14‡ | .33‡ | .20‡ | .35‡ | .14‡ | .33‡ |
| Give | (.01) | (.03) | (.03) | (.05) | (.02) | (.03) |
| Leader | 23.12† | 32.65† | 8.58 | 29.79 | 27.32† | 41.38† |
| | (8.37) | (12.88) | (7.58) | (25.95) | (10.55) | (16.26) |
| Party | 22.55 | 7.95 | 1.67 | −52.74 | 29.08 | 50.27* |
| | (15.90) | (23.54) | (13.57) | (45.20) | (20.38) | (30.52) |
| District Ideology | 20.15 | 143.51* | 14.69 | 205.16 | 1.20 | 142.48 |
| | (45.36) | (72.47) | (43.25) | (150.34) | (56.34) | (88.89) |
| Member Ideology | −.21 | −1.61† | .05 | −.08 | −.41 | −2.71‡ |
| | (.36) | (.53) | (.32) | (.94) | (.47) | (.76) |
| Challenger Spending | 1.04 | 2.46* | 1.69† | .99 | .03 | 3.96† |
| | (.78) | (1.26) | (.70) | (2.64) | (1.00) | (1.55) |
| Previous Vote | −.20 | .50 | .10 | .21 | −.32 | .66 |
| Margin | (.26) | (.38) | (.23) | (.70) | (.33) | (.48) |
| Constant | −129.83‡ | −291.29‡ | −66.02† | −259.02‡ | −129.38‡ | −342.95‡ |
| | (26.05) | (45.09) | (24.63) | (78.89) | (32.43) | (63.28) |
| Number of Cases | 725 | 725 | 163 | 163 | 562 | 562 |
| X² | 192.06‡ | 277.54‡ | 79.24‡ | 80.11‡ | 153.84‡ | 204.10 |

*p <= .05
†p <= .01
‡p <= .001

Note: The coefficients are the result of the first stage Tobit analysis. The standard errors are in parentheses (one-tailed tests of significance).

**TABLE B.18** First Stage Tobit Results, Narrow Jurisdiction Committees

| Independent Variables | All Votes | | Critical Votes | | Noncritical Votes | |
|---|---|---|---|---|---|---|
| | Support | Oppose | Support | Oppose | Support | Oppose |
| Amount Available to Give | .15‡ | .17‡ | .13‡ | .21‡ | .16‡ | .16‡ |
| | (.02) | (.01) | (.02) | (.03) | (.02) | (.01) |
| Leader | 8.53 | 6.67 | 8.56 | .75 | 11.45 | 8.29 |
| | (8.23) | (6.40) | (11.85) | (18.46) | (10.60) | (6.24) |
| Party | 32.75† | −8.87 | 67.63† | −56.31 | 29.64* | −10.94 |
| | (14.81) | (10.07) | (26.75) | (44.99) | (18.42) | (9.96) |
| District Ideology | −78.06* | 5.07 | −118.33* | 66.31 | −100.36 | 14.85 |
| | (44.29) | (39.37) | (58.66) | (89.02) | (64.10) | (46.22) |
| Member Ideology | .17 | .12 | −.89 | 2.21* | .63 | −.15 |
| | (.36) | (.24) | (.62) | (1.23) | (.45) | (.21) |
| Challenger Spending | .87 | .74 | −1.29 | 2.57 | 1.62 | .40 |
| | (.89) | (.67) | (1.85) | (1.98) | (1.06) | (.62) |
| Previous Vote Margin | .33* | −.09 | .43* | −.10 | .29 | −.08 |
| | (.17) | (.14) | (.24) | (.37) | (.22) | (.13) |
| Constant | −43.59* | −44.45* | −26.35 | −78.22* | −32.96 | −42.07* |
| | (21.81) | (20.76) | (28.75) | (46.79) | (30.53) | (22.65) |
| Number of Cases | 183 | 183 | 60 | 60 | 123 | 123 |
| X² | 127.20‡ | 259.52‡ | 62.24‡ | 74.45‡ | 75.89‡ | 199.00‡ |

*p <= .05
†p <= .01
‡p <= .001
Note: The coefficients are the result of the first stage Tobit analysis. The standard errors are in parentheses (one-tailed tests of significance).

**TABLE B.19** First Stage Tobit Results, Moderate Membership Committees

| Independent Variables | All Votes | | Critical Votes | | Noncritical Votes | |
|---|---|---|---|---|---|---|
| | Support | Oppose | Support | Oppose | Support | Oppose |
| Amount Available to Give | .20‡ | .16‡ | .19‡ | .16‡ | .21‡ | .16‡ |
| | (.01) | (.01) | (.02) | (.01) | (.02) | (.01) |
| Leader | 9.34 | 2.00 | −5.99 | −3.36 | 13.73* | 2.71 |
| | (6.25) | (4.00) | (8.80) | (7.49) | (7.98) | (4.66) |
| Party | 15.89 | −11.53* | 19.43 | −34.07* | 16.67 | −9.62 |
| | (10.90) | (6.65) | (16.07) | (15.56) | (13.73) | (7.77) |
| District Ideology | −43.04 | 55.95† | 13.17 | 52.26 | −68.90* | 67.53* |
| | (31.51) | (24.77) | (40.83) | (40.38) | (42.38) | (30.99) |
| Member Ideology | .05 | −.12 | −.29 | .44 | .14 | −.18 |
| | (.24) | (.15) | (.34) | (.42) | (.31) | (.17) |
| Challenger Spending | .37 | .88* | 1.17 | −12.16 | .15 | 1.21† |
| | (.67) | (.42) | (.99) | N/A | (.83) | (.49) |

**TABLE B.19** (continued)

| Independent Variables | All Votes | | Critical Votes | | Noncritical Votes | |
|---|---|---|---|---|---|---|
| | Support | Oppose | Support | Oppose | Support | Oppose |
| Previous Vote Margin | .04 | .07 | .04 | .26 | .01 | .05 |
| | (.15) | (.10) | (.20) | (.17) | (.19) | (.11) |
| Constant | −58.77‡ | −69.15‡ | −68.97‡ | −46.44* | −51.75† | −78.02‡ |
| | (16.21) | (14.15) | (21.65) | (21.50) | (21.36) | (17.89) |
| Number of Cases | 470 | 470 | 115 | 115 | 355 | 355 |
| X² | 277.06‡ | 309.38‡ | 105.68‡ | 67.05‡ | 185.35‡ | 253.63‡ |

*$p <= .05$
†$p <= .01$
‡$p <= .001$
Note: The coefficients are the result of the first stage Tobit analysis. The standard errors are in parentheses (one-tailed tests of significance).

**TABLE B.20** First Stage Tobit Results, Extreme Membership Committees

| Independent Variables | All Votes | | Critical Votes | | Noncritical Votes | |
|---|---|---|---|---|---|---|
| | Support | Oppose | Support | Oppose | Support | Oppose |
| Amount Available to Give | .12‡ | .35‡ | .13‡ | .32‡ | .13‡ | .36‡ |
| | (.01) | (.03) | (.02) | (.04) | (.02) | (.04) |
| Leader | 35.07‡ | 42.75† | 28.03† | 53.45* | 45.24‡ | 53.68† |
| | (10.59) | (15.16) | (12.26) | (26.91) | (14.68) | (20.25) |
| Party | 22.25 | 46.81 | 9.40 | 29.91 | 40.23 | 73.87* |
| | (22.08) | (29.43) | (22.86) | (41.27) | (30.71) | (42.17) |
| District Ideology | 82.93 | 27.96 | 53.96 | 93.36 | 52.97 | 27.62 |
| | (62.79) | (83.27) | (75.72) | (135.38) | (81.92) | (120.03) |
| Member Ideology | .20 | −1.69† | .61 | .47 | −.34 | 2.89† |
| | (.51) | (.60) | (.51) | (.90) | (.78) | (1.00) |
| Challenger Spending | 2.04* | 2.40* | 2.65† | 3.13 | 2.06 | 3.24* |
| | (.96) | (1.44) | (1.07) | (2.35) | (1.31) | (1.94) |
| Previous Vote Margin | .26 | .01 | .29 | −.14 | .29 | .29 |
| | (.32) | (.42) | (.29) | (.57) | (.45) | (.65) |
| Constant | −193.15‡ | −249.44‡ | −121.40† | −242.42‡ | −210.67‡ | −306.42‡ |
| | (36.72) | (46.78) | (43.90) | (73.11) | (49.91) | (77.47) |
| Number of Cases | 438 | 438 | 108 | 108 | 330 | 330 |
| X² | 176.35‡ | 280.05‡ | 65.92‡ | 95.96‡ | 130.09‡ | 187.15‡ |

*$p <= .05$
†$p <= .01$
‡$p <= .001$
Note: The coefficients are the result of the first stage Tobit analysis. The standard errors are in parentheses (one-tailed tests of significance).

**TABLE B.21** First Stage Tobit Results, Juice Committees

| | All Votes | | Critical Votes | | Noncritical Votes | |
|---|---|---|---|---|---|---|
| Independent Variables | Support | Oppose | Support | Oppose | Support | Oppose |
| Amount Available to Give | .15‡ | .27‡ | .18‡ | .36‡ | .15‡ | .25‡ |
| | (.01) | (.02) | (.02) | (.05) | (.01) | (.02) |
| Leader | 16.93* | 37.90‡ | 12.62 | 44.53 | 18.17* | 35.58‡ |
| | (9.02) | (10.87) | (8.16) | (28.03) | (11.25) | (11.55) |
| Party | 16.74 | 2.62 | −11.68 | −11.75 | 29.78 | 1.87 |
| | (17.47) | (18.74) | (15.71) | (51.83) | (21.90) | (19.06) |
| District Ideology | 4.86 | 100.23 | 42.33 | 176.78 | 12.74 | 88.59 |
| | (49.95) | (63.72) | (47.82) | (180.38) | (63.74) | (65.25) |
| Member Ideology | −.01 | −.88† | .33 | −.98 | −.51 | −.85† |
| | (.35) | (.37) | (.30) | (1.23) | (.46) | (.38) |
| Challenger Spending | .99 | 2.80† | 1.96† | 5.44* | .88 | 2.28* |
| | (.86) | (1.06) | (.82) | (2.93) | (1.06) | (1.09) |
| Previous Vote Margin | .03 | .58* | .32 | .42 | −.13 | .55* |
| | (.26) | (.29) | (.22) | (.72) | (.33) | (.31) |
| Constant | −115.09‡ | −239.41‡ | −78.52† | −326.12‡ | −135.48‡ | −214.77‡ |
| | (26.54) | (35.64) | (27.99) | (93.64) | (34.21) | (37.85) |
| Number of Cases | 523 | 523 | 100 | 100 | 423 | 423 |
| $X^2$ | 205.17‡ | 376.71‡ | 93.31‡ | 84.66‡ | 158.90‡ | 299.41‡ |

*$p <= .05$
†$p <= .01$
‡$p <= .001$
Note: The coefficients are the result of the first stage Tobit analysis. The standard errors are in parentheses (one-tailed tests of significance).

**TABLE B.22** First Stage Tobit Results, Nonjuice Committees

| | All Votes | | Critical Votes | | Noncritical Votes | |
|---|---|---|---|---|---|---|
| Independent Variables | Support | Oppose | Support | Oppose | Support | Oppose |
| Amount Available to Give | .18‡ | .21‡ | .14‡ | .19‡ | .21‡ | .23‡ |
| | (.02) | (.02) | (.02) | (.02) | (.03) | (.04) |
| Leader | 9.10 | −3.66 | .37 | .39 | 15.46 | −18.25 |
| | (7.95) | (9.56) | (10.34) | (12.38) | (10.84) | (15.88) |
| Party | 29.51* | −15.41 | 56.84† | −58.09* | 23.03 | −2.90 |
| | (14.17) | (16.94) | (21.53) | (35.46) | (18.49) | (26.26) |
| District Ideology | −78.04* | 42.98 | 23.76 | 23.00 | −119.26† | 67.54 |
| | (38.76) | (48.22) | (49.94) | (59.32) | (53.98) | (86.22) |
| Member Ideology | .31 | .06 | −1.01* | 1.87* | .94* | −1.25* |
| | (.36) | (.46) | (.49) | (1.04) | (.51) | (.69) |

**TABLE B.22** (continued)

| Independent Variables | All Votes | | Critical Votes | | Noncritical Votes | |
|---|---|---|---|---|---|---|
| | Support | Oppose | Support | Oppose | Support | Oppose |
| Challenger | −.29 | 1.02 | .79 | .35 | −1.23 | 2.37 |
| Spending | (.89) | (.98) | (1.18) | (1.41) | (1.21) | (1.63) |
| Previous Vote | .29 | −.09 | .09 | −.03 | .25 | −.03 |
| Margin | (.18) | (.22) | (.25) | (.32) | (.25) | (.31) |
| Constant | −61.72‡ | −83.39† | −111.85‡ | −33.76 | −43.40 | −120.45† |
| | (20.14) | (28.56) | (31.56) | (32.42) | (27.77) | (54.80) |
| Number of Cases | 385 | 385 | 123 | 123 | 262 | 262 |
| X² | 175.85‡ | 129.24‡ | 81.59‡ | 74.35‡ | 109.33‡ | 57.71‡ |

*p <= .05
†p <= .01
‡p <= .001

Note: The coefficients are the result of the first stage Tobit analysis. The standard errors are in parentheses (one-tailed tests of significance).

# Appendix C
## Questionnaire on Committee Jurisdictions

I am attempting to create a measure of committee jurisdictions that takes account of how many independent issues a committee addresses. Committees that address only a few unique issue areas are deemed "narrow" jurisdiction committees and committees that address a large number of unrelated issues are designated as "broad" jurisdiction committees.

It is important for the reliability of this measure that you not discuss your scores with others until you have finished filling out the form. Do not allow the assessments of others to influence you to change your scores after you have finished. It is critical that each person's score be an independent measure.

1. Instructions

1. Read all instructions before beginning.
2. Read all of the attached descriptions of committee jurisdictions from the 1987–88 Legislative Handbook.
3. In **Column A,** rank each of the committees listed according to how narrow or broad their jurisdictions are: one (1) is the most narrow and eighteen (18) is the most broad. In other words, which committees do you believe cover the largest number of different policy areas and which do you believe cover the least?
   **It is important that you rank each committee, even those you may not feel comfortable ranking.** The final scores will be based on a compilation

of everyone's educated guess. What is important here is each committee's position relative to the other committees.

Each committee should have its own unique number in Column A.

4. Determine how many different policy areas each committee addresses. Place that number in **Column B.**

For example, for Column B for the Agriculture and Water Committee, do you think that agriculture and water issues fall into two different policy areas? Do you think there are unique agriculture policy areas that also need to be considered? Are there different water policy areas? If you believe there are four distinct policy areas, put 4 in Column B.

Only enter a number in Column B for those committees you feel you are capable of describing.

What is your definition of a "distinct policy area?"_____

_____

_____

_____

5. When you are done, please feel free to make any comments on the comment page provided.

6. Place the committee rankings and comment pages in the attached envelope, seal, and give to Alan.

Thank you so much for giving your time to this endeavor. It is greatly appreciated.

| COMMITTEES | COLUMN A Ranking of the Committees | COLUMN B Number of Different Policy Areas |
|---|---|---|
| Agriculture and Water | _____ | _____ |
| Banking and Commerce | _____ | _____ |
| Business and Professions | _____ | _____ |
| Education | _____ | _____ |
| Elections | _____ | _____ |
| Energy and Public Utilities | _____ | _____ |
| Governmental Organization | _____ | _____ |
| Health and Human Services | _____ | _____ |
| Housing and Urban Affairs | _____ | _____ |
| Industrial Relations | _____ | _____ |
| Insurance, Claims and Corp. | _____ | _____ |
| Judiciary | _____ | _____ |
| Local Government | _____ | _____ |
| Natural Res. and Wildlife | _____ | _____ |
| Public Employees Retirement System | _____ | _____ |
| Revenue and Taxation | _____ | _____ |
| Toxics and Public Safety | _____ | _____ |
| Transportation | _____ | _____ |

**COMMENTS**

# Appendix D
## Questionnaire: Identifying "Juice" Committees in the California State Senate

Your participation in this survey is completely voluntary and, if you choose to participate, your participation will be kept anonymous. There is no list of participants and once the results are compiled, the original surveys will be destroyed. If you choose to participate, please complete the following short questionnaire and return it to the survey administrator.

Thank you.

I. Below are listed the 18 policy committees in the State Senate during the 1987–1988 legislative session. Next to each of the committees, please note whether you would consider this committee to be a "juice" committee or not..

| Committee (Chair) | Is the Committee a Juice Committee? (circle one) | |
|---|---|---|
| Agriculture | (YES) | (NO) |
| Banking & Commerce | (YES) | (NO) |
| Business & Professions | (YES) | (NO) |
| Education | (YES) | (NO) |
| Elections | (YES) | (NO) |
| Energy & Public Utilities | (YES) | (NO) |
| Government Organization | (YES) | (NO) |
| Health & Human Services | (YES) | (NO) |
| Housing & Urban Affairs | (YES) | (NO) |
| Industrial Relations | (YES) | (NO) |
| Insurance | (YES) | (NO) |
| Judiciary | (YES) | (NO) |
| Local Government | (YES) | (NO) |
| Natural Resources | (YES) | (NO) |
| Public Employees & Retirement | (YES) | (NO) |
| Revenue & Taxation | (YES) | (NO) |
| Toxics | (YES) | (NO) |
| Transportation | (YES) | (NO) |

II. In the space provided below, please explain what characteristics you believe identify a "juice" committee. Please be as complete and descriptive as possible.

Thank you for taking the time to complete this survey. If you are interested in receiving a copy of the results or know anyone else who would be interested, please contact the survey administrator at sgordon@scs.unr.edu or (775)784-4675.

# Notes

*Chapter 1*

1. This story took an even more bizarre twist when Carpenter fled the country and had to be hunted down and extradited back to the United States.
2. California had two competing initiatives on the ballot. One, Proposition 208, passed with 61 percent of the vote and the other, Proposition 212, lost with only 48.1 percent of the vote (Alexander and Weiler 1997).
3. The Nevada Constitution requires that an initiative be on the ballot and passed twice before it becomes law, so Questions 10 in 1994 and 1996 are the same initiative. Tommy Neil of the National Conference of State Legislatures kindly provided this information.
4. Some scholars argue that there are other incentives to members—besides reelection—to make policy (Arnold 1990; Fenno 1973; Krehbiel 1992) and to engage in oversight activity (Evans 1994). Still others argue that those incentives are increasing over time (Aberbach 1990; Davidson and Oleszak 1994). However, most agree that it remains a greatly overlooked task of Congress.
5. There are many reasons why small groups can avoid free-riders more easily than large groups. First, it is easier for small groups to keep an eye on other members to make sure they are participating and, if a member attempts to free-ride, they can punish or keep the member from gaining the benefits of group membership. Second, all members of small groups must often participate for their group goals to be achieved. In other words, small groups have the ability to characterize their public goods as "all or nothing." Either all members of the group participate or nothing is accomplished. Third, because of the "all or nothing" characteristic of their public goods, the law of diminishing returns does not apply to small groups. The group does not need to be concerned with the cost-benefit analysis inherent in determining whether they should focus on increasing membership or spend their resources elsewhere.
6. Political context has not been ignored in previous literature. Studies on the effect of issue visibility on the relationship are discussed in the next chapter.
7. Committee analyses were not available for this time period from the Senate Committee on Transportation, so no bills from that committee were included.

*Chapter 2*

1. In her foreword to the 1990 translation of Mauss's *The Gift*.
2. These resources include, but are not limited to, PACs who can make campaign contributions.
3. Cameron and Enelow (1992) make the case for a fifth relationship. They argue that candidates participate in rent-seeking behavior by taking positions in anticipation of receiving money from particular interest groups. I would argue that the critical vote behaviors outlined in this chapter are so subtle as to be an extremely inefficient form of rent seeking. In other words, if it were rent seeking, it probably would not be a very successful form. The visibility, access, and effort behaviors are important and observable enough to be used by legislators to attract money from interested groups. However, individual legislators are in a position to act as a critical vote for an individual donor only rarely—probably not often enough to be the only reason for interest groups to provide contributions. This does not mean that the influence of contributions on critical votes is not important in an aggregate sense. As noted numerous times previously, the change of a rare single vote, if it is critical to the outcome of legislation significantly affects policy outcomes. But, it is unlikely that a single critical vote will cause a group to give more money to a legislator. In addition, it is virtually impossible to separate this behavior from the electoral effects of contributions and, therefore, it will not be discussed in any more detail here.
4. For an exception, see Gopoian (1984).
5. Berry (1997) notes that this is not particularly true for public interest groups. "It is, to be sure, true that public interest lobbies deal most often with their friends. But it also is true that it is not always characteristic of the public interest groups to leave their opponents alone" (p. 218).
6. For example, see the 2000 *Time* magazine series by Barlett and Steele on how various donors have benefited from recent policy and why.
7. Although he also admits that "we cannot exclude the possibility that some mixed strategy is followed ..." (p. 115).
8. Even in terms of this one case, others disagree (Stern 1988).
9. This has changed in recent years. In 2000, California voters passed an initiative which places limits on campaign contributions.
10. We can begin to argue that contributions have affected a member's vote only if the member is not ideologically compatible with the group of interest. This is both a conceptual and a statistical problem and is illustrated well by this committee example. If a member generally holds the same issue positions as the contributing group, it is difficult (if not impossible) to determine if it is the contributions that caused the vote or the member's personal ideology. Once we control for ideology, the votes of compatible members cannot be affected by the contributions even if they vote consistently with the group. If a member is ideologically compatible with a group, then any contributions given to that member, by definition, have an access, effort, or electoral effect: they are not given to the member by the group with the intention of buying votes. Contributions, in this case, have no effect on voting behavior.

    It is entirely possible that, in reality, a member only voted with an ideologically compatible group because of the contributions received (and, thus, contributions independently affected votes), but there is no way to separate out this relationship in an empirical setting. Therefore, I assume here and in further discussion that votes by legislators who are ideologically compatible with the contributing group cannot be swayed by campaign contributions.
11. Campaign contributions information is published regularly by the FEC and is now available on the World Wide Web.
12. Of course, this is an empirical question that will not be addressed here. However, given the low costs of being listed, it seems to be a reasonable assumption.
13. Article IV, section 9 of the California Constitution (adopted by constitutional amendment on November 8, 1966) states that "A statute shall embrace but one subject, which shall be expressed in its title. If a statute embraces a subject not expressed in its title, only the part not expressed is void. A statute may not be amended by reference to its title. A section of a statute may not be amended unless the section is re-enacted as amended."

14. California Senate Rule 38.5 of the 1987–88 session states that "Every amendment proposed must be germane to the subject of the proposition to be amended, and an amendment is not in order which is not germane to the question to be amended."

   California Assembly Rule 92 of the 1987–88 session similarly reads "No amendment to any bill, whether reported by a committee or offered by a Member, shall be in order when such amendment relates to a different subject than, or is intended to accomplish a different purpose than, or requires a title essentially different than, the original bills.

   "No motion or proposition on a subject different from that under consideration shall be admitted as an amendment."

15. See Enelow (1981) for a discussion of the effects of "killer" and "saving" amendments.

16. These are, of course, empirical questions that will not be addressed here. Some have argued that the political environment in California might be unique for various reasons (Syer 1987, 39). However, the economic diversity, large population, and professionalized legislature make it similar to the federal legislature in many ways.

17. Clawson et al. also note that the hegemony that business enjoys in the policy process because of its various characteristics (e.g., business can affect the economy by its nonpolitical decisions, it can contribute so much money to legislators and parties) allows it to change the "social space" within which legislators make their decisions.

18. It is important to reiterate that the market analogy need not imply changes in aggregate behavior or significant numbers of votes, but the assumption that it does underlies current studies. At the least, though, if money is traded explicitly for votes, it implies an understanding by both parties that some known commodity is being traded for another. In economic terms, it is an extremely efficient form of exchange.

19. Fenno (1978) argues that members will sometimes vote against their constituents' preferences if they believe that they can explain those votes sufficiently to appease the voters. However, he also provides ample evidence that the opposite occurs as well: members often vote a particular way to avoid having to explain. At the least, he states that he agrees with Kingdon (1989) that congressmen take into account how acceptable their explanation will be to their constituents when deciding how to vote. On balance, I believe that more of the latter behavior occurs than the former, primarily because sufficient evidence has been provided from other studies that visibility appears to be an issue of concern to members when deciding whether to allow contributions to affect their votes.

20. Some have shown that contributions may affect votes on highly visible issues (Langbein and Lotwis 1990) and that members' votes may be inconsistent with constituent interests even on highly salient bills (Lascher et al. 1993). However others illustrate that constituents can, in fact, punish members for shirking their constituent's interests (Lott 1993; Wright 1993). However, because members cannot know which of these circumstances will apply, they will be less likely to shirk constituent interests if a bill is highly visible.

21. However, this literature tends to focus primarily on how stable coalitions based on swing votes are (Frohlich 1975) and the likelihood of minimum winning coalitions being created at all (Collie 1988b; Hinckley 1972; Riker 1962), not on how being part of a minimum winning coalition affects an individual legislator's behavior. Although, individual behavior clearly plays a role in explaining the nature of these coalitions (Collie 1988a; Riker 1962; Weingast 1979).

22. This is true both in the California legislature and the U.S. Congress. Although lobbyists do not have direct access to members during the course of a committee hearing or floor session, they can get messages and information to members through legislative staff.

23. This game of "counting votes" can often become very sophisticated. I once overhead a member of the California State Senate staff comment that he was afraid his member's bill would fail because he needed eight votes. He had five firm commitments, a member who was willing to be the seventh vote, and a member who was willing to be the eighth vote, but no one was willing to come out early and be the sixth vote.

24. Maltzman (1997) also believes that changes in procedures of the house and the strength of the majority party caucus are other factors that influence the power of the principals.

25. Thanks to Kip Lipper for this insight.

26. They are called juice committees because members of these committees can squeeze more money out of interest groups.

*Chapter 3*

1. In the 1990s, they changed their name to Consumer Attorneys of California.
2. For specific examples of the trial lawyers competing with business groups, see Ferguson (1996), Jacobs (1996), and Kushman (1993a, 1993b).
3. California State senators hold four-year terms. Campaigns for odd-numbered districts were held in 1980, 1984, and 1988. Campaigns for even-numbered districts were held in 1982, 1986, and 1990. Because Doolittle was placed from an odd-numbered district into an even-numbered one, he had to run in 1980 and then again in 1982. Even though he lost in 1982, he was able to retain his seat until 1984, but then had to find a new district in which to run. Block described him as "a man without a constituency" during this two-year period (1989, 106). It was in 1984 that he decided to challenge Republican Ray Johnson for the 1st District seat.
4. Doolittle was also considered to be extremely political (Block 1989)—willing to do just about anything to accomplish his own political goals. The FPPC violations mentioned occurred during the 1984 State Senate campaign for the 1st District. In the general election, Doolittle found himself running against Ray Johnson, the Republican-incumbent-turned-Independent he had defeated in the Republican primary. The Democrats, in an attempt to defeat Doolittle, actively supported Johnson's independent candidacy. In an attempt to draw Democratic votes away from Johnson, Doolittle "broke the law by providing last-minute, under-the-table help to the nominal, much-disregarded, much-ignored Democratic candidate—Jack Hornsby" and, subsequently, was fined by the FPPC for these activities (Block 1989, 106).
5. Rules Committee is probably the most powerful committee in the California Senate; it is responsible for committee referrals and rule waivers. Examples of oft-requested rule waivers are requests to allow a bill to be heard before its hearing date has been listed in the Daily File (schedule) for four days or requests to allow a bill to be heard in committee after the committee deadline.
6. This is the average contribution not including those to David Roberti.
7. This information regarding Doolittle's selection for the Republican party leadership was provided by a source who prefers that it not be specifically attributed.
8. Neither of these averages includes David Roberti.
9. Just how friendly was identified when Jackson, a contract lobbyist for insurance companies, offered Robbins $250,000 to move one of Jackson's bills to the Insurance Committee from the Industrial Relations Committee. Presumably, he believed that he would be more successful in Robbins's arena (Gladstone 1993).
10. President Pro Tempore of the Senate David Roberti said that he did not provide support to Whiteaker because he (Roberti) got along with Doolittle on the Rules Committee (Ingram 1988). This does not mean that Whiteaker received no money from the Senate Democrats. He received over $200,000 from Senate Democratic incumbents. He received an additional $82,000 from the leadership committee of the Senate Caucus Chair, Barry Keene.
11. The last variable that seems to play a part in the contributions strategies of interest groups is seniority, because the longer a member is in office, the more power we should expect him to have (Dow 1994). Therefore, the longer a member has held office, the more contributions he is expected to get (Fleisher 1993).

    Seniority should not have a significant impact on Doolittle's contributions. The mean level of seniority in the senate is about nine years and Doolittle was in his eighth year in 1988. I have not included it here because, if seniority is just another proxy for power, then the contributions he receives because of his control over the CTLA's agenda should already be captured in the Judiciary committee variable. If seniority is included as a variable in the Ordinary Least Squares (OLS) analysis presented in Appendix A, it does not change the substantive results presented. Ideology becomes insignificant, but it does not change any of the implications regarding Doolittle as an outlier.
12. See Appendix A for exact measures used and tables of OLS coefficients.
13. Figure 3.1 and Figure 3.2 suggest that heteroskedasticity may be a problem in this analysis. However, because the major concern here does not lie with the coefficients or their significance, it is not necessary to address that issue here. That being said, the heteroskedasticity seems to be driven by three observations—Doolittle, Garamendi, and Roberti.

When Garamendi and Roberti are dropped from the analysis, the heteroskedasticity seems much less obvious, the substantive results presented in the OLS table in Appendix A do not change, and Doolittle remains an outlier. When Doolittle is also dropped from the analysis, the heteroskedasticity disappears.

14. The support scores are shown in Table 3.6 and are discussed in more detail below.
15. Torres probably scored low because he was absent so much of the time. Torres, being the leading Latino in the senate, found himself with an enormously large number of committee memberships, a total of seven.
16. The other votes were Democrats Lockyer, Keene, Presley, and Torres and Republican Davis.
17. The information regarding SB 2662 was provided by Daniel Dunmoyer, advocate for the PIF.
18. Letter from the CTLA to members of the Senate Insurance Committee regarding SB 2662.
19. Doolittle's congressional office and the CTLA were contacted numerous times for interviews. Both declined to respond.
20. In fact, two individuals close to the Judiciary Committee independently identified similar behavior in that context. However, neither was willing to talk on the record until the actual bills were found. Unfortunately, even with the information they provided, I was unable to find the specific bills they were referencing.

## Chapter 4

1. Letter to Assemblyman Costa on May 7, 1987.
2. Letter to Assemblyman Costa from Consumer's Union on April 14, 1987.
3. Those in support of the bill would suggest that this consensus by newspapers against the bill was no coincidence. By far, grocery stores and other major retailers are the largest source of newspaper advertising dollars. Some might argue that the fact that those same newspapers so vigorously opposed the bill is due to their own financial interest, the same argument that the editorials were making in regards to legislative voting on the bill (Reardon 1999).
4. More extreme members are identified as those one standard deviation above the mean on the Member Ideology measure; more moderate members are identified as those one standard deviation below the mean on the same variable.
5. The Rural Caucus variable is only significant in the assembly model and not in the senate model. There are two possible reasons for this. First, the Assembly Rural Caucus took a position on the bill, but the Senate Rural Caucus did not. Second, I was able to obtain a complete list of Assembly Rural Caucus members, but had to compile Senate Rural Caucus members relatively haphazardly. This is due to the fact that the Rural Caucus in the assembly was much more organized (e.g., they met regularly, took positions on bills, had an independent staff, etc.) than the senate caucus at this time. I determined whether senators were likely to be members of the Rural Caucus based on whether they were members of the following groups: (1) the Agriculture Committee, (2) the Select Committee on Fairs and Rural Issues, or (3) a member of the Senate Rural Caucus in 1980 (the only list of Senate Rural Caucus members I could find). Because the Rural variable for the senate analysis is less reliable than that for the assembly, it is possible that that explains why contributions were significant for the senate and not the assembly if, in fact, those two variables are correlated. However, dropping the Rural variable from either analysis does not change the other substantive relationships.
6. Letter to Senator Leroy Greene from the ACLU, March 9, 1987.
7. None of the correlations in this analysis include the President Pro Tempore, David Roberti.
8. One outlier from the analysis of SB 267 has been dropped from Figure 4.2. One member of the committee received over $25,000 from supporting groups and including that observation in the chart hid the nature of the relationship. However, the analysis on which the results are based include the outlier.
9. Once again, the summary statistics presented here do not include former Senator Roberti.
10. The bill was eventually vetoed by then Governor Deukmejian. The veto was upheld in the assembly.
11. A similar bill was also introduced in 1985 by Assemblyman Hauser, AB 755, but that bill was not referred to Senate Governmental Organization. It was only referred to Senate Natural Resources and eventually failed in Senate Appropriations.

12. This was not the first lease/sale approved for the Humboldt/Mendocino area. A lease/sale approved in the 1970s was a campaign issue in the county superintendent's race during that decade (Breit 1999).

13. This quote came from a photocopy of a newsletter that was part of AB 284's committee bill file. It can be found at the California State Archives in Sacramento, California. The original source of the quote could not be ascertained from the photocopy.

14. The support and opposition information comes from letters from various groups to legislators regarding the bill and numerous committee and floor analyses of SB 3. All can be found in the bill file for SB 3 at the California State Archives in Sacramento, California.

15. Letter to Assemblyman Patrick Johnston, Chairman of the Assembly Committee on Finance and Insurance, dated June 27, 1990.

16. Note by the National Association of Independent Insurers, dated June 27, 1990.

17. Letter to Assemblyman Patrick Johnston, Chairman of the Assembly Committee on Finance and Insurance, dated July 2, 1990, from G. Diane Colborn, lobbyist for State Farm Insurance Company.

18. See the extended discussion of this issue in Chapter 3.

19. Trial lawyer contributions correlated with party at .39 and with ideology at .48 during the 1989–90 legislative session.

20. Roberti's press secretary denied that committee assignments were connected to fund-raising support (Gladstone 1993).

## *Chapter 5*

1. Not only do committees act as gatekeepers at the beginning of the process by determining what legislation makes it to the floor, but actions by legislators on floor votes may also be affected by committee preferences. This is because committee members have an "*ex post* veto." Shepsle and Weingast (1987) argue that because committee members often serve on conference committees if conference action becomes necessary, floor behavior by members may be a strategic response to possible committee actions in conference. Therefore, committee member preferences are critical at many stages in the process.

2. As stated in previous chapters, some studies attempt to control for issue visibility by controlling for the media attention given to a particular bill (Jones and Keiser 1987; Neustadtl 1990).

3. The first most requested committee in 1981, in the assembly, was the Committee on Finance and Insurance. "The F&I committee is one of the Legislature's prizes because membership on the panel guarantees healthy campaign contributions from the financial industries with a vital stake in the bills assigned to the panel.... [Former Speaker Willie] Brown responded to the requests of his colleagues by assigning 19 members—almost one-fourth of the Lower House—to seats on the committee" (Rios 1981, 109).

    In the senate, President Pro Tempore David Roberti had so many requests to the senate version of this committee that he split its responsibilities into two separate committees, Banking and Commerce and Insurance and Indemnity, "with a total membership of 16–40 percent of the Upper House" (Rios 1981, 109).

4. There is substantial anecdotal evidence that suggests that money and votes are more likely to be intimately related in these juice committees, though not in the manner theorized here. During the FBI sting in the late 1980s and early 1990s, it was in these committees where the most of the problems occurred.

    Two of the other most sought after committee assignments in the senate are the Committee on Business and Professions and the Committee on Insurance, Claims, and Corporations. The members who held the chairs of these two committees during the 1987–88 session—former Senator Joseph Montoya, Chair of the Business and Professions Committee, and former Senator Alan Robbins, Chair of the Insurance, Claims, and Corporations Committee—both served federal prison terms after being convicted of crimes related to campaign financing. Robbins had attempted to funnel money from insurance contributors to himself through the senatorial campaign committee of another former state senator (Walsh 1996). Montoya was found guilty of extortion, racketeering, and money laundering (although an appellate court overturned the extortion conviction) after "being videotaped in 1988 accepting an envelope containing $3,000 cash from an undercover [FBI] agent who was touting bogus special-interest legislation" (Walsh 1997). In addition, the member of the assembly that served as vice-chair of the Assembly Committee on Governmental Organization during this time, former Assemblyman Frank Hill, is also currently serving a prison term for an offense related to the same FBI sting operation.

5. Although Collie (1988a) argues that we miss important information about the nature of aggregate voting behavior in various Congresses over time when we drop universalistic votes (defined as votes where 90 percent or more of the members voted on the same side), most studies of the voting behavior of individual legislators do so. This is because, as Collie noted, we tend to be more interested in what explains the outcome of conflict rather than trying to predict consensus.

Collie's research shows that different variables explain when legislation is likely to be consensual than explain individual votes when legislation is conflictual. This is especially true in the context of state legislatures because legislators more often find themselves voting on legislation that is extremely narrow and/or "clean-up" legislation that fixes minor problems in previously passed bills (Rosenthal 1993). Because there is no logical reason for anyone to vote against these bills, predicting individual behavior is not theoretically interesting and, if there are too many of them, leaving them in the analysis could cause us to conclude that our independent variables are insignificant, when that lack of significance is being driven by the noncontroversial nature of the bills.

Because the votes on consent calendar bills are, by definition, always unanimous, they were dropped from the analysis as well. The consent calendar was created to move noncontroversial bills through the process more quickly by allowing the committees to vote on a large number of bills at the same time. A bill can only be "on consent" if there is no interest group opposition and the bill has not received a "no" vote at any time in the legislative process (White 1987, 358). Any member can have a bill removed from consent at any time simply by asking that it be removed.

6. The results discussed here are presented in detail in Appendix A. Interested readers will find there a detailed discussion of the variables included in the analysis and the methodological issues considered, as well as the results of the second stage probit analysis.

7. The substantive results do not change when the model is changed in this manner. The results on the contributions variables remain the same.

8. Thanks to Steve Nicholson for pointing out this particular issue.

9. I calculated these probabilities using Clarify (Tomz et al. 2003).

10. For this example, above average and below average are calculated as one standard deviation above the mean and one standard deviation below the mean, respectively.

## Chapter 6

1. Maltzman (1997) also believes that changes in procedures of the U.S. House of Representatives and the strength of the majority party caucus are other factors that influence the power of the principals.

2. Note that my definition of a broad jurisdiction committee is different than Hinckley's (1975), discussed above. She defines a broad jurisdiction in terms of how many legislators are affected by the policy content of the committee. I define a broad jurisdiction as the number of unique policy areas that make up a committee's jurisdiction. Although these two measures are obviously related—the more issues a committee addresses, the larger the number of legislators who will be affected—they are different. By her definition, a committee could have a broad scope while addressing only one policy area if the impacts of that policy affect a large majority of legislative districts. By my definition, that would be a narrow jurisdiction committee.

3. I developed a data set consisting of all 2,896 bills introduced to the California Senate during the 1987–88 legislative session. For each bill I listed the committee(s) to which it was referred and the topic of the bill as listed in the Senate Final History (California Senate 1988b).

4. The survey used is presented in Appendix C.

5. Four committees are not included in the analysis. Committee analyses were not available for the Senate Committee on Transportation for the 1987–88 legislative session, so it is not included (but was included in the survey). Neither the Senate Budget nor the Senate

Appropriations Committees are included in either the analyses or the survey because almost all bills are referred to one of these two committees. In addition, the Senate Agriculture Committee is not included in the analysis (but was on the survey) because none of the bills selected were referred to the Agriculture Committee.

6. The scores on the two measures correlate at .73 and the correlation is significant at the .001 level. Although the survey measure is based on an extremely small number of observations, it provides support for the reliability of the more concrete ranking.

7. I have not included the chart for opposition contributions to broad jurisdiction committees. Even though the general relationships between contributions and critical votes remain the same in that analysis, the baseline probability of a critical nay vote is so low that the chart is difficult to read.

8. Some might argue that ideological extremism is a characteristic of individuals, not committees. The anecdotes presented in this section suggest that that some committees may, in fact, be more extremist than others. That being said, the literature has been quite clear that contributions influence moderate legislators more than they do those that are ideologically extreme.

   Unfortunately, member ideology could not be included as an individual characteristic affecting contributions in the models presented here. To test the effect of individual ideology, one must include an interaction term between contributions and member ideology. Because the models being estimated here are so complex, when such a variable is included in the analyses, the models cannot be successfully estimated on a regular basis. In addition, when the models are able to be estimated, the standard errors are unreliable. However, by including extremism as a committee characteristic, we might be able to get at some aspect of this variable.

9. The value of 50 is an arbitrary cut-off and it was chosen because there did not appear to be an obvious middle point at which the data separated. The value of 50 placed 417 observations in extreme committees and 491 in moderate committees.

10. The survey is presented in Appendix D.

11. The correlation coefficient between the two measures is .40 and is not statistically significant.

12. I also attempted to measure the relationship between contributions and committee membership by regressing each member's contributions on their committee memberships, controlling for every other committee membership. Unfortunately, there are so many committees (twenty in all) and so few members (forty), that the coefficients cannot be trusted. Also, many committees that are clearly not money committees had positive coefficients, providing support for the previous concern.

13. I conducted each of the analysis coding these committees as nonjuice committees and the substantive results do not change dramatically. For the results on both sets of analyses, see Appendix A.

## Chapter 7

1. As quoted in Matthews (1998).
2. As quoted in Endicott (1998).
3. As quoted in O'Rourke (1999).
4. As quoted in Bernstein (1997).
5. As quoted in Sample (1999).
6. As quoted in Bernstein (1997).
7. As quoted in Bernstein (1997).
8. Thanks to an anonymous reviewer at the *Journal of Politics* for making this point.

## Appendix A

1. Note that I am referring to the SPT-III model and not the SPT-I or SPT-II models. In his 1981 article, Chappell presented three versions of his Simultaneous Probit-Tobit model. In SPT-I, he used actual contributions and, in SPT-II, he used a contributions dummy variable. In SPT-III, he used a group's "propensity to contribute" (the latent variable) instead of actual, observed contributions. In the former two models, the coefficients on contributions

were positive, but not statistically significant. In the SPT-III model, contributions were positive (as expected) and significant at the .10 level.

I am comparing my model to the SPT-III model because it is the most similar to the 2SLDV model I use here. Both the SPT-III and 2SLDV models use the latent variable from the contributions equation as the contributions variable in the probit equation rather than actual, observed contributions. However, it is important to note that I may, therefore, be overestimating the impact of contributions on voting behavior.

## Appendix B

1. Royce was coded 0 for Judiciary Committee membership even though he was placed on the committee late in the 1988 session. This is because it was probably unclear to the CTLA whether he was going to stay on the committee. In fact, Royce was replaced by Stirling in 1989, serving fewer than six months on the Judiciary Committee.
2. Voting data were collected from the *Senate Daily Journal*, 1987–88 (California Senate 1988).
3. The contributions data come from a data set compiled by Ken Mandler at Capitol Weekly, Inc. in Sacramento, California and were checked against contributions collected by the author from the California State Archives.
4. Party data were collected from the *1987–1988 Legislative Handbook* (White 1987).
5. Registration numbers were collected from the California Secretary of State's *Report of Registration* (1988).
6. The Chamber of Commerce scores had 100 as the most conservative and 0 as the most liberal. I simply subtracted each member's score from 100 to make it consistent with the other two ratings.
7. This variable takes on the value of 1 if the member is Senator William Campbell or Senator John Garamendi even though they were not members of leadership as defined above. However, Campbell was running for statewide office and so he received the larger contributions that tend to come with a statewide, rather than legislative, campaign. Garamendi had made an unsuccessful run for statewide office in 1986 and was raising large amounts of money to pay off his campaign debts. Leadership data are available in White (1987).
8. Party data are available in White (1987).
9. Party registration data are available in the California Secretary of State's *Report of Registration* (1988).
10. Challenger spending data are available at the California FPPC.
11. Election results are available in the California Secretary of State's *Statement of the Vote, General Election* (1984/1986).

# Bibliography

Aberbach, J.D. (1990) *Keeping a Watchful Eye: The Politics of Congressional Oversight,* Washington, DC: Brookings Institution.

Abramowitz, A.I. (1980) "A Comparison of Voting for U.S. Senator and Representative," *American Political Science Review* 74:633–40.

Adler, B.S. and Lapinski, J.S. (1997) "Demand-Side Theory and Congressional Committee Composition: A Constituency Characteristics Approach," *American Journal of Political Science* 41:895–918.

Alexander, H.E. and NyBlom, L.C. (1996) *Campaign Reform on the Ballot: 1972–1994,* Los Angeles: Citizens' Research Foundation.

Alexander, H.E. and Weiler, N. (1997) *Campaign Reform on the Ballot, 1972–1996: An Update to Campaign Reform on the Ballot, 1972–1994,* Los Angeles: Citizens' Research Foundation.

Alvarez, R.M. (1997) *Information and Elections,* Ann Arbor: University of Michigan Press.

Amemiya, T. (1979) "The Estimation of a Simultaneous-Equation Tobit Model," *International Economic Review* 20:169–81.

Amemiya, T. (1984) "Tobit Models: A Survey," *Journal of Econometrics* 24:3–61.

Arnold, R.D. (1990) *The Logic of Congressional Action,* New Haven: Yale University Press.

Austen-Smith, D. (1995) "Campaign Contributions and Access," *American Political Science Review* 89:566–81.

Bauer, R.A., de Sola Pool, I., and Dexter, L.A. (1963) *American Business and Public Policy,* New York: Atherton.

Baumgartner, F.R. and Jones, B.D. (1993) *Agendas and Instability in American Politics,* Chicago: University of Chicago Press.

Bee Capitol Bureau. (1998) "Helmet Exemption Bill Stalls in Senate," *The Sacramento Bee,* 17 June: 3(A).

Bernstein, D. (1997) "Contributions Corrupt Politics, Ex-Senator Testifies," *The Sacramento Bee,* 24 October: 5(A).

Bernstein, R.A. (1989) *Elections, Representation and Congressional Voting Behavior: The Myth of Constituency Control,* Upper Saddle River, NJ: Prentice Hall.

Berry, J.M. (1997) *The Interest Group Society,* 3rd Ed., New York: Longman.

Birnbaum, J.H. (1992) *The Lobbyists: How Influence Peddlers Get Their Way in Washington,* New York: Random House.

Birnbaum, J.H. (2000) *The Money Men: The Real Story of Fund-Raising's Influence on Political Power in America,* New York: Random House.

Block, A.G. (1989) "John Doolittle: The Senate's Combative Conservative," *California Journal* 20:105–9.

Block, A.G. and Carniello, S. (1987) "Putting on the Squeeze: Or, Why is Insurance So Popular?" *California Journal* 18:179–80.

Bourdieu, P. (1997a) "Selections from *The Logic of Practice*," in A.D. Schrift (ed.) *The Logic of the Gift*, New York: Routledge.

Bourdieu, P. (1997b) "Marginalia—Some Additional Notes on the Gift," in A.D. Schrift (ed.) *The Logic of the Gift*, New York: Routledge.

Box-Steffensmeier, J.M. (1996) "A Dynamic Analysis of the Role of War Chests in Campaign Strategy," *American Journal of Political Science* 40:352–71.

Breen, R. (1996) *Regression Models: Censored, Sample Selected or Truncated Data*, Thousand Oaks, CA: Sage Publications.

Breit, L. Former staff member to Assemblyman Dan Hauser. (1999) Personal interview by author, December 13. Sacramento.

Broder, D. (1999a) "Education of a Candidate," *The Washington Post*, Aug. 8, B7.

Broder, D. (1999b) "Make Realistic Goals for Campaign Reform," *The Sacramento Bee*, 3 November: 9(B).

Bronars, S.G. and Lott, J.R. (1997) "Do Campaign Donations Alter How a Politician Votes? Or, Do Donors Support Candidates Who Value the Same Things They Do?" *Journal of Law and Economics* 40:317–50.

Brooks, J.C., Cameron, A.C., and Carter, C.A. (1998) "Political Action Committee Contributions and U.S. Congressional Voting on Sugar Legislation," *American Journal of Agricultural Economics* 80:441–54.

Buchan, P. (1996) "Fighting for Civil Justice," *Trial* 32 (11): 11.

Caldeira, G.A. and Wright, J.R. (1998) "Lobbying for Justice: Organized Interests, Supreme Court Nominations, and the United States Senate," *American Journal of Political Science* 42:499–523.

California League of Conservation Voters. (1988) "1988 California Legislative Voting Chart," *The Conservation Voter*, Winter: Insert.

California Secretary of State. (1984) *Statement of the Vote, General Election 1984*, Sacramento: Secretary of State.

California Secretary of State. (1988) *Report of Registration, 1988*, Sacramento: Secretary of State.

California Secretary of State. (1986) *Statement of the Vote, General Election 1986*, Sacramento: Secretary of State.

California Secretary of State. (1996) *California Ballot Pamphlet: General Election, November 5, 1996*, Sacramento: Secretary of State.

California Senate. (1988a) *Senate Daily Journal, 1987–1988*, Sacramento: Secretary of the Senate.

California Senate. (1988b) *Senate Final History, 1987–1988*, Sacramento: Secretary of the Senate.

California Senate. (1990) Senate Floor Analysis of SB 3 (Roberti), Sacramento.

California Senate Judiciary Committee. (1987) Committee Analysis of SB 276 (L. Greene), Sacramento.

California Senate Natural Resources and Wildlife Committee. (1988) Committee Analysis of AB 284 (Hauser), Sacramento.

Cameron, C.M. and Enelow, J.M. (1992) "Asymmetric Policy Effects, Campaign Contributions and the Spatial Theory of Elections," *Mathematical and Computer Modeling* 16:117–32.

Caplow, T. (1982) "Christmas Gifts and Kin Networks," *American Sociological Review* 47:383–92.

Carmichael, H.L. and MacLeod, W.B. (1997) "Gift Giving and the Evolution of Cooperation," *International Economic Review* 38:485–509.

Carr, R. (1997) "House Probe's Outspoken Leader Finds His Own Conduct is Raising Questions," *Congressional Quarterly Weekly Report* 55:684–85.

Center for Responsive Politics. (1997) "Money and Politics Survey," Conducted by Princeton Survey Research Associates, 6 June.

Chappell, H.W. (1981) "Campaign Contributions and Voting on the Cargo Preference Bill: A Comparison of Simultaneous Equation Models," *Public Choice* 36:301–12.

Chappell, H.W. (1982) "Campaign Contributions and Congressional Voting: A Simultaneous Probit-Tobit Model," *Review of Economics and Statistics* 64:77–83.

Chong, D. (1991) *Collective Action and the Civil Rights Movement*, Chicago: University of Chicago Press.

Clawson, D., Neustadtl, A., and Weller, M. (1998) *Dollars and Votes: How Business Campaign Contributions Subvert Democracy*, Philadelphia: Temple University Press.

Clucas, R.A. (1995) *The Speaker's Electoral Connection*, Berkeley: Institute of Governmental Studies Press.

Cohen, L.R. and Noll, R.G. (1991) "How to Vote, Whether to Vote: Strategies for Voting and Abstaining on Congressional Roll Calls," *Political Behavior* 13:97–127.

Collie, M.P. (1988a) "Universalism and the Parties in the U.S. House of Representatives, 1921–1980," *American Journal of Political Science* 32:865–83.

Collie, M.P. (1988b) "The Legislature and Distributive Policy Making in Formal Pespective," *Legislative Studies Quarterly* 13:427–58.

Common Cause. (1997) "Congressional Campaign Spending," Press release.

Common Cause. (2000) Paying the Price: How Tobacco, Gun, Gambling, and Alcohol Interest Block Common Sense Solutions to Some of the Nation's Most Urgent Problems, Washington, DC: Common Cause.

Cox, G.W. and McCubbins, M.D. (1993) *Legislative Leviathan*, Berkeley: University of California Press.

Dahl, R.A. (1956) *A Preface to Democratic Theory*, Chicago: University of Chicago Press.

Davidson, R.H. and Oleszek, W.J. (1994) *Congress and Its Members*, Washington, DC: Congressional Quarterly Press.

Davis, F.L. (1993) "Balancing the Perspective on PAC Contributions: In Search of an Impact on Roll Calls," *American Politics Quarterly* 21:205–22.

Deering, C.J. and Smith, S.S. (1997) *Committees In Congress*, Washington, DC: Congressional Quarterly Press.

Denzau, A.T. and Munger, M.C. (1986) "Legislators and Interest Groups: How Unorganized Interests Get Represented," *American Political Science Review* 80:91–106.

Dexter, L.A. (1969) *How Organizations are Represented in Washington*, Indianapolis: Bobbs-Merrill.

Dow, J.K. (1994) "Campaign Contributions and Intercandidate Transfers in the California Assembly," *Social Science Quarterly* 75:867–80.

Dow, J.K. and Endersby, J.W. (1994) "Campaign Contributions and Legislative Voting in the California Assembly," *American Politics Quarterly* 22:334–53.

Dunmoyer, D. Advocate for the Personal Insurance Federation. (1998) Personal interview by author, 13 December. Sacramento.

Eaton, B. (1996) "No Joking Matter," *Newsweek* 128 (13): 20.

Endicott, W. (1997) "Doolittle: Let Freedom Reign," *The Sacramento Bee*, 12 April: 3(A).

Endicott, W. (1998) "Mulling Over Tobacco Money," *The Sacramento Bee*, 21 February: 3(A).

Enelow, J.M. (1981) "Saving Amendments, Killer Amendments, and an Expected Utility Theory of Sophisticated Voting," *Journal of Politics* 43:1062–89.

Engel, S.T. and Jackson, D.J. (1998) "Wielding the Stick instead of Its Carrot: Labor PAC Punishment of Pro-NAFTA Democrats," *Political Research Quarterly* 51:813–28.

Erikson, R.S. (1990) "Roll Calls, Reputations and Representation in the U.S. Senate," *Legislative Studies Quarterly* 14:623–42.

Etzioni, A. (1984) *Capital Corruption: The New Attack on American Democracy*, New York: Harcourt, Brace, Jovanovich.

Evans, D. (1986) "PAC Contributions and Roll Call Voting: Conditional Power," in A.J. Cigler and B.A. Loomis (eds.) *Interest Group Politics*, Washington, DC: Congressional Quarterly Press.

Evans, D. (1994) "Congressional Oversight and the Diversity of Members' Goals," *Political Science Quarterly* 109:669–87.

Evans, D. (1996) "Before the Roll Call: Interest Group Lobbying and Public Policy Outcomes in House Committees," *Political Research Quarterly* 49:287–304.

Everson, D.H. (1991) "The Impact of Term Limitations on the States: Cutting the Underbrush or Chopping Down the Tall Timber," in G. Benjamin and M.J. Malbin (eds.) *Limiting Legislative Terms*, Washington, DC: Congressional Quarterly Press.

Fenno, R.F. (1973) *Congressmen in Committees*, Boston: Little Brown.

Fenno, R.F. (1978) *Home Style: House Members in Their Districts*, New York: Harper Collins.

Ferguson, T.W. (1996) "Tort Retort," *Forbes* 157 (3): 47.

Field Institute. (1986) *Field (California) Poll, Data*. [machine-readable data file] San Francisco: The Field Institute. Field (California) Poll 86-04.

Fiorina, M.P. (1974) *Representatives, Roll Calls and Constituencies*, Toronto: Lexington Books.

Fiorina, M.P. (1981) *Retrospective Voting in American National Elections*, New Haven: Yale University Press.

Fleisher, R. (1993) "PAC Contributions and Congressional Voting on National Defense," *Legislative Studies Quarterly* 18:391–409.

Frendeis, J.P. and Waterman, H.W. (1985) "PAC Contributions and Legislative Behavior: Senate Voting on Trucking Deregulation," *Social Science Quarterly* 66:401–512.

Frohlich, N. (1975) "The Instability of Minimum Winning Coalitions," *American Political Science Review* 69:943–46.

Gallup Organization. (1999) "Public: Major Changes Needed in Campaign Finance System," Poll, 22 October 1999. Princeton, NJ: Gallup Organization. http://www.gallup.com/content/login.aspx?ci=3520.

Ginsberg, B. and Green, J.C. (1986) "The Best Congress Money Can Buy," in B. Ginsberg and A. Stone (eds.) *Do Elections Matter?* New York: M.E. Sharpe.

Gladstone, M. (1993) "Robbins Paints Sordid Picture of Politics," *Los Angeles Times*, 24 October: 3(A).

Gopoian, J.D. (1984) "What Makes PACs Tick? An Analysis of the Allocation Patterns of Economic Interest Groups," *American Journal of Political Science* 28:259–81.

Gordon, S.B. (2003) "Campaign Contributions as Gift Giving Behavior," Presented at the annual meeting of the Midwest Political Science Association, Chicago.

Gordon, S.B. and Unmack, C.L. (2003) "The Effect of Term Limits on Corporate PAC Allocation Patterns: The More Things Change …" *State and Local Government Review* 35:26–37.

Gouldner, A.W. (1973) "The Norm of Reciprocity," in A.W. Gouldner (ed.) *For Sociology*, London: Allen Lane.

Gregorowicz, P., Hegji, C.E., and Lacy, A.W. (1987) "The Economic Impact of the Beer and Wine Industries on the Alabama Economy," Unpublished manuscript.

Grenzke, J.M. (1989) "PACs and the Congressional Supermarket: The Currency is Complex," *American Journal of Political Science* 33:1–24.

Grier, K.B. and Munger, M.C. (1986) "The Impact of Legislator Attributes on Interest Group Campaign Contributions," *Journal of Labor Research* 7:349–61.

Grier, K.B. and Munger, M.C. (1991) "Committee Assignments, Constituent Preferences, and Campaign Contributions," *Economic Inquiry* 29:24–43.

Guinier, L. (1994) *The Tyranny of the Majority*, New York: Free Press.

Hall, R.L. and Wayman, F.W. (1990) "Buying Time: Moneyed Interests and the Mobilization of Bias in Congressional Committees," *American Political Science Review* 84:797–820.

Hauser, D. Former Assemblyman (D-Arcata). (1999) Phone interview by author, 13 December. Sacramento to Arcata, California.

Hayes, M.T. (1981) *Lobbyists and Legislators*, New Brunswick, NJ: Rutgers University Press.

Hinckley, B. (1972) "Coalitions in Congress: Size and Ideological Distance," *Midwest Journal of Political Science* 16:197–207.

Hinckley, B. (1975) "Policy Content, Committee Membership, and Behavior," *American Journal of Political Science* 19:543–57.

Ingram, C. (1988) "Senate Contest Focuses on AIDS, Crime Issues," *Los Angeles Times*, 24 October: section 1, 3.

Jackson, B. (1990) *Honest Graft: Big Money and the American Political Process*, Washington, DC: Farragut Publishing Company.

Jackson, D.J. and Engel, S.T. (2003) "Friends Don't Let Friends Vote for Free Trade: The Dynamics of Labor PAC Punishment Strategy over PNTR," *Political Research Quarterly* 56:441–48.

Jackson, J.E. and Kingdon, J.W. (1992) "Ideology, Group Scores, and Legislative Votes," *American Journal of Political Science* 36:805–23.

Jacobs, J. (1996) "Trial Lawyers and Their Friends," *The Sacramento Bee*, 4 August: 4(Forum).

Jacobson, G.C. (1978) "The Effects of Campaign Spending in Congressional Elections," *American Political Science Review* 72:470–78.

Jacobson, G.C. (1980) *Money in Congressional Elections*, New Haven: Yale University Press.

Jacobson, G.C. and Kernell, S. (1981) *Strategy and Choice in Congressional Elections*, New Haven: Yale University Press.

Johnston, P. Former California State Senator. (2000) Personal interview by author, 16 August. Sacramento.

Jones, W. and Keiser, K.R. (1987) "Issue Visibility and the Effects of PAC Money," *Social Science Quarterly* 68:170–76.

Keene, B. Former California State Senator. (1997) Personal interview by author, 16 May. Sacramento.

Kemper, V. (1995) "The Other Packwood Scandal," *Common Cause Magazine* 21:20–23.

Kershaw, S. (2003) "A Tale of Sex, Money and Politics, in 'Mayberry,'" *New York Times*, 27 August: 11(A).

King, D. (1997) *Turf Wars: How Congressional Committees Claim Jurisdiction*, Chicago: University of Chicago Press.

King, D.C. and Zeckhauser, R.J. (1997) "A Vote Options Model of Congress: Winning by a Little, Losing by a Lot," Unpublished manuscript.

King, G., Tomz, M., and Wittenberg, J. (2000) "Making the Most of Statistical Analyses: Improving Interpretation and Presentation," *American Journal of Political Science* 44:347–61.

Kingdon, J.W. (1989) *Congressmen's Voting Decisions*, 3rd Ed. Ann Arbor: University of Michigan Press.

Komter, A.E. (1996) "Reciprocity as a Principle of Exclusion: Gift Giving in the Netherlands," *Sociology* 30:299–316.

Krause, M. (2000) Personal interview. Sacramento.

Krehbiel, K. (1992) *Information and Legislative Organization*, Ann Arbor: University of Michigan Press.

Kushman, R. (1991) "No-Fault Vehicle Insurance Bill Killed by Panel," *The Sacramento Bee*, 29 May: 3(A).

Kushman, R. (1993a) "Tort Initiative: A Reform or a Weapon?" *The Sacramento Bee*, 24 October: 3(A).

Kushman, R. (1993b) "'Extortion' Kills Initiative Drive?" *The Sacramento Bee*, 24 November: 3(A).

Langbein, L.I. and Lotwis, M.A. (1990) "The Political Efficacy of Lobbying and Money: Gun Control in the U.S. House, 1986," *Legislative Studies Quarterly* 15:413–40.

Lascher, E.L., Kelman, S., and Kane, T.J. (1993) "Policy Views, Constituency Pressure and Congressional Action on Flag Burning," *Public Choice* 76:79–102.

LegiState Press. (1989) Who's Who in the California Legislature: Profiles of Lawmakers and Their Districts, Sacramento: LegiState Press.

Leyden, K.M. (1995) "Interest Group Resources and Testimony at Congressional Hearings," *Legislative Studies Quarterly* 20:431–39.

Lipper, K., Chief Consultant to California Senate Committee on Natural Resources. (1997) Phone interview by author, 8 May. Sacramento.

Lott, J.R. (1993) "Time Series Evidence on Shirking in the U.S. House of Representatives," *Public Choice* 76:125–49.

Madison, J. (1787 [1982]) "Federalist 10," in G. Willis (ed.) *The Federalist Papers*, New York: Bantam Books.

Maltzman, F. (1997) *Competing Principals: Committees, Parties, and the Organization of Congress*, Ann Arbor: University of Michigan Press.

Maltzman, F. and Smith, S.S. (1995) "Principals, Goals, Dimensionality, and Congressional Committees," in K.A. Shepsle and B.R. Weingast (eds.) *Positive Theories of Congressional Institutions*, Ann Arbor: University of Michigan Press.

Matthews, D.R. (1960) *U.S. Senators and Their World*, New York: Random House.

Matthews, J. (1990) "Insurance Advocate for Public Backed Senate Also Supports Tax Assessment Reform," *The Sacramento Bee*, 27 January: 4(A).

Matthews, J. (1998) "Capitol's Lone Independent Departing," *The Sacramento Bee*, 6 July: 1(A).

Mauss, M. (1923 [1990]) *The Gift*; trans. W.D. Hales. Routledge: London.

Mayhew, D.R. (1974) *Congress: The Electoral Connection*, New Haven: Yale University Press.

McCarty, N. and Rothenberg, L.S. (1996) "Commitment and the Campaign Contribution Contract," *American Journal of Political Science* 40:872–904.

*McConnell v. Federal Elections Commission* (2003) (02-1674) 251 F. Supp. 2d 176, 251 F. Supp. 2d 948.

Milbrath, L.W. (1963) *The Washington Lobbyists*, Chicago: Rand McNally and Company.

Mondak, J.J. (1995) "Competence, Integrity, and the Electoral Success of Congressional Incumbents," *Journal of Politics* 57:1043–70.

Mooney, C.Z. (1996) "Bootstrap Statistical Inference: Examples and Evaluations for Political Science," *American Journal of Political Science* 40:570–602.

Morgan, D. (1998) "Judiciary Panel: A Mix of Extremes," *The Washington Post*, 27 September: 1(A).

Munger, M.C. (1988) "Allocation of Desirable Committee Assignments: Extended Queues Versus Committee Expansion," *American Journal of Political Science* 32:317–44.

Nelson, F. and Olson, L. (1978) "Specification and Estimation of a Simultaneous-Equation Model with Limited Dependent Variables," *International Economic Review* 19:695–709.

Neustadtl, A. (1990) "Interest Group PACsmanship: An Analysis of Campaign Contributions, Issue Visibility and Legislative Impact," *Social Forces* 69:549–64.

Newey, W. (1984) "A Methods of Moments Interpretation of Sequential Estimators," *Economics Letters* 14:201–6.

Ogul, M.S. (1976) *Congress Oversees the Bureaucracy*, Pittsburgh: University of Pittsburgh Press.

Olson, M. (1965) *The Logic of Collective Action*, Cambridge: Harvard University Press.

Oppel, R.A. (2004) "Inquiry Focuses on Group DeLay Created," *The New York Times*, 16 February: 11(A).

Ornstein, N.J. (1978) *Interest Groups, Lobbying and Policy Making*, Washington, DC: Congressional Quarterly Press.

O'Rourke, L.M. (1997) "Will Lawmakers Change the Rules that Elected Them?" *The Sacramento Bee*, 27 May: 1(A).

O'Rourke, L.M. (1999). "McCain Rips Senate After It Rejects Campaign Reform," *The Sacramento Bee*, 20 October: 6(A).

Paddock, R.C. (1991) "Roberti Puts Pragmatism Above Personal Agenda," *Los Angeles Times*, 29 November: 1(A).

Parker, G.R. (1996) *Congress and the Rent-Seeking Society*, Ann Arbor: University of Michigan Press.

Pindyck, R.S. and Rubinfeld, D.L. (1981) *Econometric Models and Economic Forecasts*, New York: McGraw-Hill.

Piven, F.F. and Cloward, R.A. (1977) *Poor People's Movements: Why They Succeed, How They Fail*, New York: Pantheon Books.

Reardon, T. Chief of Staff to Senator Jim Costa (D-Fresno). (1999) Phone interview by author, 17 December. Sacramento.

Richardson, J. (1996) *Willie Brown: A Biography*, Berkeley: University of California Press.

Riker, W. (1962) *The Theory of Political Coalitions*, New Haven: Yale University Press.

Riker, W.H. and Niemi, D. (1962) "The Stability of Coalitions on Roll Calls in the House of Representatives," *American Political Science Review* 56:58–65.

Rios, D.M. (1981) "Squeezing of the Juice From Committee Assignments," *California Journal* 12:109–10.

Roeder, E. (1997) "Blank Check: The Real Fund-Raising Scandal," *New Republic* 216 (15): 19–21.

Rosen, S.J. and Nolan, T. (1994) "Seeking Environmental Justice for Minorities and Poor People," *Trial* 30 (12): 50–55.

Rosenthal, A. (1993) *The Third House: Lobbyists and Lobbying in the States*, Washington, DC: Congressional Quarterly Press.

Sabato, L. (1984) *PAC Power: Inside the World of Political Action Committees*, New York: Norton.

Sacramento Bee, The (1995) "Dole Flips to the Right," *The Sacramento Bee*, 7 September: 6(B).

Sacramento News & Review (1997) "Quote of the Week," *Sacramento News & Review*, 1 May: 16.

Saltzman, G.M. (1987) "Congressional Voting on Labor Issues: The Role of PACs," *Industrial and Labor Relations Review* 40:163–279.

Sample, H.A. (1999) "Doolittle Urges End to Campaign Spending Limits—Bill Only Requires Listing on Internet," *The Sacramento Bee*, 14 September: 4(A).

Sand, L. (1999) "No Public Outcry for Campaign Finance Reform," Gallup News Service press release, 22 February.

Scher, S. (1963) "Conditions for Legislative Control," *Journal of Politics* 28:526–51.

Schram, M. (1995) *Speaking Freely*, Washington, DC: Center for Responsive Politics.

Schroedel, J.R. (1986) "Campaign Contributions and Legislative Outcomes," *Western Political Quarterly* 39:371–89.

Schroeter, L.W. (1992) "Prospects for 'Civil Justice Reform': Trial Lawyers Play a Crucial Role in Determining the Outcome," *Trial* 28 (8): 50–54.

Shapley, L.S. and Shubik, M. (1954) "A Method for Evaluating the Distribution of Power in a Committee System," *American Political Science Review* 48:787–92.

Shepsle, K.A. (1978) *The Giant Jigsaw Puzzle: Democratic Committee Assignments in the Modern House*, Chicago: University of Chicago Press.

Shepsle, K.A. and Weingast, B.R. (1987) "The Institutional Foundations of Committee Power," *American Political Science Review* 81:85–104.

Shuit, D. (1986) "Roberti Gives Control of Key Committees to Party Conservatives," *Los Angeles Times,* 24 January: 3(A).

Simmel, G. (1950) "Faithfulness and Gratitude," in K.H. Wolfe (ed.) *The Sociology of George Simmell,* New York: Free Press.

Sinclair, B. (1988) "The Distribution of Committee Positions in the U.S. Senate: Explaining Institutional Change," *American Journal of Political Science* 32:276–301.

Smith, H. (1988) *The Power Game: How Washington Works,* New York: Ballantine Books.

Stern, P.M. (1988) *The Best Congress Money Can Buy,* New York: Pantheon Books.

Stokes, D.E. and Miller, W.E. (1966) "Party Control and the Salience of Congress," in A. Campbell, P.E. Converse, W.E. Miller, and D.E. Stokes (eds.) *Elections and the Political Order,* New York: Wiley.

Stratmann, T. (1995) "Campaign Contributions and Congressional Voting: Does the Timing of Contributions Matter?" *Review of Economics and Statistics* 77:127–36.

Syer, J. (1987) "California: Political Giants in a Megastate," in R.J. Hrebenar and C.S. Thomas (eds.) *Interest Group Politics in the American West,* Salt Lake City: University of Utah Press.

Thomas, M. (1991) "Issue Avoidance: Evidence from the U.S. Senate," *Political Behavior* 13:1–20.

Tollison, R.D. and Ekelund, R.E., Jr. (1987) "The Economic Efficiency of Geographic Restraints in the Malt Beverage Industry," Unpublished manuscript.

Tomz, M., Wittenberg, J., and King, G. (2003) "Clarify: Software for Interpreting and Presenting Statistical Results," *Journal of Statistical Software* 8 (2).

Truman, D.B. (1951) *The Governmental Process: Political Interests and Public Opinion,* New York: Knopf.

Truman, D.B. (1959) *The Congressional Party,* New York: Wiley.

Turner, J. and Schneier, E.V. (1970) *Party and Constituency: Pressures on Congress,* Baltimore: Johns Hopkins University Press.

Verba, S., Schlozman, K.L., and Brady, H.E. (1995) *Voice and Equality: Civic Voluntarism in American Politics,* Cambridge: Harvard University Press.

Walker, J.L. (1991) *Mobilizing Interest Groups in America: Patrons, Professionals and Social Movements,* Ann Arbor: University of Michigan Press.

Walsh, D. (1996) "Carpenter's Corruption Convictions are Upheld," *The Sacramento Bee,* 5 September: 4(B).

Walsh, D. (1997) "Former Lawmaker Agrees to Pay Fines," *The Sacramento Bee,* 28 March: 3(A).

Walters, D. (1993) "Jackson—Lobbyist Who Made Things Happen," *The Sacramento Bee,* 17 October: 3(A).

Walters, D. (2000) "Capitol Loves Turf Battles," *The Sacramento Bee,* 7 June: 3(A).

Wawro, G. (2001) "A Panel Probit Analysis of Campaign Contributions and Roll-Call Votes," *American Journal of Political Science* 45:563–79.

Wayman, F.W. (1985) "Arms Control and Strategic Arms Voting in the U.S. Senate: Patterns of Change, 1967–1983," *Journal of Conflict Resolution* 29:225–51.

Weingast, B.R. (1979) "A Rational Choice Perspective on Congressional Norms," *American Journal of Political Science* 23:245–62.

Welch, W.P. (1980) "The Allocation of Political Monies: Economic Interest Groups," *Public Choice* 35:97–120.

Welch, W.P. (1982) "Campaign Contributions and Legislative Voting: Milk Money and Dairy Price Supports," *Western Political Quarterly* 35:478–95.

West, D. (2000) Checkbook Democracy: How Money Corrupts Political Campaigns, Boston: Northeastern University Press.

White, D.R. (1987) *California Legislature at Sacramento,* Sacramento: Secretary of the Senate.

White, D.R. (1989) *California Legislature at Sacramento,* Sacramento: Secretary of the Senate.

Whitney, D. (2003) "House OKs flood deal: The project would include a new bridge over the American River," *The Sacramento Bee,* 25 September: 3(A).

Wilhite, A. and Theilmann, J. (1987) "Labor PAC Contributions and Labor Legislation: A Simultaneous Logit Approach," *Public Choice* 53:267–76.

Wilson, J.Q. (1989) *Bureaucracy: What Government Agencies Do and Why They Do It,* New York: Basic Books.

Woodward, B. (1994) *The Agenda,* New York: Simon and Schuster.

Wright, J.R. (1985) "PACs, Contributions and Roll Calls: An Organizational Perspective," *American Political Science Review* 79:400–414.

Wright, J.R. (1990) "Contributions, Lobbying and Committee Voting in the U.S. House of Representatives," *American Political Science Review* 84:417–38.

Wright, J.R. (1996) *Interest Groups and Congress: Lobbying, Contributions and Influence,* Needham Heights, MA: Allyn and Bacon.

Wright, M.B. (1993) "Shirking and Political Support in the U.S. Senate, 1964-1984," *Public Choice* 76:103–23.

Yamamura, K. (2002) "Foes threw $5 million at privacy bill: More money flowed to those who cast no votes, Common Cause says," *The Sacramento Bee,* 7 May: 3(A).

Zeiger, R. (1990) "Rating the Legislators," *California Journal* 21:133–41.

Zelman, W. (1988) "Beer: A Case Study in Special Interest Politics," *California Journal* 18:505–9.

# Index

## A

Aberbach, Joel D., 5, 183n
Abramowitz, Alan I., 36, 93
Abstentions, 36, 76, 80
    strategic, 13, 44, 59–62, 96–99, 152
Adler, B. Scott, 106, 134
Alcoholic Beverage Merchants, 69
Alexander, Herbert E., 3, 183n
Alquist, Al, 79
Alvarez, R. Michael, 145, 147
American Civil Liberties Union, 75, 76, 187n
Arnold, R. Douglas, 41, 154, 183n
Assembly Bill 180, 57
Assembly Bill 221, 80–82
Assembly Bill 284, 77–82, 188n
    interest group positions on, 78
    party voting on, 78–79
Assembly Bill 755, 187n
Assembly Bill 1500, 14, 67, 139, 146
    campaign contributions and voting on,
      72–74, 76, 86
    interest group positions on, 68–71
    statistical results relating to, 150–151,
      160, 167–168
Assembly Finance and Insurance Committee,
    117, 188n
Assembly Governmental Organization
    Committee, 91, 118, 189n
Assembly Health Committee, 56
Assembly Natural Resources Committee,
    78, 107
Assembly Rural Caucus, 69, 72, 146,
    151, 187n

Assembly Utilities and Commerce
    Committee, 118
Assembly Ways and Means Committee,
    78, 118
Association of California Insurance
    Carriers, 1
Association of California Insurance
    Companies, 83
Association of California State Attorneys and
    Administrative Law Judges, 75
Association of California Tort Reform, 57, *see
    also* Keene, Barry
Atlantic Richfield Company, 27, 78
Auburn Dam, 62
Austen-Smith, David, 11, 19, 20, 128
Auto insurance reform, 50, 60, 63, 82, 84, 96,
    *see also* Senate Bill 2662; Senate Bill 3

## B

Barton Beers, Limited, 69
Bauer, Raymond A., 20, 128
Baumgartner, Frank R., 106
Bee Capitol Bureau, 96
Beer distribution legislation, 67–71, 86,
    91–92, 146, *see also* Assembly Bill 1500
Bernstein, Dan, 12
Bernstein, Robert A., 155
Berry, Jeffrey M., 7, 19, 24
Beverly, Robert, 79, 80
Birnbaum, Jeffrey H., 9, 11, 20, 92, 93, 130,
    131, 139
Block, A.G., 46, 47, 91, 106, 117, 154, 186
Bourdieu, Pierre, 31, 33, 34